The Sunbeam Guide To

LED-ZEPPELIN

1

First Published in Great Britain in 2008
by Foxcote Books Ltd, London

10 9 8 7 6 5 4 3 2 1

A CIP catalogue record of this book is available from the British Library.

ISBN 1-905880-06-5

ISBN-13 978-1-905880-06-5

Designed and Typeset by Foxcote Books
Cover design by OnFire Creative, London

Illustrations by iCandy Media and Brendan Walton / © Foxcote Books Ltd, 2008

Printed and Bound by Biddles of Norfolk

www.foxcotebooks.com

The Sunbeam Guide To

LED-ZEPPELIN

by

Richard Morton Jack

foxcote

BOOKS

By the same author:

The Bumper Book of British Sleaze

(with Owen O'Rorke)

CONTENTS

LED-ZEPPELIN

A TIMELINE

1968

07/07/68	The Yardbirds play their final gig, at Luton Technical College
07/68	Jimmy Page travels to Birmingham to watch Robert Plant perform with Obstweedle. John Paul Jones contacts Page regarding joining the band
31/07/68	Page watches John Bonham playing with Tim Rose at the Hampstead Country Club, London
08/68	The quartet rehearse for the first time, in Gerrard Street, London
07/09/68	'The New Yardbirds' play their first gig, at the Gladsaxe Teen Club, Denmark
17/09/68	Scandinavian tour ends at Klub Bongo, Malmö, Sweden
20/09/68	Recording of *Led Zeppelin I* begins in Olympic Studios, London
18/10/68	First UK gig (billed as the Yardbirds), at the Marquee Club, London. The band plays several further UK shows over the next few weeks
01/11/68	Atlantic announce that it has signed the band for a $200,000 advance
09/11/68	Plant marries Maureen Wilson
10/12/68	First gig as Led Zeppelin, at the Marquee Club, London
26/12/68	First US tour begins in Denver, backing Vanilla Fudge, Iron Butterfly and others

1969

12/01/69	*Led Zeppelin I* is released in the US, eventually climbing to #10
15/02/69	First US tour ends at Miami's Thee Image Club
13/03/69	Second Scandinavian visit begins
03/69	The band tours UK clubs. 'Good Times Bad Times' / 'Communication Breakdown' peaks at #80 on the US Billboard chart
28/03/69	*Led Zeppelin I* is released in the UK, eventually climbing to #6
18/04/69	Second US tour begins at New York jazz festival, ending at the city's Fillmore East on May 31st
08/06/69	Third UK tour begins at Newcastle's City Hall, ending with two shows at the 'Pop Proms' at London's Royal Albert Hall on the 19th
05/07/69	Third US tour begins at the Atlanta Pop Festival, ending at the Dallas International Pop Festival on August 31st
17/10/69	Fourth US tour begins with two shows at New York's Carnegie Hall. It ends with two dates at San Francisco's Wonderland on November 8th
22/10/69	*Led Zeppelin II* is released, climbing to #1 in the UK and the US
27/12/69	*Led Zeppelin II* replaces the Beatles' *Abbey Road* at the top of the US chart

1970

07/01/70	Fourth UK tour begins at Birmingham's Town Hall, ending at Leeds Town Hall on January 24th
09/01/70	The band plays at London's Royal Albert Hall
01/70	'Whole Lotta Love' / 'Living Loving Maid' 45 hits US #4
24/2/70	Scandinavian tour begins at Helsinki's Kulturhous, ending at the Montreux Jazz Festival on March 14th
28/2/70	Eva von Zeppelin threatens to sue if the band uses her family name in Denmark. They play Copenhagen's K.B. Hallen billed as 'The Nobs'
21/03/70	Fifth US tour begins at Vancouver's Coliseum, ending on April 18th at Phoenix's Coliseum
05/70	Page and Plant visit Bron-Yr-Aur and write songs
22/06/70	The band travels to Reykjavik, Iceland
28/06/70	The band headlines the UK's Bath Festival
15/08/70	Sixth US tour begins at New Haven's Yale Bowl, ending at New York's Madison Square Garden on September 19th
19/09/70	The band topple the Beatles as 'top international group' in the Melody Maker Poll
05/10/70	*Led Zeppelin III* is released and climbs to #1 in the UK and the US

1971

01/71	'Immigrant Song' / 'Hey Hey What Can I Do' reaches #16 in the United States
05/03/71	'Back To The Clubs' tour begins at Belfast's Ulster Hall, where they debut 'Stairway To Heaven'. The tour ends at London's Marquee Club on March 23rd
03/71	The band plays the Montreux Jazz Festival
01/4/71	The band plays a live BBC session at London's Paris Theatre
04/71	The band is given the keys to the city of Memphis
05/07/71	Fans riot at a concert in the Vigorelli Stadium, Milan, Italy
19/08/71	Seventh US tour begins in Vancouver's Pacific Coliseum, ending in Honolulu's International Center on September 17th
23/09/71	First Japanese tour begins at Tokyo's Budokan Hall, ending at Osaka's Festival Hall on the 29th
08/11/71	Untitled fourth album is released, climbing to UK #1 and US #2
11/11/71	Sixth UK tour begins at Newcastle's City Hall, ending at Salisbury's City Hall on December 15th
20/11/71	First 'Electric Magic' show at London's Wembley Empire Pool, with the second a day later

1972

16/02/72	First Australasian tour begins at Perth's Subiaco Oval, ending at Brisbane's Festival Hall on the 29th
02/72	'Black Dog' / 'Misty Mountain Hop' peaks on the US singles chart at #15
03/03/72	Third European tour begins in Copenhagen, ending in Paris on April 2nd
04/72	'Rock And Roll' / 'Four Sticks' climbs to US #47
06/06/72	Eighth US tour begins at Detroit's Cobo Hall, ending at Tucson's Community Center on the 28th
02/10/72	Second Japanese tour begins at Tokyo's Budokan Hall, ending in Kyoto's Kaikan #1 Hall on the 10th
30/11/72	Seventh UK tour begins in Newcastle City Hall, ending in Preston's Guild Hall on January 30th 1973

1973

02/03/73	Third European tour begins at Copenhagen's K.B.Hallen, ending at Paris's Palais des Sports on April 2nd
28/03/73	*Houses Of The Holy* is released, and climbs to #1 in the UK and US
05/73	'Over The Hills And Far Away' / 'Dancing Days' reaches US #51
04/05/73	Ninth US tour begins at Atlanta's Braves Stadium
05/05/73	Their gig at Florida's Tampa Stadium breaks US attendance / box office record set by the Beatles in 1965, with an audience of 56,800 and a take of $309,000
30/05/73	A gig at LA's Forum is cancelled after Page sprains his finger
02/06/73	A gig at San Francisco's Kezar Stadium breaks their own newly-set world record for a gross at a single gig, taking $325,000
27/07/73	They play the first of three gigs at New York's Madison Square Garden, filmed for *The Song Remains The Same* movie
29/07/73	On the last day of their ninth US tour, $209,000 in cash is stolen from their safety deposit box at the Drake Hotel, NYC. It is never traced
09/73	'D'yer Mak'er' / 'The Crunge' reaches US #20

1974

04/04/74	The NME announces the creation of the band's own label, Swan Song, to be distributed through Atlantic
05/74	Swan Song is launched at parties in the US and the UK
14/08/74	Page and Bonham join Stephen Stills, Graham Nash and Neil Young for an impromptu jam at Quaglino's restaurant, London
31/10/74	The band hosts a lavish party in Kent's Chislehurst Caves

12/74	Page traps his finger in a train door en route for rehearsals in London, forcing him to develop a new three-digit technique until it heals

1975

18/01/75	Tenth US tour begins at Minneapolis's Metro Sports Centre, ending at the LA Forum on March 27th
24/2/75	*Physical Graffiti* is released and quickly climbs to #1 in the UK and the US
04/75	'Trampled Under Foot' / 'Black Country Woman' reaches US #38
17/05/75	The band plays the first of five shows at London's Earls Court Arena
06/75	The band enters tax exile in Switzerland, later moving to Jersey and Malibu
04/08/75	Plant is involved in a serious car accident in Rhodes, causing planned US dates to be cancelled
11/75	The band enters Musicland Studios, Munich, Germany to record *Presence*
10/12/75	In tax exile from the UK, the band plays an impromptu gig in Behan's nightclub, Jersey

1976

31/03/76	*Presence* is released, and climbs to #1 in the UK and US
18/06/76	'Candy Store Rock' / 'Royal Orleans' is released as a single in the US, but does not chart
28/09/76	*The Song Remains The Same* soundtrack LP is released, later climbing to UK #1 and US #2
20/10/76	*The Song Remains The Same* film premieres at Cinema One in New York
04/11/76	*The Song Remains The Same* film premieres simultaneously in London's Warner West End and ABC Shaftesbury Avenue cinemas

1977

01/04/77	Eleventh US tour begins at Dallas's Memorial Auditorium
30/04/77	A gig at the Silverdome in Pontiac, Michigan breaks their own world attendance record, attracting 76,229 people
23/07/77	The so-called 'Oakland Incident' occurs backstage at the Oakland Coliseum, San Francisco
24/04/77	The band plays its last-ever US gig, also at the Oakland Coliseum
25/07/77	Plant is told of his son Karac's death, and returns to the UK. The band enters a hiatus

1978

02/78	Bonham, Peter Grant, Richard Cole and John Bindon plead *nolo contendere* to charges relating to 'the Oakland incident' and are fined
05/78	The band reconvenes for rehearsals at Clearwell Castle, in the Forest of Dean
11/78	They record *In Through The Out Door* at Abba's Polar Studios in Stockholm, completing it in December

1979

04/08/79	The first of their two Knebworth shows
11/08/79	The second of their two Knebworth shows
15/08/79	*In Through The Out Door* is released and climbs to #1 in the UK and the US
29/12/79	Plant, Jones and Bonham appear with Paul McCartney at the 'Rock For Kampuchea' concert in London's Hammersmith Odeon

1980

02/80	'Fool In The Rain' / 'Hot Dog' reaches US #21
17/06/80	Their first full-scale European tour since 1973 begins at Dortmund's Westfalenhalle
07/07/80	They play their final gig, at Berlin's Eissporthalle
24/09/80	They reconvene in Berkshire to rehearse for their forthcoming twelfth US tour
25/09/80	Bonham is found dead in bed at Page's Windsor home, having choked in his sleep after a vodka binge
10/10/80	Bonham is buried at St Michael's Church, Rushock, Worcestershire
04/12/80	Led Zeppelin issue a statement announcing their decision to disband

1982

19/11/82	*Coda* is released, and climbs to UK #4 and US #6

1995

21/11/95	Peter Grant dies of a heart attack, and is buried on December 4th

LED-ZEPPELIN

A - Z

Abba

Swedish pop sensations led by Benny Andersson and Bjorn Ulvaeus, in whose Polar Studios Led Zeppelin recorded *In Through The Out Door* in November and December 1978. "Their women were horrified at us taking their boys out in their hometown to the sort of clubs we'd go to," Robert Plant told the Mirror newspaper in November 2003. "We were on the run with Benny and Bjorn, trying to steer clear of their wives."

Abbey Road

The Beatles' final studio album, released in late September 1969. It immediately went to the top of the charts on both sides of the Atlantic, where it seemed set to remain well into 1970. *Led Zeppelin II*, however – released in late October 1969 – dislodged it from the top of the Billboard chart on December 27th, meaning that Led Zeppelin started the new decade as usurpers of the Liverpudlians' crown. As Robert Plant told a US press conference in 1970, it was "A shock and very elating, a really good feeling. But we've been in the middle of a tour for about four weeks in the States and we took a week off in England, so we really haven't had time to sit back and realise what's happened."

Aberystwyth

Welsh town in whose King's Hall the band played a memorable gig on January 16th 1973. As Page explained to Disc that June: "We spent a lot of time songwriting in Wales, and Aberystwyth was the nearest large town... we felt quite warm vibes about the whole place, so when we set up our last tour we said 'wouldn't it be a gas if we did Aberystwyth?' Like a nostalgic thing. So we did it... it was a really tiny place, it had only had about 800 people and it was a real folly to do it... they were just aghast. They were all sitting down, just sort of regimented in these rows... That's what I mean about an audience being really uptight about a situation. It's never happened to us anywhere else, this is the only time. It was quite funny". Robert Plant evidently bore no grudge against the place: he returned at the end of the year to film part of his 'fantasy sequence' for the *Song Remains The Same* movie.

Acheson, Revd. David

Enterprising vicar of St. Mary's, Studley, Warwickshire, who befriended John Bonham in the local pub, the Duke of Marlborough. In 1970 he asked the drummer to sign autographs at the village fete, which took place on Saturday July 11th. Bonham agreed, and arranged for Atlantic to send a hundred assorted albums to be sold on the cheap, while his wife Pat judged the 'Queen of the Fayre' pageant. The day was a great success, and – according to Bonham's brother Mick – 'after the event we joined the Vicar of Studley for a spot of refreshments back at the Duke, emerging in the early hours of the following day'.

Achilles Last Stand

The hard rock tour-de-force that opens 1977's *Presence*. Inspired by Page and Plant's travels around Morocco in the summer of 1975 and written by them in Malibu that autumn, it has been suggested that the title obliquely refers to Plant's broken ankle (an injury sustained in his car accident on Rhodes on August 4th), though the lyrics are more preoccupied with matters of the heart. "There were basically two sections to the song when we rehearsed it," Page told Trouser Press in October 1977. "I know John Paul Jones didn't think I could succeed in what I was attempting to do. He said I couldn't do a scale over a certain section, that it just wouldn't work. But it did. What I planned to try and get that epic quality into it, so it wouldn't just sound like two sections repeated, was to give the piece a totally new identity by orchestrating the guitars, which is something I've been into for quite some time." The finished song features up to twelve overdubbed guitars (all recorded in one night at Munich's Musicland Studios in late 1975), as well as some of Bonham's most powerful drumming. During a playback, Plant became so animated that he got up from his wheelchair and began to dance, before falling over, accompanied by a cracking sound from his bad leg. As he told Melody Maker in February 1976, "I was hobbling around in the middle of this great track when suddenly my enthusiasm got the better of me... There was an almighty crack and a great flash of light and pain, and I folded up in agony. I'd never known Jimmy to move so quickly. He was out of the mixing booth and holding me up, fragile as he might be, within a second." Fortunately, no lasting damage was done and the track became a live staple for the rest of their career.

Affinity

Progressive jazz-rock band whose sole album, *Affinity* (Vertigo 6360 004, June 1970), features two arrangements by John Paul Jones, on 'I Am And So Are You' and 'I Wonder If I'll Care As Much'. These are of especial interest to Led Zeppelin collectors, as he had supposedly ceased such work in favour of his band commitments by that time.

Alexandra Palace

Cavernous London venue known as 'the Ally Pally' that Led Zeppelin played in on December 22nd and 23rd 1972. Its acoustics did not meet their standards, and they subsequently regarded the shows as some of their most disappointing.

All My Love

This unabashedly emotional song appears on 1979's *In Through The Out Door*, and is widely considered to have been inspired by Robert Plant's late son, Karac. Penned by Plant and John Paul Jones, it's one of only two songs by the band not to feature a Jimmy Page writing credit (the other being 'South Bound Saurez'). "That one just came from Robert and me, really," Jones later recalled. "We came in one morning and just started playing something and it was written as it went, as it were, right on the spot. Even the lyrics – Robert came out with a few lines and we had it finished quite quickly." Page wasn't especially enthusiastic, telling Guitar World magazine in 1993: "I wasn't really keen on 'All My Love'. I was a little worried about the chorus. I could just imagine people doing the wave and all of that, and I thought, that's not us. That's not us. In its place it was fine, but I wouldn't have wanted to pursue that direction in the future." Nonetheless, it was the only song to be debuted on their 1980 'Led Zeppelin Over Europe' tour, where it was well-received. A much longer out-take of the track exists, with an extended final chorus and extra guitar solo.

All Right Now

Tyne Tees TV show presented by comic Billy Connolly, which featured the last TV interview John Bonham ever gave. Screened on Tuesday March 4th 1980, it consisted of footage from *The Song Remains The Same* of the drummer playing 'Moby Dick', followed by a short exchange. "John was in great shape, but he was a bit uptight," Connolly told Mojo magazine in October 2005. "He'd had a couple of brandies, then decided that he didn't want to do the interview… So I said to him, 'Look, why don't I ask you really lengthy, confusing questions and you can just shrug as if you don't know the answer, or just say yes. That way we still get to do the interview, but you don't actually have to do it, it'll just seem like you're mercilessly taking the piss'. So we did it and it was funny." After the recording, the duo headed out together. "We went for dinner at this place in Newcastle that did rabbit pie. When we got there John was a bit fired up, and he started shouting, bawling

and breaking things. Then he said 'I've had enough! I'm going for a lie-down'. He found a chaise-longue and the next thing, we heard him snoring."

All Your Own

Long-running UK children's TV talent show on which Jimmy Page appeared in April 1958, playing guitar with the Epsom-based JG's Skiffle Group. They performed two songs (including 'Mama Don't Wanna Play No Skiffle No More'), after which Page told the remarkably condescending presenter Huw Wheldon that he wished to become a 'biological researcher'. The band was formed by Joe Gardiner, though he had left by the time the programme was taped. Their rehearsals took place at Page's home, but they broke up soon after the broadcast. A photograph of them can be seen in Bourne Hall Museum in Ewell, Surrey.

America

By the end of their career, the Yardbirds were considerably more popular in the US than at home, so it was there that Peter Grant focused his campaign to break Led Zeppelin in 1968 and 1969. They first visited it in late 1968, touching down in California on Christmas Eve. "Bonzo and I were amazed," Plant later recalled. "We'd barely even been abroad, and here we were. It was the first time I saw a cop with a gun, the first time I saw a 20-foot-long car. The whole thing was a complete bowl-over." They soon found their feet. On April 5th 1969 Jimmy Page told the NME that "In America the audiences get into their music more. They are more appreciative. They will listen to the sort of patterns you are playing. In Britain all they are interested in is the way to the bar." John Bonham concurred, telling Record Mirror in June 1970 that "America gave us our chance. When we formed, we couldn't get a gig here worth playing. America wanted us because Jimmy came from the Yardbirds... it was the Fillmores that made us, and the kids have been great ever since." The band toured with Vanilla Fudge for a week before playing gigs in Seattle, Portland and Denver, reaching LA at the start of January. Page had a raging temperature, but they went down a storm and felt at home in the city ever after. They moved on to San Francisco for three gigs at the Fillmore West from January 9th – 11th. "I can tell you when I knew when we'd broken through, which was in San Francisco," the guitarist told the NME in September 1973. The city also held special resonance for Plant, who told Melody Maker in September 1970: "When I finally got to San Francisco and saw the Youngbloods and the remnants of that 1966 spirit, it was a cross between being in tears and giggling all the time, because I saw that air that I knew I'd see one day".

John Paul Jones, meanwhile, though he disliked the group's hectic touring schedule, told the NME in February 1973: "America has always been very good for us. I can't really recall a place that hasn't accepted us". Plant had different memories, however, telling Blender magazine in 2002 that "The brutality of the police in the southern states in the early 70s was unbelievable. In either Memphis or Nashville, the police brutalized the fans every time they stood up, so I did a Roger Daltrey spin with the mic and hit a cop on the back of the head. That caused a few problems." When visiting Detroit in 1969, Plant was very upset when a motorist spat at him for having long hair, a salutary reminder that the country was by no means all about peace and love. "The restaurant scene in the South can be unbelievable," Bonham remarked in 1970. "We've stopped for a coffee and watched everybody else in the place get service, people who came in after we did. Everybody sits and glares at you, waiting and hoping that you'll explode and a scene will start... We even had a gun pulled on us in Texas." Page griped to journalist Ritchie Yorke that "I'm fed up with people making nasty comments [about long hair]. We're discriminated against all the time. If we were coloured, we'd really be able to kick up a stink about it." Nonetheless, the country did offer the band a chance to create an alter ego – as Richard Cole wrote, 'Back in England, Zeppelin lived quite normal lives with storybook-like families or girlfriends. But the road – particularly Los Angeles – was a place of excess'.

They eventually played eleven tours of the US (four in 1969, two in 1970, and one each in 1971, 1972, 1973, 1975 and 1977), but the charge of focusing on the American market to the exclusion of others always infuriated them in interviews. "It's complete rubbish that we concentrate our attention on the States," stated Page to the NME in December 1972. "If people could be bothered to examine just how much time we spend in one country at a time you'd find that we measure out our touring schedule to take in as many countries as we can." They played their final US gig at San Francisco's Oakland Coliseum on July 24th 1977, though they had announced plans to return shortly before Bonham's death in September 1980.

Anger, Kenneth

b. Feb 3rd 1927

US underground author, movie-maker and occult dabbler for whose ill-fated film *Lucifer Rising* Jimmy Page agreed to compose original music. The two met at a Sotheby's auction of Aleister Crowley books in 1973, and soon reached what Anger later described as 'a gentlemen's agreement' concerning the project, which had already been seven years in the making and had suffered numerous setbacks in the US. Page also offered Anger the use of his Kensington basement as an editing suite, as he had equipment there for use on Led Zeppelin's *Song Remains The Same* footage. He told the NME in December 1974 that "I've always got on very well with Anger. He's a good friend... I saw him recently and he was playing my soundtrack against some of the rushes, and it came together really nicely."

In mid-1976, however – by which time Page had only completed about 23 minutes of droning, synthesized guitar sketches – Anger was allegedly ejected from the guitarist's home, whose locks were allegedly changed to prevent his re-entering. Anger swiftly announced that he had sacked Page from the project, griping to the NME in 1977: "The way

he's been behaving is totally contradictory to the teachings of Aleister Crowley and totally contradictory to the ethos of the film... I've left messages on his Kafka-esque answering machine. All I've had is promises that the soundtrack is on its way, but nothing's materialized. I've got a fucking film to finish. I'm beginning to think Jimmy's dried up as a musician. He's got no themes, no inspiration, and no melodies to offer." Page, meanwhile, countered that "I've lost a hell of a lot of respect for Anger... at one point he was writing silly letters to everyone he thought I knew... God, it was all so pathetic... I just don't know what he's playing at." The ensuing spat would rumble on for years to come, though Page seemed more bemused than aggrieved. The 29-minute film was finally finished in 1980, with a soundtrack by convicted murderer and Charles Manson acolyte Bobby Beausoleil.

see *Lucifer Rising*

Antiques

Jimmy Page, Peter Grant and Richard Cole were all keen collectors of antiques, especially Victoriana and art nouveau. As Cole told Howard Mylett for his book *Led Zeppelin* in 1974: "We're all collectors, it's like a sort of competition between us to see who can pick up the biggest bargain – I usually do worst, of course, because I have less money than the other two. If any of us finds a really good shop it becomes a carefully-guarded secret from the others. When we're on tour we have a routine of booking in at the hotel in the morning, going on an antiques expedition in the afternoon and then doing the gig in the evening. When the customs people at London Airport used to see all the stuff they nearly had heart attacks, but now they just say 'Oh, it's only Led Zeppelin'." Jimmy Page apparently refused to allow his finds to be carried in the holds of aeroplanes, booking them seats instead, sometimes as 'Mr. Carson' – a reference to Atlantic executive Phil Carson. In Cole's memoirs he claims that on tour in Europe he 'had arranged for a five-ton truck to travel with us… I sensed that the band would be accumulating new belongings along the way. That's what new money does for you.'

Appice, Carmine
b. Dec. 15th 1946

Drummer with Vanilla Fudge (who toured with Led Zeppelin in late 1968 and early 1969) and a great admirer and advocate of John Bonham, for whom he arranged sponsorship with Ludwig drums in 1969. According to John Paul Jones, "Carmine and Bonzo became like brothers." Nonetheless, Appice had some cool words to say about the band in Melody Maker of September 19th 1970: "Basically, what they have done is to take a little of Hendrix, Fudge and Jeff Beck and come up with a formula. They just had to happen, because America was looking for a replacement for Cream." He went on to gripe that "This third album of theirs, which I hear is being released sometime in September, is really weird. Most of it is acoustic, nothing at all like they have done in the past, and it doesn't work. Robert Plant is a screamer and his voice doesn't fit on these quiet numbers."

After Bonham's death in 1980, Appice remarked: "I loved Bonzo. He was a beautiful man. He was a really respectful guy, and always treated me with courtesy. Even when he had a few drinks, he always treated me with respect."

Arabella Hotel

Munich hostelry whose basement housed Musicland Recording Studios, where *Presence* was recorded in November and December 1975.

Atlantic Records

Led Zeppelin's record label until 1974, and the distributor of Swan Song thereafter. Having recorded their debut at Jimmy Page's expense, at the end of October 1968 Page and Peter Grant flew to New York (tapes and artwork in hand) for an audience with Jerry Wexler and Ahmet and Nesuhi Ertegun, the heads of Atlantic. They were adamant that they should be signed to Atlantic proper, not the Atco subsidiary (typically the repository for rock acts) – as Page told Guitar World magazine in 1993, "I didn't want to be lumped in with those people, I wanted to be associated with something more classic."

On November 1st it was reported that they had got their wish, and an advance of $200,000. Ertegun stated that "The first album Peter Grant brought us absolutely bowled myself and Jerry Wexler over because it was so powerful. Naturally we knew that we had a band that was going to be extremely popular on radio and in person." Initially the deal excluded the UK, but when Mo Austin at Warner Bros. and Louis Benjamin at

Pye both deemed the £17,500 advance Grant demanded too high, he assigned the British rights to Atlantic too. The label expressed a desire to remix the album, but Page resisted and it was duly released as it stood in January 1969. The label was wise to concede the point: by the end of 1974 Swan Song's publicity department was announcing that 'Led Zeppelin is the best-selling group in the history of Atlantic Records'.

Auger, Brian
b. July 18th 1939

Arguably Britain's leading exponent of the Hammond organ in the 1960s and 1970s. Along with Jimmy Page, saxophonist Joe Harriott, drummer Micky Waller and others, he backed Sonny Boy Williamson for some sessions in 1965. Williamson died shortly afterwards, and the results didn't appear till 1969, when they were released as *Don't Send Me No Flowers* (Marmalade 608004). Page's contribution is fairly muted and unremarkable, however. Auger's band, the Trinity (featuring vocalist Julie Driscoll) went on to tour the US as support to Led Zeppelin on their second US visit in 1969, along with the Colwell-Winfield Blues Band.

Aungier, Cliff
b. 1941 / d. 2004

Croydon-born folk singer who played in a duo with Royd Rivers in the mid-1960s. Their sole LP, 1965's *Wanderin'* (Decca LK 4696), was an early production by Jimmy Page, who is also credited with writing the perfunctory sleevenotes ('Royd and Cliff's personal appearances have proved by the fantastic following they have acquired just what monster talents they are' etc). The record is a stark affair based on their club act, and the deal seems to have had something to do with Page's involvement with Immediate Records.

Australasia

The only Led Zeppelin tour down under was in February 1972. Their first gig was on February 16th, at Perth's Subiaco Oval, where they performed in front of an estimated 5% of the city's population. The event was marred by crowd violence and inadequate policing, and the following morning the band was awoken by drug police in their Scarborough hotel, allegedly acting on a tip-off. They went away empty-handed. There was further unrest at their performance in Adelaide on the 19th, which had in fact been scheduled for the 18th, but was postponed for 24 hours owing to rain. This presented rock fans with an appalling dilemma, as Creedence Clearwater Revival were also in town on the 19th. According to Richard Cole in *Stairway To Heaven*, 'Creedence's drummer, Doug Clifford, had a practice drum kit in his hotel room, and Bonham and he took it in turns pounding out a thunderous beat until almost daybreak. Amazingly, no one from the hotel complained.'

When the gig did take place, it was also chaotic. Plant later told the local Go-Set magazine that "there were people shrieking and shouting and fights ten feet from the stage, and I was getting really upset because this is the last thing any of us in the group like to see."

On the 24th they visited New Zealand, where 25,000 fans saw them at Auckland's Western Springer Stadium. 500 of these had chartered a train dubbed 'the Zeppelin Express' in order to reach the gig, an idea copied by Grant for their Earl's Court shows in London in May 1975. On the 27th they played before 26,000 fans in Sydney, before the tour ended in Brisbane's Festival Hall on the 29th.

Autumn Lake

Tune Jimmy Page is seen playing on a hurdy-gurdy beside a lake in 1976's *The Song Remains The Same* film, as the camera approaches through his grounds at Plumpton Place. The song was listed on the film credits, but never recorded by Led Zeppelin. According to Page in Mojo magazine in December 2007: "It sounds excruciating. Absolutely excruciating."

Babe I'm Gonna Leave You

The second track on the band's debut, and the first indication of their interest in folk music. The original version is credited to US folk singer Anne Bredon, who wrote it in the 1950s. Though Led Zeppelin's demented version is radically different (and adapted from Joan Baez's rendition), a credit was added for Bredon in the 1980s when her son inadvertently discovered that the song had been penned by her. Page and Plant have stated that they listened to the Baez version together at their first proper meeting, at the guitarist's Pangbourne home in August 1968. The singer's improvised assertion that he intends to 'go walking through the park every day' with the very babe he plans to leave has disquieted pedants for decades. The band only played the song live in 1968 and 1969.

Back To The Clubs

Tour of UK clubs and ballrooms undertaken by the band from the 5th to the 24th March 1971, shortly after completing the sessions for their untitled fourth LP. The idea was twofold: to perform for fans who couldn't make it to larger venues, and to remind themselves of what it was like to play in more intimate surroundings. As Bonham told Melody Maker in February: "It'll be great because the atmosphere is always much better than a big place like the Albert Hall. We wanted to do a tour where the greatest number possible could come and see us, at the places that made us when we started out." Richard Cole, however, later wrote that the tour was 'much better as a concept than as reality. None of us particularly enjoyed it.' As Page told Mojo magazine in December 2007, "We'd gone back and tried to play smaller places, and it was absolutely ridiculous, with streets closed off and too many people who couldn't get in."

They charged the same appearance fees they had originally received, on the basis that ticket prices were commensurately low. The press were also discouraged from tagging along. As Page told Record Mirror at the time: "The audiences were becoming specks on the horizon at concerts. It made you feel you were looking through the wrong end of a telescope. In the clubs, you are close enough to people to pick up on their reactions – you can see their faces and establish some sort of contact." Ironically, though the initiative had been motivated by respect for their fans, so many were turned away that letters of complaint appeared in the music press, criticising them for not choosing larger venues. The poor sound systems, cramped dressing rooms and low remuneration made the band less nostalgic than they had anticipated, and the experiment was not repeated (though they did play one further club date in December 1975 – see *Behan's*). Immediately after the 'Back

To The Clubs' tour, the band recorded their famous final BBC session, on April 1st (aired on April 4th).

Backward masking

The alleged practice of concealing words or messages backwards during songs. It has long been rumoured that Led Zeppelin did just that in 'Stairway To Heaven', with 'If there's a bustle in your hedgerow' supposedly transforming into 'Oh here's to my sweet Satan' when played backwards. The band has not often dignified the claim with a riposte, though a statement from Swan Song crisply stated: 'Our turntables only play in one direction.' Robert Plant has remarked that "To me it's very sad, because 'Stairway To Heaven' was written with every best intention, and as far as reversing tapes and putting messages on the end goes, that's not my idea of making music," while engineer Eddie Kramer posed the question: "Why would they want to spend so much studio time doing something so dumb?"

Backwards echo

Also known as reverse echo, this studio technique was developed by Jimmy Page with the Yardbirds, and can be heard at the end of 'You Shook Me' on Led Zeppelin's debut, as well as on 'Whole Lotta Love', 'When the Levee Breaks', 'The Wanton Song' and 'Sick Again'. "I pioneered that effect," the guitarist told Guitar Player magazine in 1993. "When we recorded 'You Shook Me', I told the engineer, Glyn Johns, that I wanted to use backwards echo on the end. He said, 'Jimmy, it can't be done'. I said

'Yes, it can. I've already done it.' Then he began arguing, so I said, 'Look, I'm the producer. I'm going to tell you what to do, and just do it.' So he grudgingly did everything I told him to, and when we were finished he started refusing to push the fader up so I could hear the result. Finally, I had to scream, 'Push the bloody fader up!' And lo and behold, the effect worked perfectly. When Glyn heard the result, he looked bloody ill!"

Bad Company

Hard rock act formed by singer Paul Rodgers and drummer Simon Kirke of Free, along with guitarist Mick Ralphs (ex-Mott the Hoople) and bassist Boz Burrell (ex-King Crimson). Managed by former Zeppelin roadie Clive Coulson, they were signed to Swan Song by Peter Grant, who later described Rodgers as "probably the most difficult person I ever had to work with". Jimmy Page was an admirer of theirs, telling the NME on September 14th 1974: "You know, there really is a comparison to be made with this band and Zeppelin. Paul and Simon played together before, like Bonzo and Robert did, and all of them came together from other bands, like we did. And the combined fusion of all the musical forces has just worked out so well — and it's such good, strong, virile music." Bad Company's self-titled debut album (Swan Song SS 8410) was the label's first release, in June 1974, and topped the US charts. Page joined them onstage in the US twice that September (in Texas and New York, jamming on 'Rock Me Baby'), as well as at London's Rainbow Theatre on December 16th (along with John Paul Jones). Page and

Plant joined them onstage at the LA Forum on May 23rd 1976 to sing 'I Just Want To Make Love To You' (one of Plant's first public performances since his car accident the previous August). The gesture was reciprocated by Ralphs at a Led Zeppelin gig in Fort Worth, Texas on 22nd May 1977 and by Kirke on July 5th 1980 – the band's penultimate performance. Page later formed The Firm with Rodgers.

Badgley, Larry
Harvard-educated doctor who toured with the Rolling Stones in 1972, and was employed to join Led Zeppelin in the US in 1973, 1975 and 1977. Robert Plant told Mojo magazine in October 2005 that "the only reason we ever had a doctor around in Led Zeppelin was to get some Quaaludes. We never had anybody checking us up… We had no thought about that then. It was a very, very large whisky and coke and on with the show." It has been suggested that Page and Bonham developed a tendency to help themselves to Badgley's supply of Quaaludes, which strained relations between them, with Badgely openly accusing Page of pilfering after their gig at the Minneapolis Sports Arena on April 12th 1977, much to the guitarist's annoyance. According to journalist Jan Uhelszki, writing in Creem in July 1977, Badgley appeared 'to do little more than administer the occasional throat spray and aspirin, in addition to picking up as many willing young lovelies as medically possible'.

Baja / A Foggy Day In Vietnam
Low-selling solo single by John Paul Jones, issued in the UK in April 1964 by Pye (7N 15637) and in the US by Parkway (P-915) the same year. 'Baja' was a surf-type instrumental written by Lee Hazelwood, while the orchestral B-side, written by Andrew Oldham and Mike Leander, may well have been a demo by the Andrew Loog Oldham Orchestra, and probably doesn't feature Jones at all. The NME described it as 'a beaty instrumental with novel tambourine effects', while Jones told Record Mirror on April 25th: "I'd been planning a solo career for myself but I hadn't really got around to deciding exactly what to do. Then recording manager Andrew Oldham came up one day and said he had just the right number for me. It was quite a session. We used a ten-piece orchestra, but the disc started with just bass and drums. Then it just started building – we even had a choir on it later on. My main hobby now is buying records. Anything by Dionne Warwick, Sarah Vaughan or Tony Bennett is great by me. The only thing I really dislike is having to rush about." Simultaneously released (and no more successful) was the Kinks' 'You Still Want Me' / 'You Do Something To Me' (Pye 7N 15638).

Baldwin, John
John Paul Jones's real name. The change had been suggested by Andrew Loog Oldham by April 1964, when Jones's one-off solo single appeared on Pye. Jones still received occasional credits under his real name later in the decade, however, such as on Mark Wirtz's 1967 *Mood Mosaic* LP.

see *Jones, John Paul*

Ballantine Ale

Popular brand of American beer whose logo looked remarkably similar to the 'interlocking drums' symbol John Bonham chose to be represented by on the band's untitled fourth LP in 1971.

Banana

Curved yellow fruit which, eaten in moderation, supplies slow-burning energy and a range of nutritional benefits. John Bonham collapsed fifteen minutes into the band's concert at Nuremberg's Messezentrumhalle on June 27th 1980, after eating 27 of them.

Banana daiquiri

Alcoholic beverage upon which Jimmy Page largely sustained himself in 1976 and 1977. "I prefer to eat liquid food, something like a banana daiquiri," he told Focus Rock Entertainment in Ohio during the band's 1977 US tour. "And I put all this powdered vitamin in it – sort of the thing that they would give invalids. I'm not into solid foods very much. I can't remember when I last had a steak… That blender thing is great. I mean, I know I'll never turn down some alcohol, so a banana daiquiri with all the food protein is the answer to the problem." The guitarist's gaunt appearance was much remarked upon at the time.

Band Of Joy

Midlands club act that existed from January 1967 to March 1968 and featured Robert Plant and John Bonham in its ranks, alongside a revolving cast of musicians including Kevyn Gammond (guitar) and Paul Lockey (bass). Plant was sacked from the first line-up by their manager (the organist's father), so he formed his own rival Band Of Joy, which played gigs at London clubs including Middle Earth and the Marquee, earning around £65 a pop – barely enough to cover their expenses. Their sound was US West Coast-influenced, and local audiences just weren't ready for them. According to Howard Mylett's 1976 *Led Zeppelin* book, the group 'went through three line-ups, including one when it was all kaftans and bells, and the group had painted faces before Arthur Brown's 'Fire' era; the big bass player would come running onstage and dive straight off, and the music was all howling vocals'. One publicity stunt involved Plant being enrolled as a member of the Noise Abatement Society, but it achieved little.

The band released no material, but they did make some demos at Regent Sound in 1967. These included covers of 'For What It's Worth' and 'Hey Joe', as well as originals 'Adriatic Sea View' and 'Memory Lane'. Plant has stated that the latter was only song he ever wrote before joining Led Zeppelin (he has also given its title as 'Dagger Lane'), adding to Circus magazine in January 1976: "It was really quite funny, something about a chick on the back of a motorbike with a chrome horse between her legs." The demo was to prove unexpectedly important in the summer of 1968, when Plant gave a copy to Jimmy Page – as the guitarist told ZigZag magazine in November 1972, "having listened to a demo he

26

had given me, I realised that, without a doubt, his voice had an exceptional and very distinctive quality."

Plant went on to tell Q magazine in March 1988: "The Band Of Joy could play better than a lot of the groups we were listening to." Bonham only played in the final line-up, and it was while they were supporting Tim Rose at the Marquee on February 23rd 1968 that the drummer was talent-spotted by the US singer. Following the band's split the following month, Plant began to sing with Alexis Korner. Lockey and Gammond later issued an LP with a revised Band Of Joy in 1978.

Bannister, Freddie

Leading 1970s UK rock promoter, who had known Robert Plant since his early days on the Midlands pub circuit. He promoted Led Zeppelin's famous appearances at the 1969 and 1970 Bath Festivals, but his relationship with the band ended on a sour note when Peter Grant challenged him over the true size of the audience at Knebworth in August 1979. The licence was only for a 100,000-strong crowd, but Grant was convinced that fraud was afoot. As such, he had aerial photographs of the crowd analysed by experts in Nassau and claimed that 218,000 had come on the 4th and 187,000 on the 11th. Despite Bannister releasing a statement on September 20th stating 'There have been some misconceptions reported in the press… at all times, Led Zeppelin, their manager and his staff have been completely co-operative', the ongoing row forced his company, Tedoar Ltd,

into liquidation. In his subsequent memoirs, *There Must Be A Better Way*, he wrote: 'Why did we retire abruptly? In a word – fear. Peter Grant was in such a terrible state, both mentally and physically, we thought he was on his way out and would be delighted to take us with him.'

Barclay, Eddie

b. Jan. 26th 1921 / d. May 13th 2005
Proprietor of Barclay Records and the most powerful man in the French music industry. Jimmy Page had recorded numerous sessions for him in the mid-1960s, and in October 1969 he invited Led Zeppelin to play a showcase gig in Paris for the local media. The band reluctantly agreed (according to Grant, "Jimmy only wanted to go so he could meet Brigitte Bardot"), only to refuse to play when they realised that the stage was to be a boxing ring. Nonetheless, the 'performance' was ecstatically reviewed in the French press the next day, indicating how influential Barclay was.

Bath Festival Of Blues / Bath Festival Of Progressive Blues

Music festival first held on Saturday June 28th 1969, in front of up to 30,000 people. Acts included Led Zeppelin, Fleetwood Mac (the headliners), Ten Years After, the Nice and Blodwyn Pig. The following year promoter Freddy Bannister expanded the concept, adding the word 'progressive' to the billing and attracting 150,000 fans to Shepton Mallet over the weekend of June 27th – 28th. Led Zeppelin headlined the second day, supported by Frank Zappa, the Byrds, the Flock, Santana, Dr. John, Country Joe and Hot Tuna. The band had declined lucrative offers in America in order to play it, and received a fee of £20,000. Their set began at around 8:30 pm, after Grant cannily calculated that their performance would be more dramatic if it coincided with the sunset. They only started on time because Richard Cole began unplugging the Flock's equipment as their set over-ran. The band was received rapturously, though Peter Grant wasn't concentrating: he famously drenched some bootleggers' equipment during it. According to Disc on July 4th 1970, 'As soon as Zeppelin ripped into their first number the living sea of people exploded. Zeppelin immediately seemed to be in top gear. But then, they don't use any lower ones… The pitch of excitement they achieved was frightening." The gig would remain in the band's memory far longer than many others – Page singled it out in the NME in December 1972 as 'truly magic', stating: "It was quite incredible, because everything seemed to be right for us. The energy was quite phenomenal."

The Battle Of Evermore

Mandolin-led tune on the band's untitled fourth LP, fondly described by Page as 'a let's dance round the maypole number' and by Robert Plant as 'really more of a playlet than a song'. Its musical basis emerged when Page began improvising on Jones's mandolin for the first time during a tea break at Headley Grange in early 1971. Plant had already written the lyrics, their inspiration variously attributed to a book on Scottish battles

or the Battle of Pelennor Fields in Tolkien's *Lord Of The Rings*. In order to lend the words the desired dramatic effect, the band invited their friend Sandy Denny (of Fairport Convention and Fotheringhay) to contribute the second voice – as Plant told Melody Maker in April 1972, "I sang the events in the song, Sandy answered back as if she was the pulse of the people on the battlements." The song was not performed live until their 1977 US tour, when Jones bravely handled Denny's part.

BBC sessions

Given their disdain for both singles and TV appearances, in their early days the band were aware of the need to perform on the radio. Their debut appearance was recorded on the afternoon of Monday, March 3rd 1969 for John Peel's *Top Gear* show, in the BBC's Playhouse Theatre in Northumberland Avenue, London. The band set the template for future BBC appearances by playing a selection of album material, fleshed out by extemporisations. Plant told Mojo magazine in December 1997 that "the whole thing was very quaint: the politeness of the audience, technicians fumbling about, proper, almost hallowed, low-key introductions…" On June 27th they recorded another performance at the Playhouse, which was aired as the first in the popular In Concert series. Other 1969 BBC appearances included Alexis Korner's Rhythm & Blues show (World Service, aired 14/4/69), Chris Grant's Tasty Pop Sundae (aired 22/6/69), another Top Gear (aired 29/6/69) and a pilot called One Night Stand (aired as part of Top Gear on 10/8/69). The band returned in 1971, performing a legendary set for In Concert, presented by John Peel and aired on the evening of Sunday April 4th 1971. After decades of bootlegging, which much confused the details of the original sessions, an official double CD (and vinyl boxed set) was finally released as *BBC Sessions* in November 1997, with some judicious edits overseen by Page.

The Beast

Popular nickname for John Bonham, allegedly given to him by a French employee of Atlantic, Benoit Gautier, on their third European tour, when he observed the drummer's tendency to groan when drunk. The moniker may also have been inspired by Bonham's single-handed destruction of the Frenchman's Volvo.

Beat Club

Germany's leading rock music TV show in the late 60s and early 70s. Led Zeppelin appeared on it on March 28th 1970, performing 'Whole Lotta Love' and 'Babe I'm Gonna Leave You'. Also seen in the episode were Ashton Gardner & Dyke, Marsha Hunt, The Beatles, Mott The Hoople and The Edgar Broughton Band. On their way back to the UK, their plane made a crash landing at Stansted Airport. As the Herts and Essex Observer wrote at the time, 'The well-known pop group were amongst 87 passengers who took part in a dramatic escape down safety chutes after a British European Airways Comet made an emergency landing'.

The Beatles

Unquestionably the most successful pop act of the 1960s, this Liverpudlian quartet's crown was symbolically passed to Led Zeppelin at the close of 1969, when *Led Zeppelin II* replaced *Abbey Road* LP at the top of the US chart on December 27th. In September 1970 Led Zeppelin toppled the Beatles from their long-held places as top British and international group in the Melody Maker Polls, something that made headlines around the world. "I think they're great, they've done some fantastic statements," Page told a US press conference that month, while Plant added: "The fact that they got through to so many millions and millions of people has been an inspiration for every performing group in England, and I should think in the whole world." John Bonham, meanwhile, told Melody Maker in November 1970 that "There was an unbelievable rumour about a year ago. They said I was leaving to join George Harrison. Well, I've never even met the guy. That's how much I know him. I'd like to meet him." His wish was granted on May 31st 1973, when the Beatle joined the band for the drummer's riotous birthday celebrations in Laurel Canyon.

Page, meanwhile, was friendly with Paul McCartney, and met him in New York in 1970 while they were both working on new albums. John Paul Jones and John Bonham both played on McCartney's *Back To The Egg* LP as part of his so-called 'Rockestra', recording two tracks at Abbey Road on October 3rd 1978. Jones, Bonham and Plant also appeared onstage with the Rockestra at the

Concert For Kampuchea (organised by McCartney) in London's Hammersmith Apollo on Sunday December 29th 1979. The performance is thought to have been Bonham's last on a UK stage, and when he died McCartney described him as 'one of the greats'. Ringo Starr, meanwhile, had been a frequent drinking partner of Bonham's, and the two of them appeared in the execrable 1974 comedy film *Son Of Dracula*. Oddly, none of the members of Led Zeppelin are known to have socialised with John Lennon, though Page told Guitarist magazine in December 2003: "I actually saw The Beatles' first London concert, at Walthamstow Baths, I think. 'Love Me Do' was just scraping into the charts and they played 'Please Please Me' that night, before it had been released. But they didn't go down too well, and I actually heard John Lennon going past, saying 'Fuck these London audiences'."

Beck, Jeff

b. June 24th 1944

Mercurial lead guitarist in the Yardbirds from mid-1965, and a schoolfriend of Jimmy Page's in Epsom from the age of eleven. They were introduced by Beck's older sister, and Beck promptly attempted to sell Page a guitar he'd made. Having remained friends, they played together in the Yardbirds between June and December 1966, when Beck departed after a fractious US tour. "When he's having a shining night, he's fantastic," Page told Melody Maker in April 1970. "He plays things of sheer genius." Though Page always went out of his way to praise him, Beck was less effusive, perhaps because he suspected Page had

copied the arrangement of 'You Shook Me' that appeared on his *Truth* LP a few months before *Led Zeppelin I* (a charge Page has categorically denied and which Beck seemed to have forgotten by June 1971, when he told Rolling Stone that he was 'quite honoured, really').

"We used to hang out a hell of a lot when he was in the Yardbirds and I was doing studio work," Page told Trouser Press in October 1977. "He had the same sort of taste in music as I did. That's why you'll find on the early LPs we both did a song like 'You Shook Me'. It was the type of thing we'd both played in bands… It's a classic example of coming from the same area musically, of having a similar taste. It really pissed me off when people compared our first album to the Jeff Beck Group and said it was very close conceptually. It was nonsense, utter nonsense. The only similarity was that we'd both come out of the Yardbirds, and we both had acquired certain riffs individually from the Yardbirds." John Paul Jones, meanwhile, joked to Guitar Player that July: "I did one Jeff Beck single ['Hi Ho

Silver Lining'] and he's never spoken to me since." In fact, coincidentally, Jones also played organ on another track on *Truth*, 'Ol Man River' .
see *the Yardbirds*

Behan's

Jersey nightspot owned by Irish-born Hughie Behan, in which Led Zeppelin played a surprise gig on December 10th 1975, along with resident pianist Norman Hale. Jones and Bonham had sat in with him a week earlier, and promised to return with Page and Plant. Entrance cost 25p a head, and the show (introduced by Behan) featured several 50s covers as well as a handful of Led Zeppelin songs. It was the first performance Plant had given since his car accident in Rhodes that August (he was obliged to perform on a stool) and was rapturously received by the 350-strong crowd (half the club's capacity). Plant reportedly enjoyed it a great deal, and told the NME in February 1976: "It was like a dance hall that was like some place ten years gone by, in the best old English tradition. Guys with dickey bows and evening jackets ready to bang your head against a wall if you stepped out of line…" The venue closed in the mid-1990s, and has since been converted into flats.

Bell, Madeline

b. July 23rd 1942
American-born soul singer who became close friends with John Paul Jones on London's session circuit, where she was a leading vocalist in the 1960s. The bassist and his wife spent Christmas 1968 with Bell and her family in America

before he flew on to join his bandmates in California for their first US tour. Her 1973 funk / soul LP *Comin' Atcha* (RCA SF8393) was produced by Jones, and recorded at his own Dormouse Studio. He also wrote or co-wrote all of the ten tracks, as well as contributing keyboards, synthesizer, bass guitar, guitars and backing vocals. He appeared with Bell to perform the title track on the TV special 'Colour Me Soul', screened in the UK on December 6th 1973, but the album didn't chart on either side of the Atlantic.

Bell, Maggie

b. Jan 12th 1945
Lead singer of Stone The Crows (co-managed by Peter Grant) and an early signing to Swan Song in 1974. Jimmy Page was a long-term admirer of her voice, and contributed guitar to two tracks on her 1973 LP *Suicide Sal* (Polydor 2383 313), 'Coming On Again' and 'If You Don't Know'. She later remarked that "I didn't want to become a cabaret singer at 27, and I thought Peter failed me a bit. He was so busy with Led Zeppelin that I couldn't sit him down to talk for an hour."

Berlin Eissporthalle

Venue for the band's last-ever show, on Monday July 7th 1980, at the end of their short European tour. It lasted for two and a quarter hours, and opened with 'Train Kept A-Rollin' – appropriately enough, one of the very first songs they ever played together. The set included epics like 'Since I've Been Loving You', 'Nobody's Fault But Mine' and 'Stairway To Heaven', alongside shorter numbers including 'Hot Dog' and 'Rock and Roll'. They finished with a 17-minute rendition of 'Whole Lotta Love', before Plant said: "I thank you. Thank you very much, Berlin. Thank you very much everyone who's worked for us and put up with us, and all those sort of things, and, er... Goodnight!"

Bindon, John

b. Oct 4th 1943 / d. Oct 10th 1993

Described by Jimmy Page in Q magazine in 2003 as "a very scary person to be around", this remarkably unpleasant London thug was employed as head of security for the band's 1977 US tour. His tenure has often been cited as a symbol of the tour's joylessness. After stints in Borstal, Bindon worked as an antiques dealer before finding bit-parts as an actor, including appearances in Ken Loach's *Poor Cow*, Nicolas Roeg's *Performance* and Mike Hodges' *Get Carter*. In 1974 he started a security business and gained employment for actors Ryan and Tatum O'Neal. His old crony Richard Cole ill-advisedly invited him to join Led Zeppelin's entourage for their much-anticipated US live comeback in 1977, when he mainly worked as protection for Page. Bindon's aggressive style was soon noted, but his true colours didn't come through until the notorious 'Oakland incident' on July 23rd, when – having already knocked out stage crew chief Jim Downey by banging his head against concrete – he savagely beat one of Bill Graham's security men, Jim Matzorkis, in a trailer (assisted by Cole, Peter Grant and John Bonham). Charged with assault, Bindon returned to the UK, where was prosecuted for murder in 1979. Having been acquitted (on grounds on self-defence) he spent his remaining years tending to cocaine and heroin addictions and died of an AIDS-related illness.

Birmingham Water Buffalo Society

Name under which Led Zeppelin appeared onstage for encores at a Fairport Convention gig at LA's Troubadour in September 1970.

Black Beauty

For many years Jimmy Page's favourite guitar was a 1960 Les Paul 'Black Beauty', which he bought for £185 in 1962 and played on innumerable sessions, as well as Yardbirds and early Led Zeppelin classics. He didn't often use it live, though it featured at their famous Royal Albert Hall gig on January 9th 1970. That April, during their fifth North American tour, however, it was stolen at an airport en route from the US to Winnipeg. On July 19th 1973 an ad was placed in Rolling Stone stating 'Missing guitar. Reward for return of British musician's lost or stolen black Gibson guitar. Les

Paul Custom with Bigsby arm, #06130 with extra switches. Missing in US for about one year. No questions asked. Contact Ted Rosenblatt, 444 Madison Ave. NY…', but the instrument was never recovered. Page told the NME in October 1974: "I was starting to use it more than anything else. It got nicked off the truck at the airport – we were on our way to Canada. Somewhere there was a flight change and it disappeared. It just never arrived at the other end. I advertised for it in Rolling Stone. Just a photograph – no name – and a reward. No luck though, even though it was very recognisable for all the custom work that Joe Jammer had done on it."

Black Country Woman

This punchy acoustic track was taped in the garden at Stargroves (Mick Jagger's home) during the *Houses Of The Holy* sessions in 1972, but ended up as the penultimate song on 1975's *Physical Graffiti*. At its start engineer Eddie Kramer can be heard saying "Shall we roll it Jimmy? We're rolling on, uh, what one? No, one again… Gotta get this aeroplane off," to which Plant replies "Nah, leave it, yeah." At one stage it was sub-titled 'Never-Ending Doubting Woman Blues' (after a final spoken line from Plant, left off the album – 'What's the matter with you mama? Never-ending, nagging, doubting woman blues'), but took its final name from the common nickname for the West Midlands (owing to its industrial history), where Plant and Bonham grew up. It was played in a medley with 'Bron-Y-Aur Stomp' on the band's 1977 US tour, with Jones on upright bass.

Black Dog

The first track on the band's untitled fourth LP was built around a mighty riff devised by John Paul Jones, inspired by 'Tail Dragger' on Howlin' Wolf's *New Album* LP from 1969. As he told Mojo magazine in December 2007, it was "a blues lick that went round and round and didn't end when you thought it was going to. My dad had taught me this very easy notation system using note values and numbers, so I wrote it on a bit of paper on the train coming back from rehearsal in Jimmy's house in Pangbourne."

The song owes its title to a stray labrador that wandered in and out of Headley Grange, where the band was recording in early 1971. As Jones later recalled, "There was an old black dog around the Grange that went off to do what dogs did and came back and slept. It was quite a powerful image at the time". Plant's vocal interjections call to mind Fleetwood Mac's 'Oh Well', while the song's complicated rhythm (devised by Bonham) makes it almost impossible to cover. "We struggled with the turnaround

33

until Bonzo figured out that you could just count four-time as if there's no turnaround," explained Jones. It was released as a 45 in the US and Australia in December 1971 (backed with 'Misty Mountain Hop'), climbing to US #15 in mid-February 1972. It was a frequent feature of the band's live set for the rest of their career, with the exception of their 1977 US tour. On their final tour, 1980's 'Led Zeppelin Over Europe', the normally taciturn Page introduced the song, an unexpected development.

Black magic

"My interest in the occult started when I was 15," Jimmy Page told Gig magazine in May 1977, by which time rumours of his obsession with the dark arts had come to dominate coverage of the band – greatly to his frustration. "I do not worship the devil, but Magick does intrigue me," he continued. "Magick of all kinds. I read *Magick in Theory and Practice* when I was about 11 years old but it wasn't for some years that I understood what it was all about." Page became a considerable collector of materials relating to occultist Aleister Crowley, and opened an occult-themed bookshop named Equinox in London in 1975, but chose not to discuss his own beliefs with the press. This encouraged them to speculate wildly, and even to imply that the band's latter-day misfortunes (Plant's car accident in August 1975, the death of Plant's son Karac in July 1977, the death of engineer Keith Harwood a month later, the death of John Bonham in September 1980) were in some way attributable to his interest. As Plant told Q magazine in March 1988, "all

that crap came from Page collecting all the Crowley stuff. Page had a kind of fascination with the absurd, and Page could afford to invest in his fascination with the absurd, and that was it."

Groupie Pamela Des Barres later wrote 'I believe that Jimmy was very into black magic and probably did a lot of rituals, black candles, bat's blood, the whole thing', but her opinion was not widely held. According to road manager Richard Cole's autobiography, 'He never talked about it much with the band, and he never tried to get any of us to become believers in a particular metaphysical concept. So, even though it all seemed a little weird to us, none of us ever interfered with whatever wavelength Jimmy might be on at the moment.' The guitarist confirmed this in an interview with Rolling Stone in March 1975, stating: "I'm not interested in turning anybody on to anybody that I'm turned onto... if people want to find things, they find themselves. I'm a firm believer in that." As for claims that the band (excluding Jones) had made a pact with the devil at the outset of their career, Plant remarked to Q magazine: "The only deal I think we made was with some of the girls' high schools in San Fernando Valley."

Black Mountain Side

Adapted by Jimmy Page from the folk instrumental 'Black Waterside' for the band's debut, this instrumental gave the guitarist an early opportunity to showcase his prowess on the acoustic guitar, accompanied by Viram Jasani on tablas. "I wasn't totally original on that riff," he conceded to Guitar World magazine in 1993. "It had been done in folk clubs a lot. Annie Briggs was the first one that I heard do that riff. I was playing it as well, and then there was Bert Jansch's version." He frequently played the piece at Led Zeppelin concerts (together with 'White Summer') as a solo acoustic showcase.

Blakeshall Bashers

Kidderminster-based football team formed by Robert Plant and some local friends in the 1970s, which played regular Saturday games throughout the decade.

Blue Star Trio

The first band in which John Bonham drummed onstage, along with singer-guitarists Terry Beale and Mick Ellis. Their regular gig was Wednesday nights at Redditch Youth Club in 1963, when Bonham was fifteen.

Boleskine House

Jimmy Page's long-time Scottish retreat, bought in 1971. Located on the shores of Loch Ness, it consists of a hall, a drawing room, a dining room, a playroom, a kitchen, a utility room, five bedrooms, three bathrooms and cellars,

as well as a gate lodge and approximately 47.5 acres of land. It had been the home of Aleister Crowley from 1899 until the 1920s, accounting for the guitarist's interest in acquiring it. Page set about restoring it to the state it had been in during Crowley's tenancy, and hired self-professed satanist Charles Pace to paint murals in it. "The house was built on the site of a Kirk dating from around the 10th century that had burned down with all of its congregation inside," he told Melody Maker in September 1974. "Nobody wanted it, it was in such a state of decay. I hadn't originally intended to buy it, but it was so fascinating. It's not an unfriendly place when you walk into it. It just seems to have this thing..." In the same interview he expressed contempt for the local authorities, stating: "I was just so upset that they wanted to put pylons in this magnificent countryside, and I really got involved, doing up petitions and all that."

Nonetheless, Page never spent much time there (though his climbing sequence for *The Song Remains The Same* was filmed around the property in December 1973). Instead he installed a childhood friend, Malcolm Dent, to act as caretaker, and made it available to his friends.

"You see, people are not used to total quiet and that's what it is there," he explained to Rolling Stone on August 12th 1976. "It's a really interesting house, and a perfect place to go when one starts getting wound up by the clock. I bought it to go up and write in. The thing is that I never get up that way. Friends live there now." According to William Burroughs, writing in Crawdaddy magazine in June 1975, 'At one time the house had also been the scene of a vast chicken swindle indirectly involving George Sanders, the movie actor, who was able to clear himself of any criminal charges.' Fed up by media speculation about his motives for buying it, and by the endless stream of fans visiting it, Page sold it in the early 1990s.

see *Dent, Malcolm*

Bombay Orchestra

Robert Plant and Jimmy Page visited Bombay together in mid-February 1972, following their failure to enter Singapore (owing to their long hair). They played an impromptu gig in a club there, for which they were paid a bottle of Scotch. Both loved the experience, with Plant telling Australia's Go-Set magazine soon afterwards that "sometimes I think I'd like to live there... I find it really relaxing and I find it very near to the right way to live." Having fallen for its atmosphere, they returned in March en route home from their antipodean tour to record versions of 'Friends' and 'Four Sticks' with the Bombay Orchestra, who employed tabla drums and sitars. The collaboration is said to have come unstuck as the orchestra didn't keep time

in the Western style, and drank to excess. Plant told the NME in June 1973 that the tracks would not be released, adding: "We were just checking out, sussing how easy it would be to transpose the ideas that we've got into the musicians' minds." True to his word, the recordings have never been officially released

Bonehead

Early 1970s Midlands band featuring Robert Plant's former Band Of Joy bandmate Paul Lockey on bass. In January 1971 Record Mirror speculated that Plant would be producing their debut album, but no such project was ever undertaken.

Bonham, Jason

b. July 15th 1966

John Bonham's cherished son, whom he sat behind a miniature kit as soon as he was old enough to play. His father told Disc in June 1970 that Jason "has got his mother's looks, but in character he's just like me. He's always drumming. Even when we go out in the car he takes his sticks to bash on the seats. He hasn't got much technique, but he's got a great sense of time." In the late 1970s Jason became a scrambling / motocross fanatic, and his father proudly attended meetings of the West Mercia Schoolboy Scrambling Club, as well as sponsoring events. His drumming had come on as well – according to Jimmy Page, at a Knebworth soundcheck in August 1979 "I was onstage concentrating on the guitar, and I didn't even realise until I turned around that it was Jason playing the drums: Bonzo was out front checking the balance." By December

2007 he had evidently developed enough technique to fill his father's mighty seat at the band's 'reunion' gig, having also joined the three surviving members of Led Zeppelin at Atlantic Records' 40th anniversary concert in New York in May 1988.

Bonham, John

b. May 31st 1948 / d. Sept. 25th 1980
John Henry 'Bonzo' Bonham was born without a heartbeat after 26 hours of labour in Redditch, Worcestershire, but went on to become Led Zeppelin's drummer, as well as developing a reputation for hard living that few rock musicians have equalled.

A childhood fixation with rhythm led the young Bonham to hit anything in sight, and he was much influenced by a family friend, Charlie Atkins, who drummed in a dance band and taught him the basics of drumming, as well as giving him his first gig (at a caravan park dance when he was 11). His mother, Joan, and father, John Sr. ('Jacko'), who ran a small shop and a building business respectively, finally bought him a simple drum kit when he was 15. A write-off at Lodge Farm County Secondary School and at agricultural school, Bonham left school in 1964, apprenticed as a carpenter and began to play in local bands, going on to appear with the Blue Star Trio, Terry Webb & the Spiders (distinguished by their loud jackets), the Nicky James Movement, Steve Brett & the Mavericks, Danny King & the Mayfair Set, Pat Wayne & the Beachcombers and Locomotive. At this time he was also given encouragement by a slightly older local amateur jazz drummer, Garry Allcock, with whom he'd practise.

Aged 16 he abandoned building for work in a local gents' outfitters named Osborne's, but drummed as often as he could. His recording debut came in June 1964, with the Senators' *She's A Mod / Lot About You* 45 on the tiny Dial label (DSP 7001), but he'd soon joined the more progressive A Way Of Life and then the Crawling King Snakes, in whose ranks he befriended Robert Plant. "He was very good at leaving groups without them realising he was gone," Plant joked to Mojo magazine in October 2005. "He'd say he had to get his drums out of the van to clean them, and that would be the last you'd see of him." His early years of playing for a living were extremely lean, and when he married Pat Philips in February 1966 they initially lived with her parents on Dudley's Priory Estate, and also with his parents. With the imperative to support a child, he briefly left music for hod-carrying and factory work in 1967, and the family moved into a 15-foot caravan outside his family's home when their son Jason got a little older. He was so miserable away from music, however, that he soon abandoned other work.

The break he was waiting for finally came when US folk-rocker Tim Rose offered him a place in his band at £40 a week in June 1968, having seen him playing with the Band of Joy at the Marquee Club on February 23rd. By then Jimmy Page and Robert Plant were forming the New Yardbirds, and – at

Plant's urging – Page, Peter Grant and Chris Dreja went to watch him play with Rose at the Hampstead Country Club on July 31st. He was swiftly offered a place in Led Zeppelin at an initial £50 a week, but didn't jump at it: after years of living hand-to-mouth he was earning a regular living for the first time, and also had offers from Joe Cocker and Chris Farlowe to consider. As he told Disc on June 27th 1970, "It wasn't just a question of who had the best prospects, but which was going to be the right kind of stuff." After a blizzard of telegrams from Grant he finally agreed, allegedly offering his services as driver for an extra £30 a week.

He told Melody Maker on June 6th 1970: "When I first joined the group I didn't know Jimmy and felt a bit shy. He was the big star and had been around for ages with the session thing and the Yardbirds." John Paul Jones's impression was different – as he told Bonham's brother Mick in 2005: "The first thing to strike me about John was his confidence, and you know he was a real cocky bugger in those days." They quickly gelled, however, with Bonham's musical importance being acknowledged at once. As he went on to tell Melody Maker in November 1971, "I'm not governed by them in what I play. They ask me how a drum thing should be played, and that's the way we all work." Indeed Bonham contributed considerably to their arrangements – as Jones later stated, "He had a lot of input into the riffs we played – more than he was credited for, I'd say. He would change the whole flavour of a

piece, and lots of our numbers would start out with a drum pattern." Bonham also contributed vitally to their onstage dynamism. "I yell out when I'm playing," he told Disc in June 1970. "I yell like a bear to give it a boost."

He was quickly hailed as the world's finest rock drummer, but was dismissive of such praise, telling Melody Maker in November 1971: "I'm a simple, straight-ahead drummer and I don't pretend to be anything better than I am… There's always something another drummer can play that will knock me out. I watch all drummers in groups, and I always learn from them." He expanded on this theme to the same paper the following July, stating: "When I have a solo I don't ever imagine drummers around watching me. I don't try to impress people who play the drums. I play for people." Jones went on to assess his approach thus: "He only used a small kit, but he used to play large drums. He never played a large kit in terms of the number of drums - he only ever used four drums most of the time, and never had racks of stuff, like other people did. He could do most of what he wanted on a small amount of equipment. It didn't matter what drums they were: I'd hear him sit down on all sorts of strange drum kits and he'd immediately sound like him. It was just the way he hit them, plus an impeccable sense of timing." Bonham's own taste in music was wide, with an especial liking for US soul. His favourite drummers included legends like Gene Krupa and Joe Morello, contemporaries such as Carmine Appice, Bartholomew Smith-Frost, Ringo Starr, Keith Moon and Ginger Baker, and the cream of the next generation, including Stewart Copeland. He also enjoyed the work of contemporary artists such as Supertramp and Joni Mitchell, though punk left him cold: he famously managed to be ejected from a Damned gig in 1977, after becoming too abusive.

When the band hit big in 1969, the Bonham family moved to a flat in Eve Hill, Dudley, then a detached house in Hagley, a village east of Birmingham. They eventually settled for good at the Old Hyde, a farm in Worcestershire, where Bonham began to breed cattle. Away from the band, he also enjoyed DIY, gardening, fishing and cars. From his youth he'd had a predilection for fast driving – as his former Way Of Life bandmate Reg Jones recalled in 2001: "He drove like a maniac – whenever he borrowed his dad's van he would do handbrake skids on the gravel." When he began to earn large sums with Led Zeppelin he built up a considerable car collection, starting with a Jaguar in February 1969, to which he'd soon added a Rolls Royce, an Aston Martin, a Jensen Interceptor and a souped-up Model T Ford acquired from Jeff Beck and nicknamed 'the Boston Strangler'. As Richard Cole put it, "One day he'd turn up in a Maserati and the next day it would be a Jensen, an E-Type Jaguar or a Rolls Royce. If he'd see Tony Iommi of Black Sabbath with a new car, he'd say 'I've got to get one of those'. The car dealers in Birmingham loved him." The local magistrates were less enthusiastic: in June 1975 he was banned from driving for 6 months, just before his daughter Zoë was born. In the same year he famously tore down LA's Sunset Strip in a hot rod (alongside Mick Ralphs of Bad Company), but managed to talk his way out of the consequences when the police stopped him.

Bonham was also a familiar figure in licensed premises all over the globe. "I like people around me all the time, parties, going out and general looning," he told Disc on January 10th 1970. "I suppose I'm a bit of a noisy person – in fact, I'm probably the noisiest of the four of us... I'm still as hot-headed as ever. I'm a bit quick-tempered – I never sit down and think about things." This aspect of his personality had full play when the group was on tour, with homesickness often cited as an explanation for his boorish conduct. "Anything to do with the hotel part of touring I don't like," he told Beat Instrumental in August 1970. "It's so much easier to play in England. You get the motor out of the garage and toddle off, and you're so at ease all the time. Whereas if you're in America, you're all day in a hotel somewhere, having arguments with bloody rednecks and turdheads and everything, and then you've gotta go to the gig. And it does affect you." His boredom was closely allied to heavy drinking, leading to his drunken alter ego of 'the Beast'. Tales of his rampages are legion, and often took place in hotels or mid-air. As John Paul Jones put it, "He drank at the airport because he knew he had to get on a plane, and then when he was on the plane he'd create a bit because he was drunk. He was boisterous rather than abusive. He just got loud, so we had to calm him down." According to Richard Cole's autobiography, Bonham's japes included urinating over a disc jockey in a Japanese club from above, defecating in groupies' shoes and purses, and 'methodically demolishing his hotel suite'.

Bonham suffered from bad nerves before going onstage, and began to drink more and more heavily. By the late 1970s he had become an alcoholic, a problem compounded by heroin abuse. What was once youthful hell-raising had become aggressive and intimidating, and was described by the NME in 1980 as 'a capacity for quite malicious debauchery which would often terminate with him bursting into tears'. His taste for violence reached its nadir with the notorious 'Oakland incident' of July 1977, resulting in his arrest and subsequent conviction for assault (alongside Peter Grant, Richard Cole and John Bindon). As Bev Bevan, drummer with the Move

and a friend of Bonham's since the mid-60s, later remarked: "He was such a smashing guy when he wasn't drinking – a lovely, big, huggable, friendly sort of bloke – but when he had too much to drink he did get quite aggressive and started picking fights. He wasn't a friendly drunk – he went the opposite way". As Richard Cole put it in *Stairway To Heaven*, 'When you can play drums the way he could, people are willing to put up with a lot more crap than they would from someone with less talent.'

Perhaps chastened by the ignominious and tragic ending to the band's final US tour, in September 1977 'JH Bonham Developments' opened for business, with the intention of renovating old farms in the Worcestershire area. In all, three projects were carried out by the firm, superintended by the drummer (amidst much merriment). His other major preoccupation in the late 70s was watching his son taking part in motocross / scrambling events (a floral tribute in the shape of a motorbike was sent to his funeral). He was more than usually nervous in the run-up to the band's 1980 European tour, and his normally sturdy constitution wasn't as reliable as it had once been: he collapsed at Nuremberg's Messezentrumhalle on June 27th 1980, falling off his stool fifteen minutes into the performance, after eating an estimated 27 bananas. By the summer of 1980 he was attempting to get his substance abuse under control, and remained a devoted family man. "The last time I saw him [in July 1980] he was packing up little dolls he had collected from different countries for his daughter, Zoë," Bad Company drummer Simon Kirke later reminisced. "So this image of the wild man eating maids for breakfast was wiped out." Bonham spent the whole of that August on holiday with his family in the south of France, before returning invigorated and looking forward to the band's forthcoming US tour. He is thought to have conquered his heroin problem, though he was still drinking heavily.

He spent the morning of Wednesday, September 24th washing and polishing his cars at the Old Hyde, before his assistant, Rex King, turned up at lunchtime to take him to rehearsals at Bray Studios, after which he was to stay at Jimmy Page's new home nearby in Windsor, The Old Mill House. They stopped en route at the local Chequers pub for lunch, and Bonham downed four quadruple vodkas. Plant joined him for the drive to the studios, and later recalled him seeming downcast about his drumming abilities: "We were driving in his car, and he pulled off the sun visor and threw it out of the window as he was talking. He said, 'I tell you what, when we get to the rehearsal, you play the drums and I'll sing'. And that was our last rehearsal."

His drinking continued all afternoon and evening – over a 12-hour period he had consumed an estimated forty measures of vodka, as well as ham rolls, three pizzas and a curry – and around midnight he nodded off on a sofa. In a stupor, he was carted off to bed in a guest room by Page's assistant, Rick Hobbs, who positioned him on his side, supported by pillows. When he still hadn't surfaced by the next afternoon (a Thursday), John Paul Jones and Plant's assistant Benji Le Fevre went to rouse him and found him dead. He was 32.

On October 8th the East Berkshire coroner, Robert Wilson, ruled it an accidental death due to pulmonary oedema, 'due to consumption of alcohol'. His funeral was held on October 10th in St Michael's Church in the nearby parish of Rushock. It was attended by fellow Midlands musicians including Roy Wood, Denny Laine, Bev Bevan and Jeff Lynne, with wreaths from drummers Carl Palmer, Phil Collins, Carmine Appice and Cozy Powell, as well as Paul McCartney. Bevan later stated: "His wife and family were utterly distraught. There was much weeping. The church was jammed, and there were so many people outside. It was very, very sad." Bonham's body was cremated at Worcester Crematorium, and his ashes were buried in Rushock. His headstone reads: 'Cherished memories of a loving husband and father / John Henry Bonham / Who died September 25th 1980 aged 32 years / He will always be remembered in our hearts / Goodnight, my love, God bless'.

Following his death, the band went to Jersey and unanimously decided not to continue. Upon their return they had tea at London's Savoy hotel with Peter Grant, who concurred, and on December 4th 1980 the following statement was released: "We wish it to be known that the loss of our dear friend, and the deep respect we have for his family together with the sense of undivided harmony felt by ourselves and our manager, have led us to decide that we could not continue as we were."

Bonham, John Henry Sr.

Known as 'Jacko', John Bonham's father bought him his first drum kit when he was fifteen. The drummer later described it as 'almost prehistoric. Most of it was rust'. Jacko worked for his own father's building business, giving his son early employment, and eventually moving to his farm, the Old Hyde, whose cottage he occupied. He died in 1989.

Bonham, Mick

b. 1951 / d. Jan 14th 2000

John Bonham's younger brother, and the author of the 2005 volume *John Bonham: The Powerhouse Behind Led Zeppelin*. In the 1970s he was employed by his famous sibling (who was frequently generous to him) on a variety of building and maintenance projects at the family farm, the Old Hyde, in Worcestershire. Though he loved and respected him, the drummer's violent temper prompted periods of estrangement in the 1970s. Mick later worked as a DJ and photographer.

Bonham, Pat

b. Feb 24th 1948

Born Pat Philips, John Bonham's wife since February 19th 1966. "After all we've gone through, our marriage should survive anything," the drummer told Disc on January 10th 1970. They met at a dance in Kidderminster's Old Hill Plaza club in 1965, and married soon afterwards, when she was already several months pregnant with their son Jason (Bonham spent his stag night watching the Move play at the Railway pub in Kings Heath). Led Zeppelin provided the entertainment at her 21st birthday party in Wolverhampton's Lafayette Club in February 1969, and though she largely stayed away from the rock world she did inspire 'Pat's Delight', the lengthy drum excursion that was eventually recorded as 'Moby Dick'. The couple had two children, Jason (b. 1966) and Zoë (b. 1975). "Underneath all the brash bravado and all that stuff, he was very reliant on Pat," Robert Plant told Mojo magazine in October 2005. "They fought like cats and dogs, but they loved each other tremendously."

Bonham, Zoe

b. June 10th 1975

John Bonham's only daughter. The drummer opted not to go into tax exile with his bandmates in order to be present at her birth, commenting: "There was no way, for any money in the world, I was going to go away. I wanted to stay at home, and missed out as far as the last tour was concerned." She is now a singer-songwriter.

Bonzo

Nickname by which John Bonham was universally known throughout Led Zeppelin's career.

Bonzo's Montreux

Percussion blowout recorded by John Bonham and Jimmy Page in Mountain Studios, Montreux, in September 1976, engineered by John Timperly. The collaboration quickly gave rise to rumours of a Bonham solo LP, but in fact the track went unreleased until 1982's posthumous *Coda* compilation, where it was credited to the 'John Bonham Drum Orchestra'.

Boogie With Stu

Recorded at Headley Grange in early 1971 as part of the sessions for the band's untitled fourth LP, this playful jam ended up on 1975's *Physical Graffiti* and may have been originally titled 'Sloppy Drunk'. It's based on Ritchie Valens's 'Ooh, My Head' (itself an adaptation of Little Richard's 'Ooh, My Soul') and took its name from Ian 'Stu' Stewart, the pianist and 'sixth Rolling Stone', who was on hand at the time. Over an odd slapping rhythm from Bonham, Page plays mandolin as Stewart lays down flowing barrelhouse piano. It has even been rumoured that Plant plays guitar on the track. Initially considered a throwaway, when it was dusted down for inclusion on *Physical Graffiti* a co-writing credit was given to Valens's mother. As Page explained, "What we tried to do was give Ritchie's mother credit, because we heard she never received any royalties from any of her son's hits, and Robert did lean on that lyric a bit. So what happens? They tried to sue us for all of the song! We had to say bugger off." The band never performed it live.

Bootlegs

Led Zeppelin, and Peter Grant in particular, fought a constant battle against bootleggers, or suspected bootleggers. The band's rise coincided neatly with the growth of the home-taping industry, however, and a flood of cheaply-packaged LPs appeared almost as soon as the band reached the top in 1969. Part of the allure of such recordings was the band's fault, it can be argued: they not only starved fans of TV appearances and singles, but (often as part of onstage medleys) also performed songs that weren't on official LPs. Jimmy Page was, at least in the short term, fairly ambivalent about bootlegs, as he enjoyed listening to them himself. What he objected to, however, was their expense in view of their poor quality. Peter Grant was implacably opposed, however, and is known to have had bootleggers' equipment destroyed during gigs. On one memorable occasion in Vancouver in August 1971 he mistook a noise pollution expert (working for the Canadian government) for a bootlegger and had his $2500 sound monitor smashed (earning himself a 12-month ban from the country in the process). He is also known to have visited shops carrying bootlegs to remonstrate in person with their owners. It wasn't only concert bootlegs he was on the lookout for, either: as he told Melody Maker of October 10th 1970, "I've often been very unpopular with engineers because I always insist that tapes come away from the studio after all our sessions. That cuts down the risk." In the aftermath of the band's career, however, bootlegs came to be an invaluable source of information about the band's live history. "I've heard some dreadful bootlegs, but then I've heard some good ones," John Paul Jones told Blow By Blow magazine in 1992. "I think there's a place for them."

Boston Tea Party

Legendary rock venue in Massachusetts in which the band played a legendary residency between January 23rd and 26th 1969, thereby setting the seal on their reputation in America. "We played for hours," John Paul Jones later recalled. "We did old Beatles numbers, Chuck Berry, anything. It was the greatest night. We knew we had definitely done it by then." Rihard Cole concurred, writing in *Stairway To Heaven*: 'If any doubt still existed about the power of Zeppelin, it vanished at the end of January at the Boston Tea Party."

Bray Studios

Film studios that served as the venue for the band's Knebworth rehearsals for three weeks in June and July 1979. In the fierce summer heat, they worked up a variety of old and new numbers, as well as rehearsing 'Wearing And Tearing' ahead of its possible release as a 45. It was also used for technical rehearsals, and for the filming of numerous promotional video clips.

Bredon, Anne

American folk singer who wrote 'Babe I'm Gonna Leave You' in the 1950s. As such she has latterly been credited on Led Zeppelin's version, though it is not especially reminiscent of the original, owing more to Joan Baez's interpretation.

Bring It On Home

Adapted from a Willie Dixon song made famous by Sonny Boy Williamson, this closes *Led Zeppelin II*. Starting as an eerie psychedelic blues, it later veers into violent hard rock powered by a typically meaty Page riff, and gave the guitarist and John Bonham a chance to duel onstage in 1969 and 1970. The song also offers Plant a rare showcase for his harmonica playing skills.

Brittle, Phil

Respected drummer on the West Midlands circuit who was reportedly considered by Robert Plant for inclusion in the New Yardbirds in mid-1968, when it seemed that John Bonham would be joining Joe Cocker's band.

Bron-Y-Aur Stomp

Driven by Plant and inspired by the time he and Page spent at Bron-Yr-Aur in 1970, this rollicking, folk / country tune appears on *Led Zeppelin III* (where its title was misspelt). It was first attempted by the band in late 1969 as an instrumental entitled 'Jennings Farm Blues', with a tune bearing similarities to 'The Waggoner's Lad' by Bert Jansch (which opened his 1966 LP *Jack Orion*). Its lyrics pay tribute to Plant's blue-eyed Merle dog, Stryder. Bonham plays spoons and castanets behind Page's flowing acoustic guitar work on the recording, which is lighter-hearted than much of the band's work. It was featured onstage from 1971-73, at Earl's Court in May 1975 and on their 1977 US tour.

Bron-Yr-Aur (place)

Simple 18th Century cottage on the River Dovey, outside Machynlleth in Gwynedd, Wales, in which numerous Led Zeppelin classics were written by Robert Plant and Jimmy Page in May and October 1970.

44

Plant had spent happy childhood holidays in the stone-walled cottage (whose name means 'golden hill' or 'golden breast' in Welsh), and revealed his plan to return there with Page to Melody Maker that March. By the end of their fifth US tour on April 18th the band was unassailably the world's biggest rock act, but they were also exhausted.

"After the intense touring that had been taking place through the first two albums, working almost 24 hours a day, basically, we managed to stop and have a proper break, a couple of months as opposed to a couple of weeks," Page told Trouser Press in October 1977. "We decided to go off and rent a cottage to provide a contrast to motel rooms." As Plant told *Rolling Stone* in 1975, "it was time to step back, take stock, and not get lost in it all. Zeppelin was starting to get very big, and we wanted the rest of our journey to take a pretty level course. Hence the trip into the mountains and the beginning of the ethereal Page and Plant."

Joining them were Maureen and Carmen Plant, the family's blue-eyed Merle dog Stryder, Page's French girlfriend Charlotte Martin and roadies Clive Coulson and Sandy MacGregor. The house was only accessible via fields (negotiated in a yellow ex-army jeep), and had no central heating, running water or indoor lavatory – the party was obliged to visit the Glyndwr Hotel in Machynlleth if they wanted a bath. "It was freezing when we arrived," Coulson told Mojo magazine in April 2000. "We collected wood for the open-hearth fire, which heated a range with an oven on either side. We had candles and I think there were gaslights. We fetched water from a stream and heated it on the hot plates for washing." Nonetheless, Page and Plant thoroughly enjoyed themselves. Plant told Uncut magazine in May 2008 that "There was no electricity, outside toilets, the smell of woodsmoke and alcohol. I don't think we even smoked dope then," while Page has commented: "It was the first time I really came to know Robert. Actually living together at Bron-Yr-Aur, as opposed to occupying nearby hotel rooms."

The duo went on long walks together, carrying tape recorders, and had a couple of memorable encounters – one when they had to deny their identities when recognised by some local lads restoring an old house, and again when a rowdy group of youths were roaring around on motorbikes one evening. Nights were spent mellowing by the fire, drinking cider heated by warm pokers and recharging their tape machines' batteries by grilling them. As Plant told Blender magazine in 2002, "They'd just invented the cassette machine with speakers, so during the sexual act – with the women, not the dog – we could play the tape really loud." Page's daughter Scarlett was even conceived there, shortly after 'That's The Way' was written (or so Plant claimed onstage in 1994).

They didn't go there specifically to write songs, but it the atmosphere did prove conducive to creativity. As Page told ZigZag magazine in November 1972, "Though it wasn't planned as a working holiday, some songs did come out of it". These are thought to include 'Hey, Hey, What Can I Do?' (a non-LP B-side), 'Friends', 'Celebration Day', 'That's The Way', 'Bron-Y-Aur Stomp' and 'Hats Off To (Roy) Harper' (all of which appeared on their next LP, Led Zeppelin III), as well as 'Over The Hills And Far Away' and 'The Crunge' (which showed up on Houses Of The Holy in 1973). Upon leaving the cottage, the band entered Headley Grange for a month (as of May 18th) to record the songs they had been working on at the cottage. They returned to Bron-Yr-Aur at the end of October to work on further material, including 'The Rover' and 'Down By The Seaside' (which ended up on Physical Graffiti in 1975) and 'Poor Tom' (which only saw the light of day posthumously on 1982's Coda compilation).

Looking back on their time there, Plant told Mojo magazine in June 2004: "No matter how cute and comical it might be now to look back at, it gave us so much energy, because we were really close to something. We believed. It was absolutely wonderful, and my heart was so light and happy. At that time, at that age, 1970 was like the biggest blue sky I ever saw." Contrary to popular belief, the cottage was never owned by Plant. It was bought in 1972 by the Reverend John Dale, who is not a fan of the band. "We've had more than one break-in and once a photograph was taken near the fireplace and posted on the web," he told the BBC website in December 2007. "It is a beautiful place, but people must remember that it is a private house surrounded by private farmland, although there is a footpath at the top of the field behind the house."

Bron-Yr-Aur (song)
This pretty acoustic instrumental appears on 1975's Physical Graffiti, but was originally recorded during the Led Zeppelin III sessions in 1970. It only features Jimmy Page, and is a tribute to the Welsh cottage in which he and Plant penned several Led Zeppelin classics in May and June of that year. At just over two minutes, it is the band's shortest studio recording, and

was rarely performed live, though it was occasionally incorporated into the acoustic section of their set on their sixth US tour in August and September 1970. It can also be heard briefly as background music in their 1976 film, *The Song Remains The Same.*

Browne, Carole

Peter Grant's secretary and the manager of Swan Song's UK office (484 King's Road, London SW10) in the 1970s. Having run the Walker Brothers' fan club and worked for the Beatles at Apple, she met Peter Grant through her previous employer, Don Arden. She went on to work in a general capacity at RAK Music Management for acts including Jeff Beck, Terry Reid, Stone the Crows and Rory Gallagher. For Led Zeppelin her jobs ranged from general admin to house-hunting for Jimmy Page, but devoted the majority of her time to putting off the many callers wishing to communicate with Grant.

Brumbeat

Name given to a short-lived music industry hype centred on Birmingham in 1964. John Bonham made his recording debut with the Senators on an obscure compilation also entitled *Brumbeat* (Dial DLP1, 1964), contributing the track 'She's A Mod', penned by his bandmate Terry Beale. Also appearing on the LP were the Crescendos, the Shakes, the Grasshoppers, the Solitaires, the Fortunes, the Sinners and the Renegades. Though Brumbeat didn't catch on, the city did eventually yield the Moody Blues, the Spencer Davis Group and the Move.

Burroughs, William

b. Feb. 15th 1914 / d. Aug. 2nd 1997
American 'beat' writer who memorably interviewed Jimmy Page for the June 1975 issue of Crawdaddy magazine, having first attended a Led Zeppelin gig ('There was a palpable interchange of energy between the performers and the audience which was never frantic or jagged'). Their conversation took place at Burroughs' apartment in New York's Franklin Street and over dinner at the city's Mexican Gardens, and touched on magic, Scotland, film-making, stage effects and various other abstruse topics. "We had a lengthy discussion on the hypnotic power of rock, and how it paralleled the music of Arabic cultures," Page told Guitar World magazine in 1993. "This was an observation Burroughs had made after hearing 'Black Mountain Side', from our first album. He then encouraged me to go to Morocco and investigate the music first hand, something Robert and I eventually did."

Bush, Mel

Veteran UK live promoter who put on the band's legendary run at London's Earl's Court in 1975. Peter Grant later commented: "Mel Bush did a great job with those dates and Earls Court was fantastic. Nobody sat behind the stage. We had the video screen and the whole Showco stage set up. It took half a jumbo jet to get it over. Mel Bush did a super job in presenting those gigs. He presented us with souvenir mirrors afterwards, depicting the 'Physical Rocket' idea used for the advertising."

Butterfield Court

Twenty-storey tower block in Dudley (in the UK's West Midlands) that can be seen on the back cover of the band's untitled fourth LP.

By Invitation Only

Double album of Atlantic tracks nominally compiled by UK DJ Alan 'Fluff' Freeman in 1976 (as Atlantic K60112), containing Led Zeppelin's 'Whole Lotta Love' and 'Immigrant Song', as well as tracks by the Rolling Stones, Buffalo Springfield, Yes and others.

see *The Summit / Supertracks*

and you would know that through thick and thin he would fight with you all of the way… If you were his friend, then to you he would give his all."

Candy Store Rock

Short, 1950s rock and roll-influenced track included on the band's 1976 *Presence* album, with lyrics supposedly inspired by numerous Elvis Presley songs. It was written quickly whist the band was in Munich's Musicland Studios in late 1975, and Robert Plant has said it is one of his favourite Led Zeppelin tracks. It was released as a 45 in the US in June 1976 (backed with Royal Orleans, as Swan Song SS 70110), but failed to chart and the band never played it live.

Caesar's Chariot

45-seat Boeing 707 aeroplane owned by Caesars Palace Hotel in Las Vegas and chartered by the band for their 1977 US tour (following the grounding of the Starship). According to journalist Steven Rosen, 'the plane is fitted with huge, overstuffed-chair type seating. There is also a bar and private rooms for each member.'

Callan, Alan

Old friend of Jimmy Page's who served as Peter Grant's vice-president of Swan Song in the UK from 1977 to 1983. As well as overseeing the label's existing acts, he made efforts to sign artists including John Lennon and Vangelis. He went on tour with the band four times, and later commented that they were "like four medieval princes cavorting across Europe, indulging their every whim". In December 1995 he delivered the eulogy at Grant's funeral, stating: "His greatness was that he was a man of many parts. He was as adept at the ominous glance as he was at the disarming remark. He was a man whose mythology was a never ending treasure trove to the story teller in each of us. He could engage you in the greatest conspiratorial friendship

Car accidents

The band had been involved in several car accidents before Robert Plant's near-fatal crash in August 1975 (see *Rhodes*). Page had to miss a presentation from the Board of Trade at the Savoy in December 1969 owing to a car accident en route on the M4. On February 1st 1970 Plant and his wife Maureen were injured in Kidderminster when their Jaguar collided with another vehicle on their way home from a Spirit concert in Birmingham. Plant suffered cuts and bruises, but chose only to stay in hospital overnight. As a result a gig in Edinburgh that weekend had to be cancelled, and Page told Melody Maker three weeks later: "He's still in a bad way and we had to cancel some work, though he said he would appear onstage in a wheelchair. He can't raise his arm above his shoulder and has a cut above his eye." At home that June, an Aston

Martin Plant had jacked-up while he worked beneath it fell onto him, bruising his ribs, and in January 1973 a Bentley in which Plant and Bonham were travelling to a gig in Sheffield broke down, forcing them to hitch-hike the rest of the way (and causing Plant to catch flu, and thus postpone gigs in Preston and Bradford). In June 1975 Bonham lost his licence for six months, but it did little to curb his appetite for speed: Melody Maker reported on August 20th 1977 that he had been hospitalised with two broken ribs after crashing a car near his home in Kidderminster.

Carlo, Phil

Road manager for Bad Company who was drafted in to do the honours for Led Zeppelin's European tour in 1980 (along with Rod Stewart roadie Billy Francis) when Richard Cole was deemed unfit for the task, owing to his drug addiction. As Grant told *Tight But Loose* in 1993: "He had a massive problem, so I thought the only way to shake him up was to blow him out."

Carnegie Hall

Prestigious New York concert venue, in which Led Zeppelin played two celebrated shows at the end of October 1969. Plant told the NME soon afterwards: "It was a prestige thing for us to play Carnegie Hall, because you have to wait until you're asked to play at the Hall by a committee that runs the place." Though both dates were instant sell-outs, the management was reportedly concerned at the possible ravages of their fans, as was the Royal Albert Hall in London.

Gary Carnes

Showco's lighting chief, who had a bird's eye view of every show on the band's 1977 US tour. He later claimed that he'd overheard muttered exchanges between Page and Plant: "Quite often Robert would announce a song and Jimmy would go, 'Robert, how does that go?' And Robert would sort of turn around and hum it to him. And Jimmy would go, 'Oh yeah, oh yeah, I got it, I got it.' Or Robert would announce a song and Jimmy would go into the wrong song... it was very, very rare, but it did happen."

Carouselambra

Lengthy progressive-styled song that opens side two of 1979's *In Through The Out Door*. It was conceived at the band's May 1978 rehearsals at Clearwell Castle, and is dominated by Jones's synthesizer work, meaning that Page plays an uncharacteristically modest part in it. Plant's vocals are also unusually low in the mix, causing him to tell Mojo magazine in May 2004: "I rue it so much now, because the lyrics on 'Carouselambra' were actually about that environment and that situation. The whole story of Led Zeppelin in its latter years is in that song... and I can't hear the words!" The band never played it live.

Carpenter, Karen

b. March 2nd 1950 / d. Feb. 4th 1983
Carpenters drummer who was placed higher than John Bonham in Playboy's 1975 music poll, much to his disgust. As he fumed to the NME that February: "She couldn't last ten minutes with a Led Zeppelin number."

Carry On Columbus
Released in 1992, this amazingly bad late entry in the British comedy film series features a cameo from Peter Grant as a cardinal.

Carson, Phil
Former bass player with the Springfields who became General European Manager for Atlantic Records from October 1969. Soon afterwards he inadvertently became responsible for one of the band's leading rarities, by approving the pressing of 500 copies of the UK 'Whole Lotta Love' 45, which were apparently shipped to Manchester before Peter Grant got wind of the fact. Carson was the executive who worked closest with the band from their earliest days with the label, even joining them onstage for an encore of 'Summertime Blues' in Dublin on March 6th 1971, and again (on bass) for Barrett Strong's 'Money' at Frankfurt's Festhalle on June 30th 1980. He also went on tour with them from time to time, accompanying them to Japan in 1971, for example (and being abandoned naked in the lobby of the Tokyo Hilton for his pains). He was often the butt of the band's jokes, including having bills for exotic expenses sent to him care of Atlantic's offices. Grant later commented that Carson "sometimes took too much of the limelight. Phil went blabbing a bit too much." Nonetheless, he went on to a successful career in management himself, with clients including Jimmy Page's mid-80s act The Firm.

Cartoone
Scottish pop band formed in 1967, who signed to Atlantic shortly after Led Zeppelin in late 1968 and whose sole album (Atlantic SD 8219, May 1969) featured guitar support from Jimmy Page. They were managed by Peter Grant's sometime partner Mark London, and flew to the US to support Led Zeppelin in April and June 1969, but their chart-orientated sound did not go over well with audiences, and when their album failed to sell they were dropped by the label.

Cattini, Clem
b. Aug. 28th 1937
Prolific session drummer briefly considered for a place in the New Yardbirds' in 1968. Unfortunately he was too busy to attend the relevant meeting with Peter Grant, and the opportunity had soon gone.

Celebration Day
Uplifting hard rock song included on *Led Zeppelin III*. It begins with a sinister swirling effect (provided by a Moog synthesizer), included to mask damage accidentally done to the start of the recording on the master tape. As Page explained to Guitar World in 1993, "I forget what we were recording, but I was listening through the headphones and nothing was coming through. I started yelling 'What the hell is going on?!' Then I noticed that the red recording light was on what used to be the drums. The engineer had accidently recorded over Bonzo! And that is why you have that synthesizer drone from the end of 'Friends' going into 'Celebration Day', until the rhythm track catches up." The song concerns Plant's initial impressions

of New York, and was occasionally introduced by him onstage as 'the New York song'. The band played it live throughout late 1971 and 1972, and were still throwing it in as late as their Knebworth gigs in 1979.

Chevry, Bernard
b. 1922

Organiser of MIDEM, the music industry's annual conference in Cannes, France. He came a cropper in January 1972 when he wrote to Peter Grant informing him that 'the artist committee for the gala evenings organised by [MIDEM] has selected Led Zeppelin and his musicians to participate in an International Groups Night... of course, Led Zeppelin and his group would be our guests during their stay in Cannes'. Grant was so tickled by this that he reproduced it as a full page ad in trade publication Record Retailer on January 15th (the week of the conference), headlined 'Mr. Zeppelin Regrets...'

Chislehurst Caves

22-mile long network of tunnels that were used as a music venue in the late 60s (acts that performed there included David Bowie, Jimi Hendrix and Pink Floyd) and which served as the venue for the launch party for the Pretty Things' first Swan Song LP, *Silk Torpedo*, on Halloween night 1974. The bash was attended by all Swan Song artists (Led Zeppelin, Maggie Bell, Bad Company) as well as random celebrities including Adam Faith (a neighbour of Jones's), George Melly and Peter Wyngarde. Peter Grant sported a sailor's cap for the occasion, and guests feasted on venison

and mulled wine as they were entertained by Bob Kerr's Whoopee Band and John Chilton's Feetwarmers (to say nothing of jelly-wrestling nuns), before a food fight broke out. According to Howard Mylett's 1976 book *Led Zeppelin*: 'The candles filling the caves flickered as old movies were projected onto the walls; sword-swallowers and fire-eaters lined the cave, and slides of ancient paintings were projected onto another wall, where inebriated 'nuns' roamed around. No one there could ever forget it.'

The event had an important resonance for the band, too. Having spent much of 1974 resting, without playing any concerts or releasing any new material, they met at the party for the first time in months. As Plant told the NME in February 1975: "At that Chislehurst Caves function I realised I really missed the unity of the four of us. I realised that above everything else, above record companies, above films, we were Led Zeppelin – above everything. From that moment on we started rehearsing and getting into full gear."

Chkiantz, George

Engineer who worked on *Houses Of The Holy*, and was also responsible for recording the band's 1979 Knebworth shows, using the Rolling Stones' mobile studio.

Christian, Dick

Jersey-based lawyer who had Robert Plant to stay in the summer of 1975, when the singer was in tax exile and recovering from his car accident on Rhodes. According to Richard Cole,

'Christian was a thoroughly cordial host. He was a tall, middle-aged man with blond hair and glasses... he made us feel as though we could stay as long as we wanted.' When it was time for the band to fly to Malibu and rehearse for the *Presence* album, Cole continues, 'Dick genuinely seemed sad we were leaving. To show our gratitude, Peter had engraved the names of Dick's children on Led Zeppelin gold records, and gave them to the kids as gifts.'

Christian, Neil
b. Feb. 4th 1943

Born Christopher Tidmarsh, this singer heard the young Jimmy Page playing in a local hall in Surrey in 1959, and swiftly offered him a job at £15 a week (once Page's father had agreed). "His parents wanted him to stay on at school and not leave for some rock and roll band, but I talked them into it," Christian told Disc on November 17th 1973. Together they formed Neil Christian and the Crusaders, the first professional combo Page played in. Christian later remembered Page as "a nice kid, quiet, shy, well brought-up". The band largely played Chuck Berry, Gene Vincent and Bo Diddley covers, and their hectic touring in 1960-61 took a toll on Page's health. As he told ZigZag magazine in November 1972, "all the travelling to one-nighter gigs made me ill – I used to get sick in the van." He'd departed by the time their debut 45, 'The Road To Love' (produced by the eccentric Joe Meek), appeared in November 1962. As Page told the NME in October 1974, "it was just disheartening to go up to, say, Rushden or somewhere like that, and find ten people having a punch-up."

Soon afterwards Christian moved to the continent and played mainly in France for a couple of years. By April 1966 he was back in the UK, with a #14 hit single out on the tiny Strike label, 'That's Nice'. "I've just reformed the Crusaders with Jimmy Page on lead guitar," he told *Melody Maker* on April 30th, but this proved to be wishful thinking – on June 25th the paper's front page announced that Page had become a Yardbird.

Clapton, Eric
b. March 30th 1945

Alongside Jimmy Page and Jeff Beck, arguably the UK's leading electric guitarist of the 1960s, and a founding member of the Yardbirds. He'd known Page since the early 60s, when they were both regulars at clubs such as the Marquee, the Flamingo and the Ricky Tick. Page later said of that time "Eric and I became very close, I think. We got on very well and we used to go out and have dinner. We talked about a variety of subjects... Eric was concentrating solely on blues guitarists in those days, whereas I was and still am interested in other types of music." In 1965 Andrew Oldham, manager of the Rolling Stones and co-founder of Immediate Records, suggested to Page that he collaborate with Clapton on a blues album, which Page would produce. He agreed, so the duo rehearsed and laid down four tracks - 'Telephone Blues', 'I'm Your Witch Doctor', 'Sittin' On Top Of The World' and 'Double Crossin' Time'.

When Clapton signed to Decca as part of John Mayall's Bluesbreakers shortly afterwards, Immediate demanded that

Page surrender all tapes the duo had made together while under contract to Immediate, including home rehearsals of tracks including 'Miles Road', 'Freight Loader', 'Choker', 'Draggin' My Tail', 'West Coast Idea', 'Tribute To Elmore and 'Snake Drive', with the idea of releasing them as an album and on compilations. No royalties were paid, and – as Page put it – "Immediate hustled together those albums. I was really embarrassed. I think that everyone thought that I had been somehow responsible. Of course, I wasn't."

Either way, the incident soured the friendship between the guitarists, though Page never lost respect for Clapton, telling the NME in April 1969 that "I don't play anything like Eric. I am nowhere near as good. I am still learning." Clapton, meanwhile, told Australian rock journalist Ritchie Yorke in early 1970 that he thought Led Zeppelin "were very loud – I thought it was unnecessarily loud. I liked some of it, I really did like some of it. But a lot of it was just too much. They over-emphasised whatever point they were making, I thought." In January of the same year Page had embarked on a long affair with Charlotte Martin, who had been Clapton's girlfriend in the late 1960s.

Clarke, Arthur C.
b. Dec. 16th 1917 / d. March 19th 2008
Fantasy novelist, the ending of whose 1953 novel *Childhood's End* served as inspiration for the *Houses Of The Holy* artwork, conceived and designed by Hipgnosis.

Clearwell Castle
Following three days of meetings in London in mid-March 1978, it was agreed that the band should ease into playing again, following the death of Plant's son Karac the previous July. This mock-Gothic pile in the Forest of Dean served as the location for their tentative May 1978 rehearsals, ahead of the *In Through The Out Door* sessions. "It was Bonzo that brought me back to piece together something that became *In Through The Out Door*," Plant told Mojo magazine in October 2005. "He worked on me. Until then, all I was doing was parading around with a shotgun and a bottle of Johnnie Walker, trying to shoot at the press." As well as jamming, the band wrote songs including 'Carouselambra' there and recorded demos (using bluesman John Mayall's mobile studio) which have subsequently been bootlegged.

Clifton, Peter
b. 1945
Sydney-born film-maker who took over the troubled *Song Remains The Same* project from Joe Massot in March 1974. A seasoned director of pop shorts and promo films, he'd first met Jimmy Page and Peter Grant in 1970, when he was considered as editor for the footage Stanley Dorfman had shot at their Albert Hall gig. Four years later, en route to Jamaica with his family, he was summoned to Swan Song's office in the King's Road and offered the *Song Remains The Same* job. He was promised artistic freedom and an equal share of the film's copyright to Grant and the band members (equating to

17%), but was refused a contract. He prepared a report for the band, and his suggestions (including extensive reshoots of Massot's concert footage) were accepted. All seemed well, but the honeymoon was brief. Synching the film was nightmarish, and cutting together coherent live sequences proved almost impossible. Clifton did manage to marshal the band at Shepperton Studios in the summer of 1975 for some secretive reshoots of concert footage, and later claimed that he'd also had to film Page's nocturnal climbing segment again because the guitarist was worried that his backside looked too large in Massot's version.

By 1975, however, the band had largely lost interest in the project, so calls began to go unreturned and meetings were frequently cancelled. Frustration soon rotted Clifton's enthusiasm for working with Grant and Page. "The pair of them turned breaking appointments into an art form," he later griped. "They did just whatever they wanted at whatever time of day... Peter had created this incredible aura around them, which partially obscured the fact that they were all *arseholes!*" In fairness, Clifton was quick to exclude Jones from that judgement, but he was fast running out of patience in any case. A row over his use of a limo in LA prompted the paranoid Grant to have Clifton's London home searched in his absence (in case he had squirreled away any footage), and after the premiere he had nothing more to do with the band. A final insult came when his name was left off the publicity materials, and Clifton

later concluded that the band and Grant were 'the rudest, most arrogant and inhumane people I ever encountered in my 25 years of filming music'.

A Clockwork Orange

1962 novel by Anthony Burgess, filmed by Stanley Kubrick in 1971. It centres on the exploits of one Alex and his band of 'droogs', vicious thugs who thrive on sex and violence. On Led Zeppelin's 1975 US tour, John Bonham took to performing and socialising in their distinctive uniform of a white boiler suit and bowler hat.

Cocker, Joe

b. May 20th 1944

British soul belter who offered John Bonham a place in his band shortly before the drummer was invited to join Led Zeppelin. Cocker's June 1969 debut album, *With A Little Help From My Friends* (Regal Zonophone SLRZ 1006), featured guitar playing from Jimmy Page on five tracks. These were recorded in London shortly before Led Zeppelin formed.

Coda

Retrospective collection of out-takes that appeared in November 1982, to fulfil the band's contract with Atlantic. According to Jimmy Page in the August 2004 edition of Mojo magazine, shortly before John Bonham's death the two musicians had agreed that the next Led Zeppelin LP would be more "hard-hitting and riff-based" than *In Through The Out Door*, in whose genesis they had played a smaller part than Plant and Jones.

Sadly, no new music was ever recorded by the band. Instead they agreed with Atlantic's Ahmet Ertegun that if the album Page compiled was sub-standard, then the deal would be abandoned. As it was, however, enough decent material was salvaged to present an interesting postscript to their career. There was another motivation too, as Page later confirmed: "*Coda* was released, basically, because there was so much bootleg stuff out. We thought, 'Well, if there's that much interest, then we may as well put the rest of our studio stuff out'."

Its working title was 'Early Days And Latter Days', but John Paul Jones suggested 'Coda' (meaning the final section of a piece of music). It purported to span recordings made between June 1969 and late 1978, though the extent to which Page tampered with the tapes and added overdubs has never been clear. It opens with 'We're Gonna Groove', supposedly recorded in June 1969, though its similarity to the band's performance of the song at the Albert Hall on January 9th 1970 has been commented upon. 'I Can't Quit You Baby' was certainly taken from the Albert Hall gig, but may have been edited to sound like a soundcheck recording (as claimed in the original artwork). 'Poor Tom' is a leftover from the *Led Zeppelin III* sessions. Closing side one is 'Walter's Walk', from the 1972 *Houses Of The Holy* sessions, though Plant's vocal was in fact recorded at Page's Sol Studios in early 1982, owing to the changed timbre of his voice.

Side two features three out-takes from the *In Through The Out Door* sessions, 'Ozone Baby', 'Darlene' and 'Wearing and Tearing'. The latter had been mooted for release as a 45 in August 1979, as a souvenir of the band's Knebworth shows, though time constraints caused the plan to be abandoned. 'Bonzo's Montreux' is a recording made by Page and Bonham in Switzerland in August 1976, with electronic effects added by the guitarist. The album's overall running time was little over thirty minutes, and its outer artwork was sober, though the inside of the gatefold sleeve showed a plethora of photographs of the band throughout their career. It was released in November 1982. Publicity was muted, in contrast to previous Led Zeppelin releases, and sales were commensurately lower. It reached #4 in the UK that December and #6 in the US, but wasn't in the charts for long.

Cole, Richard
b. Jan 2nd 1946

Generally known as 'Ricardo', this controversial individual served as the band's road (and later tour) manager throughout their career. Born in London's Kensal Rise, Cole worked as a scaffolder and a boxer, as well as a fashion designer (briefly). A dedicated mod by night, he found work as a roadie for Ronnie Jones & the Nighttimers in late 1964, and soon graduated to humping gear around for beat bands such as Unit 4+2, the Searchers and the Merseybeats, as well as briefly acting as a driver for John Entwistle and Keith Moon of the Who. His big break came when Grant took him on as road manager for the New Vaudeville

Band's 1967 American tour. The novelty act had hit US #1 in December 1966 with Winchester Cathedral, and Cole was charged with shepherding them around the US at a wage of £30 a week. After that he toured Germany with the Creation, but his competence, brashness and raucous sense of fun had endeared him to Grant, who invited him to road-manage the Yardbirds from 1967. He pioneered the practice of taking a band's own equipment and road crew on tour instead of relying on local services, later explaining that "it was much easier to bring you own stuff and know what you're getting every night, than to take a chance on things being wrong. Some of the smaller cities just didn't have the right equipment we needed." Having briefly worked for Vanilla Fudge, Cole was invited by Grant to road-manage Led Zeppelin, starting with their first US tour in December 1968.

As well as vetting venues (to ensure they were up to the standard required for the band to perform) and ensuring that accommodation and travel arrangements ran smoothly (he was responsible for hiring the Starship in 1973), he also arranged security for the band. A capable and often proactively violent protector of his charges, Cole also had a prodigious appetite for merry-making and substance abuse. His partner-in-crime was usually John Bonham, though at different times every band member was involved in the antics he devised, including the infamous 'shark incident'. He had no input into their musical development, though as a mark of respect he was frequently invited to play congas with them onstage during 'Whole Lotta Love'. His status took a knock on July 29th 1973, when $203,000 of the band's money was stolen from a safety deposit box in New York's Drake Hotel, but he was absolved of any involvement and by 1975 had become their personal manager. "He's such a rock on the road, such a unique man," Robert Plant told Melody Maker in February 1976. "Ricardo knows what he's doing all the time – at least during the time he's supposed to."

As time went on, however, Cole didn't feel sufficiently rewarded by the band. As he wrote in *Stairway To Heaven*, 'With Swan Song up and running, I thought I might be given a shot at a top position within the new company, or perhaps a small percentage of the band's record royalties... But no such offers were ever forthcoming. It just didn't seem fair.' Instead, he left to work for Eric Clapton in 1974, but had returned in time for Led Zeppelin's 1975 US tour. By the end of it, the stress of his work and the temptations of the road had made him into a confirmed heroin addict. By 1980 he was deemed unfit to road-manage the band's European tour – as Grant later commented, "He had a massive problem, so I thought the only way to shake him up was to blow him out... He was shattered and he spoke to Jimmy, but I had made the decision." When news of Bonham's death reached Cole in September 1980, he was in Italy's Rebibia prison, on suspicion of blowing up Bologna railway station following a bizarre misunderstanding. He underwent forced cold turkey behind bars, and was released the following autumn, without charge.

Having cleaned up, he found making a living outside the band tough, and began to grant interviews for money, much to his former employers' consternation. The most notorious of these was granted to Stephen Davis for *Hammer Of The Gods*. In March 1988, soon after its publication, Robert Plant told Q magazine: "Richard just possesses an inherent bitterness, because he was in a constant position of absorbing and reflecting glory without ever being given the reins of authority because he was always second in command to Peter Grant. So when it all ended he decided to get his own back on a bunch of guys who were just shambling their way through the universe." Before long, Cole had decided to pen his own memoirs, published as *Stairway To Heaven* in 1992. An affectionate but extremely indiscreet volume, it further alienated his former employers. "He went into AA as a chronic alcoholic and came out a chronic liar," Jimmy Page quipped to Mojo magazine in December 1994. The guitarist also told Guitar World magazine in 1993: "There's a book written by our former road manager, Richard Cole, that has made me completely ill. I'm so mad about it that I can't even bring myself to read the whole thing. The two bits that I have read are so ridiculously false, that I'm sure if I read the rest I'd be able to sue Cole and the publishers. But it would be so painful to read that it wouldn't be worth it."

Though Cole remains a controversial figure in the band's history, Peter Grant paid him this tribute in 1993: "I can't take away what he did for us in the peak years. He was always there and always reliable. He was always employed by me."

Coleby, Barrington

Artist and old friend of Jimmy Page's, whose drawing 'The Hermit' fills the gatefold of the band's fourth album. His name is misspelt as 'Colby' on the sleeve, and he is now thought to be resident in Switzerland.

Collins, Jeffrey

London record dealer and a notorious purveyor of bootlegs. In a famous incident in 1969, Peter Grant visited his shop incognito and personally removed his entire stock of Led Zeppelin items. "The funny thing was, he rang me up the next day and said Polydor had sent these people down and it was really disgusting how they'd treated him, he'd been terrified," Grant delightedly told Melody Maker on June 22nd 1974. "He said one of the men was six feet three, weighed eighteen-and-a-half stone, had a beard and was really vicious. 'It just shows you what the industry's coming to', I said... Then the next day he rang back and said, 'Oh, all right, I know you've made a cunt of me.' 'Well, we did have a laugh', I said, 'cause we recorded you on the phone.' We hadn't, but it was a parting shot."

Colson, Glen

John Bonham's drum roadie for the band's earliest UK shows, in late 1968. Colson was a friend of another of their roadies, Kenny Pickett (formerly the singer in the Creation), and later remarked: "I did about six or seven gigs with them. I wasn't on the payroll, Kenny just gave me 20 quid for helping out, and because I was a drummer I knew how to set up Bonzo's kit. Basically Kenny and I had to do everything. We had a Transit van and between us we had to carry a Hammond organ, a PA, a drum kit and two Marshall stacks.... They were only getting £300 quid a gig, because I can remember picking up the money one night. It was £300 for Liverpool University (October 19th 1968)."

He also stated that at that time "Grant and Page had it all tied up. As far as I could see, Jimmy was the boss and none of the others said a word... They'd sit around the dressing room saying nothing. I guess they were sort of smouldering, ready to explode on stage. The gigs were phenomenal. I'd never seen anything like it." Colson later became a promoter and press officer for Charisma and Stiff Records.

Communication Breakdown

This intense hard rock song, featured on the band's debut, would quickly become recognised as one of their signature pieces. Built around a basic, up-tempo Page riff, it was a live staple throughout their career. Page revealed to Guitar World in July 1977 that the song's claustrophobic sound came from being recorded "in a small room. A little tiny vocal booth-type thing, miked from a distance." Page, unusually, contributed backing vocals to the recording as well. It was performed at most of the band's concerts, and was issued as the B-side to the US 'Good Times Bad Times' 45, released on January 12th 1969.

Concert For Kampuchea

Series of four charity gigs held at London's Hammersmith Apollo in December 1979. At the final show, on Sunday December 29th, Robert Plant sang 'Little Sister' with Rockpile (fronted by Swan Song artist Dave Edmunds), before Jones and Bonham joined him for the encore, as part of Paul McCartney's so-called 'Rockestra', playing 'The Rockestra Theme', 'Let It Be' and Little Richard's 'Lucille'. The performance is thought to have been Bonham's last on a UK stage.

Concerts West

Founded by Tom Hulett and Jerry Weintraub in 1967, these Dallas-based live music promoters started by handling tours by acts including Jimi Hendrix and Creedence Clearwater Revival, and went on to present many of Led Zeppelin's US appearances, as well as those of other superstars including Elvis Presley.

Condliffe, Brian

John Paul Jones's long-term roadie, responsible for setting up and tuning his bass and keyboards onstage.

Continental Hyatt House

Hotel on LA's Sunset Boulevard nicknamed 'the Riot House' on account of Led Zeppelin's antics there. "The Riot House, aka the Hyatt House, was basically a kind of youth club where you had to pay to get in," Plant told Blender magazine in 2002. "And you had to pay even more when you left. I can't check in anymore, because I was banned in 1972. They lift the ban only when the staff who banned you die." On their 1975 tour armed guards were posted outside each member's room on the notorious ninth floor in a bid to keep out groupies and hangers-on. From the hotel the band would venture forth at night to clubs such as the Roxy and the Rainbow Bar and Grill. Richard Cole found the effort required to walk between the different suites too much, so he used a small motorcycle instead. 'Rather than walk along the corridor I used to keep the motorbike handy, and I'd drive it into the elevator and then up to their floor,' he wrote in *Stairway To Heaven*. 'Then, if I wanted to go out, I'd just go downstairs in the elevator and drive it straight through the lobby.'

Coulson, Clive

b. 1948 / d. 2006

Led Zeppelin's road manager until late 1973, when he departed to help manage Bad Company. The New Zealand native had sung in bands down under such as the Rayders and Mecca, before travelling to the UK in 1967 and finding employment with Peter Grant, whose right-hand man he soon became, along with Richard Cole. Having worked for Rod Stewart and Jeff Beck, he became a key member of Led Zeppelin's road crew in 1968 and was the only man ever to share vocals onstage with Plant (in Japan in September 1971). Alongside roadie Sandy MacGregor, he was present for Plant and Page's legendary sojourn at Bron-Yr-Aur in May 1970, telling Mojo magazine in April 2000: "Me and Sandy were the cooks, bottle-washers and general slaves. Pagey was the tea man. Plant's speciality was posing and telling people how to do things! No, everyone mucked in really. I wouldn't take any of that superior shit. They were wonderful people to work for – normal blokes. They weren't treated as gods."

In 1974 Cole took over as the band's tour manager, while Coulson focused on Bad Company (also a Swan Song act). Asked by Circus magazine that December to recall the most bizarre request he'd ever had to fulfil for a musician, he replied: "I once had to drive a wild goat from London to Wales so Robert Plant could keep a pet on his new estate." He subsequently moved back to New Zealand, where he bought coastal property and farmed cattle, but returned to the UK to act as a pall-bearer at Grant's funeral in 1995. He died of a heart attack aged 58.

Crawling King Snakes

Formed in 1967 and named after a John Lee Hooker song, this Birmingham-based blues outfit was the first band in which Robert Plant and John Bonham played together. According to Plant years later, "It was pretty debatable at first whether John would join us. It was a fairly long way to go and pick him up for a gig, and we never knew whether we'd have the petrol money to get over there." The band gigged around the West Midlands while Bonham took a break from A Way Of Life, but made no recordings. Other members included Ian Watts (lead guitar), Bruce Oakes (bass) and Johnny Pasternak (guitar).

Crowe, Cameron
b. July 13th 1957
The youngest contributor in the history of Rolling Stone magazine, for which he interviewed Jimmy Page and Robert Plant in 1975. As the magazine's then-editor Ben Fong-Torres told the San Francisco Chronicle: "He covered the bands that hated Rolling Stone." Led Zeppelin was certainly one of those. A series of negative reviews and references had led them to refuse all invitations to be interviewed for it. Crowe's youthful and guileless approach, however, finally won them over. As he writes on his website, 'The quest to land Rolling Stone's first interview with Led Zeppelin was a rough one… While touring with the band for the Los Angeles Times, I attempted to talk them into speaking with me for Rolling Stone too. One by one they agreed, except for Page. I stayed on the road for three weeks, red-eyed from no sleep, until he finally relented… out of sympathy, I think.' The resulting interview (published in March 1975) was one of the more revealing the duo ever gave, and led to Crowe being asked to

contribute liner notes to the soundtrack LP to *The Song Remains The Same*. Crowe went on to write and direct Hollywood films. *Almost Famous* (released in 2000) is a semi-autobiographical account of his experiences as an adolescent rock journalist, and features numerous incidents based on his time with Led Zeppelin.

Crowley, Aleister
b. Oct. 12th 1975 / d. Dec 1st 1947
Controversial British mystic, occult writer, racist, misogynist and drug addict whose life and work fascinated Jimmy Page.

"It goes without saying that Crowley was grossly misunderstood," the guitarist informed the NME in December 1974. "I began being interested in him in school, after having read this ridiculous book called *The Great Beast*, where the author hadn't the faintest idea of what Crowley was all about and was totally condescending, so I took it from there."

By 1970 he was an avid collector and student of Crowley, and bought his former home, Boleskine House (on the shores of Loch Ness) in 1971. In 1975 he funded a London bookshop and publishing imprint called Equinox, partly in order to make Crowley's work more readily available. "I feel Aleister Crowley is a misunderstood genius of the 20th century," he told Sounds on March 13th 1976, "because his whole thing was liberation of the person... The further this age we're in now gets into technology and alienation, a lot of the points he's made seem to manifest themselves down the line."

see *Black Magic / Boleskine House / Equinox*

The Crunge

Light-hearted, James Brown-influenced funk piece on *Houses Of The Holy*, and the song – alongside 'D'Yer Mak'er' – most singled out for criticism by reviewers of the album. "Bonzo and I were both James Brown freaks," John Paul Jones explained to journalist Ritchie Yorke at the time. "We used to play his records all the time on the tour plane... onstage we'd get into funk grooves quite a lot." Robert Plant went on to recall to Melody Maker on August 4th 1973: "Bonzo and I were going to just go into the studio and talk Black Country through the whole thing – you know, 'Ah, bloody hell, how you doin', y'all right, mate?', and it just evolved there and then." Page added that "Bonzo started the groove. Then John Paul Jones started playing that descending bass line, and I just came in on the rhythm. You can hear the fun we were having." Jones told Blow By Blow magazine in 1992 that "We were originally going to do those feet patterns they have to show people how to do dances, showing how to do 'The Crunge' in a way which would guarantee that you would at least fall over and injure yourself severely." The song was never performed live in full by the band, though it was occasionally incorporated into 'Dazed and Confused' in 1972 and 'Whole Lotta Love' in 1975.

Cullderstead

Company name registered in reserve by Peter Grant before settling on Swan Song in 1974. Cullderstead Ltd. eventually became the US management wing of Grant's operation, helping to handle Led Zeppelin's business affairs there. It was run by Danny Goldberg, who was also Swan Song's US Vice-President from 1974-76.

Custard Pie

The funky hard rock track that opens 1975's *Physical Graffiti*. Its sexually-charged lyrics echo blues classics 'Drop Down Mama' by Mississippi Fred McDowell, 'Shake Em On Down' by Bukka White, 'I Want Some Of Your Pie' by Blind Boy Fuller and 'Custard Pie Blues' by Brownie McGhee. The recording features John Paul Jones on electric clavinet and a memorable guitar solo from Page, incorporating a wah-wah pedal put through an ARP synthesizer. The song was apparently rehearsed for the band's 1975 US Tour, but they never performed it in public.

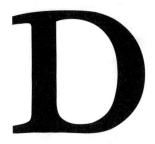

D

the band were so pleased with it that they spontaneously danced on the lawn during its playback. Like 'Over the Hills and Far Away', it was played live before its appearance on record, making its debut in Seattle on June 19th 1972 (when they even played it twice). Having been played often throughout the remainder of the year, it was dropped soon after the album was released, though a shortened acoustic rendition occasionally cropped up on their US tour in 1977.

The Damned

UK punk pioneers of whom Robert Plant and Jimmy Page were outspoken admirers, having seen them live in January 1977. In an interview with Melody Maker on June 25th that year the singer stated: "I went to the Roxy and got frightened to death, but at the same time I stood my ground for all we dinosaurs, and I saw the Damned. I found them very exciting, thrilling." The guitarist, meanwhile, told the paper in November that the band "are a knockout... Exactly what rock and roll is all about, sheer adrenaline music." John Bonham was less impressed when Page and Plant took him to see them a week later: following their set he drunkenly clambered onstage and attempted to demonstrate how real music should be played, before being bundled out of the club, hurling insults all the while.

Dancing Days

Positive, upbeat song that opens side two of *Houses Of The Holy* and was inspired by Page and Plant's visit to Bombay in March 1972. It was recorded at Stargroves later that year, and engineer Eddie Kramer has recalled that

Dansette Damage

Midlands-based punk / new wave act whose February 1978 debut single, 'The Only Sound' / 'NME' (Shoestring LACE 001, recorded at the Old Smithy Studios in Kempsey) was produced by Robert Plant, who also contributed backing vocals. He is referred to on the sleeve as 'The Wolverhampton Wanderer' and 'Uncle Bob'. Their connection with him came through their keyboard player, Eddie Blower, a noted photographer and friend of the singer. The release was billed as 'the world's first double B-side', and was not a hit.

Darlene

Rock number taped on November 16th 1978, during the *In Through The Out Door* sessions in Stockholm, but not released until 1982's *Coda* compilation. It was the only track from the sessions to be credited to all four band members, but was never performed live.

Davies, Cyril

b. Jan 23rd 1932 / d. Jan 7th 1964
Blues harmonica player and early figurehead of British R&B, who offered

the young Jimmy Page a place in his band, the Cyril Davies All-Stars, in 1962 – but was turned down after a couple of rehearsals, as Page wished to avoid the demands of touring and continue at Sutton College of Art instead. Davies therefore offered him the chance to play in the intervals of his Marquee gigs, during one of which he was talent-spotted by Decca producer / arranger Mike Leander, leading to his prolific session career in the years ahead. Davies – who was also an inspiration to the Rolling Stones and the Yardbirds – died of leukaemia.

Dazed and Confused

Written by New York folkie Jake Holmes, this downbeat tune appeared in an epic, multi-partite arrangement on Led Zeppelin's debut album. The Yardbirds had played alongside Holmes in New York in 1967, and promptly incorporated the track into their repertoire as 'I'm Confused'. The lyrics were amended for Led Zeppelin's treatment, which also showcased Page's famous violin-bowing technique. It was a live staple throughout their career, allowing the band to extemporise at length, as well as to throw in snippets of other songs as the mood took them. These included popular hits by their contemporaries, fifties classics and even their own material. As Page told Disc in June 1973, "it changes every night, so it's really a vehicle for exploring and getting off, for me personally." A gruelling 29-minute rendition was included in the film soundtrack *The Song Remains The Same* in 1976.

Denny, Sandy

b. Jan. 6th 1947 / d. April 21st 1978
Lead singer with Fairport Convention and Fotheringay, who contributed vocals to 'The Battle Of Evermore' in 1971, becoming one of the only outsiders to feature on a Led Zeppelin recording, and the only one to sing. Jimmy Page told ZigZag magazine in November 1972 that Fairport Convention's "*Liege & Lief* for me was the best album of 1969". The band's bassist, Dave Pegg, was a lifelong friend of Plant and Bonham, and they had supported Led Zeppelin in 1970, as well as being joined onstage by them at LA's Troubadour in 1970. A final connection came on August 4th 1979, when they provided support at the first of Led Zeppelin's Knebworth dates. Denny, tragically, had died over a year earlier, of head injuries sustained after falling downstairs, following years of substance abuse.

Dent, Malcolm

b. 1944

Surrey-born schoolfriend of Jimmy Page, who invited him to become caretaker of Boleskine House in 1971. "He caught me at a time in my life when I wasn't doing a great deal and asked me to come up and run the place," Dent told the Inverness Courier on November 3rd 2006. "I never did establish why he fixed on me." Dent's duties included overseeing the restoration of the house, which was virtually a ruin, as well as opposing a plan to install pylons in its grounds. He was no acolyte of Aleister Crowley ("I knew Jimmy had some weird interests, but that was about it"), and was not much troubled by supernatural activity there ("doors would be slamming all night, you'd go into a room and carpets and rugs would be piled up... we just used to say that was Aleister doing his thing"). He'd been less dismissive in an interview with the Highland News on February 8th 1997, however, when he claimed to have heard "a huge beast, snorting, snuffling and banging" one night, adding: "Whatever was there, I have no doubt it was pure evil."

Dent's tenancy came to an abrupt end in 1991, when he accepted payment from the Scottish Sun to allow them overnight access to the property. The resulting spread did not impress Page, who had not given permission and sold up soon afterwards. Dent has since griped to the tabloids that the guitarist failed to honour a promise to give him six acres of land as severance payment, thereby shattering his dream of opening a caravan park there. The duo are not thought to have remained friends.

Denver

Location of Led Zeppelin's first-ever US gig, on December 26th 1968. "I remember pulling up to a theatre and the marquee said, Vanilla Fudge, Taj Mahal and support," Plant told Rolling Stone in May 2005. "I thought, Wow, here we are: Support!" In fact, it was Spirit and not Taj Mahal who joined them and Vanilla Fudge on the date. The Rocky Mountain News had this to say of them: "Singer Robert Plant – a cut above the average in style, but no special appeal in sound. Guitarist Jimmy Page, of Yardbirds fame – exceptionally fine. Used a violin bow on the guitar strings in a couple of tunes with resultant interesting, well-integrated effects. Bassist John Paul Jones – solid, involved, contributing. John Bonham – a very, effective group drummer, but uninventive, unsubtle and unclimactic in an uneventful solo."

Des Barres, Michael

b. Jan. 24th 1948

British-born lead singer of US hard-rockers Detective, who signed to Swan Song in 1975. "I had super high power management and they contacted Zeppelin, who had just started Swan Song Records," he told Juice magazine in April 2007. "I'd known Jimmy, so it was a very natural thing that we were the first American band to be signed by Swan Song." Late that year, as Robert Plant recovered from his car accident, the band found itself rehearsing at the same Malibu facility as Led Zeppelin, SIR. As Plant told Circus magazine in January 1976: "I had to sit in an arm chair with my leg up in the air while the band was on the stage. And I'd go into another room where Detective were playing, and Michael Des Barres was singing, aping all of my movements and looking in the mirror at the same time... we figured that if I don't go out on the road again, we'd just change his name quickly and send him out as me." Page is widely believed to have produced their debut LP under the pseudonym 'Jimmy Robinson'. As Des Barres has stated: "Jimmy produced the record. We recorded it twice. It cost millions of dollars. And we just sat in the jacuzzi with the record playing and smoked coke and had the girls give us massages. It took six months to get a drum sound. It was insane." It was finally released in April 1977. Three months later Des Barres married Page's former lover, whom he'd known as 'Miss Pamela' (see below).

Des Barres, Pamela

b. Sept. 9th 1948

Born Pamela Ann Miller, this self-professed 'queen of the supergroupies' served as Jimmy Page's on-off lover in the US from July 1969. A member of Frank Zappa's girl-group the GTOs (Girls Together Outrageously), she met Page at an aftershow party and went on to boast: "We held hands, we had wild sex ... I sat up on his amps when the band played." She was also charged with the onerous task of safeguarding the band's jewellery while they played, but their relationship ended when Page's interests switched to 14-year old Lori Maddox in 1972. 'Miss Pamela' went on to marry UK-born Michael Des Barres, singer with Swan Song signings Detective. "I believe that Jimmy was very into black magic and probably did a lot of rituals,

black candles, bat's blood, the whole thing," she later stated. "I believe he did that stuff."

De Shannon, Jackie

b. Aug. 21st 1944

Born Sharon Lee Myers, this Kentucky-born singer-songwriter penned numerous hits in the 1960s. Having toured the US with the Beatles in 1964, she spent time in England in 1965 and embarked on a passionate affair with Jimmy Page. The duo collaborated on several songs and Page travelled to the US with her in 1966, but their relationship didn't last long. He is thought to have written an unreleased Yardbirds track for her, 'Knowing That I'm Losing You', which was later reworked by him as 'Tangerine' for *Led Zeppelin III*.

Digby Smith, Richard

Youthful engineer and assistant to Andy Johns, who found himself on the nightshift at Headley Grange when 'Stairway To Heaven' was recorded in January 1971. "I can recall the take," he later remembered. "It was a very large room. Page was playing acoustic guitar sat at the front with four tall baffles that completely enclosed him... Jones was to the right of him playing Moog bass which was the industry standard at the time... Bonzo just sat at the back, you know, waiting for that bit where he comes pounding in, which is about ten minutes into the song. There were these big orange speakers with Page standing between them, and we played him back through them as loud as possible, and he just leaned up against the speakers with his ear virtually pressed against them, with a cigarette hanging out of his mouth, and rattled out that solo… I sometimes get people coming up to me saying 'I know someone who assisted on 'Stairway To Heaven', but I was the only assistant that night."

'Discover America'
Long-running scheme operated by TWA, which greatly assisted the band's first trek around the States in 1968 and 1969. As Richard Cole explains in *Stairway To Heaven*, it 'allowed us to buy airline tickets that routed us through the US, saving us 50% on every connection. It cut our travel expenses by thousands of dollars.'

Dixon, Willie
b. July 1st 1915 / d. Jan 29th 1992
US bluesman whose songs 'I Can't Quit You Baby' and 'You Shook Me' featured on the band's debut album. In addition, *Led Zeppelin II's* 'Whole Lotta Love' contains lyrics from his 1950s classic 'You Need Love', though its riff is undoubtedly Page's. In 1985 Dixon sued the band, who admitted what Plant called 'a nick' and settled out of court.

Dorfman, Stanley
Prolific and distinguished music film-maker who shot the famous footage of the band performing at London's Royal Albert Hall on January 9th 1970. In July 2007 he recalled in a Huffington Post blog: "I called Zeppelin's manager Peter Grant to see if I could tape them for my BBC 'In Concert' series. This was of no interest to them, but what they did want was to document the concert for their archives. This would mean that the footage would belong to the band, and the BBC would not agree. So I decided to moonlight and to do it myself!" The spectacular results were taped under duress by Dorfman, documentary-maker Peter Whitehead and an assistant, and were deemed too dark by Peter Grant. They languished for 35 years until they were restored for the band's live DVD set in 2003.

Dormouse Studio
John Paul Jones's home studio in Hertfordshire, set up in 1972, where he recorded Madeline Bell's 1973 LP *Comin' Atcha*.

Double-necked guitar
Jimmy Page is closely associated with the Gibson EDS-1275, an unorthodox guitar with two necks which he used onstage for performances of songs including 'Stairway To Heaven', 'The Rain Song', 'The Song Remains The Same' and 'Gallows Pole'. It meant that he didn't have to stop mid-song to switch between six and twelve-string guitars. He rarely used it in the studio (one definite appearance was on 'Carouselambra', included on 1979's *In Through The Out Door*), and later told the BBC: "I had to get the double neck to handle 'Stairway', because even though I had played six-string acoustic, electric and twelve-string electric, I couldn't do it on one or the other. The double neck was the only way of being able to handle it."

Down By The Seaside
This contemplative, evocative song was written at Bron-Yr-Aur on Page and

Plant's second stay there in October 1970, and recorded at their brief sessions in London's Island Studios that December. They chose to leave it off their untitled fourth LP, however, and finally included on 1975's *Physical Graffiti*. It was never performed live.

Drake Hotel

Exclusive New York hostelry, located on Park Avenue, from which approximately $203,000 of the band's money was stolen on July 29th 1973. The cash was kept there to pay for members of their staff as well as expenses such as running the Starship, because their US management company (Entertainment Overseas Ltd.) did not have a US bank account. It had been held in safe deposit box #409, whose key Richard Cole was entrusted with. This, coupled with the fact that Cole discovered the theft (at 7:15 that Sunday morning), led him to be suspected of involvement. He was interrogated for an hour by the FBI, but – according to his memoirs – 'if I appeared nervous during the interview it was because I was desperately trying to drag it out for as long as possible to make sure the housecleaning upstairs was completed'. He was cleared following a lie detector test the same day ("I had nothing to fear and I think it was the right thing to do," he commented).

The media initially speculated that it was a staged publicity stunt, but despite Peter Grant's offer of a $10,000 reward, the cash was never recovered and no one was ever charged with its theft. The band weren't overly fussed – as Page told the NME in September 1973, "It

had reached the point where we couldn't really care too much. I mean, if the tour had been a bummer, then that would have been the last straw, but it wasn't." Bonham, meanwhile, told the press: "If we'd have said we were not upset, they would have thought we were so rich it meant nothing to us, and if we say we're upset about it, they'll say money is all we care about." The day had an especially unpleasant conclusion for Grant, who was arrested for assaulting a Daily News photographer, after he'd forcibly removed the film from his camera. The band subsequently sued the hotel over the theft and received what Cole describes as 'a reasonable settlement'.

Dreja, Chris

b. Nov 11th 1946

Founding member and rhythm guitarist with the Yardbirds who was initially involved with the formation of Led Zeppelin, and travelled to Birmingham with Jimmy Page and Peter Grant to watch Robert Plant performing with Obbstweedle in July 1968.

When John Paul Jones expressed an interest in joining, however, he was only too happy to step aside. "I'd had enough of the music biz by then," he told Q magazine in 2003. "I wanted to be independent and not have to rely on loonies." He took up photography instead, serving an apprenticeship with US photography guru Irving Penn and going on to shoot the picture that appears on the back of *Led Zeppelin I* (in a studio in Putney). Since 1992 he has been playing with reformed Yardbirds line-ups.

Drew, Richard

Artist and former lecturer in fine arts at Leeds Polytechnic who had been friends with Jimmy Page at Sutton College of Art in 1962. In 1970 Page invited him to design the complex artwork for *Led Zeppelin III*, which he did under the pseudonym 'Zacron'. The initial concept was Page's, based on gardening catalogues – as he told Disc in October 1970, "you'd turn it to 'roses' and see what kind of manure to use." To Drew's bemusement, he later professed himself dissatisfied with the result (which featured a large number of disparate images and a rotating wheel), telling Guitar World in 1998: "I thought it looked very teeny-bopperish. But we were on top of a deadline, so of course there was no way to make any radical changes to it. There were some silly bits - little chunks of corn and nonsense like that."

Driving to Kashmir

Original title for 'Kashmir', as named by Robert Plant when he penned the lyrics in 1973, during a driving holiday in Morocco, immediately after Led Zeppelin's 1973 US Tour.

Drugs

"I can't speak for the others," Jimmy Page told Guitar World magazine in 1993, "but for me drugs were an integral part of the whole thing, right from the beginning, right to the end." Led Zeppelin emerged from the 1960s counter-culture, where hallucinogens, hashish and marijuana were the drugs of choice. Their years of greatest fame, however, coincided with the rise in popularity of cocaine and heroin, both of which would play a considerable part in their touring and personal lives. On their first US visit, however, alcohol was the drug of choice. 'Substance abuse eventually became part of the Led Zeppelin legend, and we got off to a fast start on that initial tour,' Richard Cole wrote in *Stairway To Heaven*. 'Alcohol became our constant companion. We had plenty of marijuana too, and occasionally a snort or two of cocaine. But alcohol was nearly an everyday indulgence.'

Robert Plant has commented of his and Page's stay at Bron-Yr-Aur in May 1970 "I don't think we even smoked dope then", but by their ninth US tour in 1973 the band was reportedly employing a so-called 'coke lady' backstage, whose job it was to supply a hit of cocaine with her little finger, followed by a pinch of cherry snuff and a sip of Dom Perignon as and when required. UK newspaperman Bob Hart flew out for part of the tour, and later commented that "some of it was incredibly and outrageously funny.

However, we were appalled by some of the things we saw. It was mainly driven by cocaine. Led Zeppelin was a band of great wealth, even at this point, but also a band of incredible decadence. I think that degree of decadence had a lot to do with the amount of coke that was going down. I saw quantities of coke on that tour that were truly remarkable." Shortly after that tour ended on July 29th 1973, Page told the NME that "everyone went over the top a few times. I know I did and, to be honest with you, I don't really remember much of what happened. The thing is that even when we were totally fucked, we'd somehow be able to perform onstage."

According to Cole's memoirs, 'With the passage of time, Zeppelin continued to become more enamoured with cocaine... people were constantly offering us cocaine, and it seemed silly to say no.' By the time they congregated in Malibu to rehearse for *Presence* in the autumn of 1975, the element of control that Page had referred to was beginning to shake, and heroin had entered the scene. "We were all up to no good, one way or another," Plant told Uncut magazine in May 2008, referring to the period surrounding the recording of *Physical Graffiti* in 1974. "It's just a question of how much you're doing and how the constitution will take it." By 1975 Page and Cole had begun to use heroin frequently, and in 1977 – when the band finally toured the US again – the guitarist's frailty was widely remarked upon, and his performances started to become sloppy. This affected his creative relationship with Robert Plant (who was always a moderate drug user, and gave up altogether when his son died that July). By the time that the band convened in Stockholm to record *In Through The Out Door* in late 1978, Bonham is also thought to have started using heroin, meaning that Jones and Plant were frequently left to their own devices in the studio.

Asked in 2003 by Q magazine whether he regretted his drug-taking, Page replied: "I don't regret it at all, because when I needed to be really focused, I was really focused. That's it. Both *Presence* and *In Through The Out Door* were only recorded in three weeks: that's really going some. You've got to be on top of it." Richard Cole, however, had a different view. 'The booze and drugs became a desperate way to keep the fun alive and the boredom from becoming too oppressive,' he wrote in *Stairway To Heaven*. 'In the end, rather than keeping the fun alive, it destroyed so much of what was good about the band.'

Dunbar, Aynsley
b. Jan. 10th 1946
Liverpool-born drummer and leader of UK blues-rockers Aynsley Dunbar's Retaliation, who was seriously considered as a possibility for the nascent Led Zeppelin before Jimmy Page encountered John Bonham. Dunbar went on to play with Frank Zappa, Jefferson Starship, Whitesnake and others.

Dunwoody, Gwyneth
b. Dec 12th 1930 / d. April 17th 2008
Longstanding British MP who was serving as Parliamentary Secretary to the Board of Trade in 1969. In that capacity

she presented Led Zeppelin with two platinum discs and one gold disc (representing US sales equivalent to $5 million) in a ceremony at London's Savoy Hotel on December 11th, quipping: "You seem to be gas rockets rather than lead zeppelins." The following day the Financial Times explained to its appalled readership that 'their earning power goes to the assistance of the British balance of payments'.

see *Grant, Anthony*

D'yer Mak'er

"We were fiddling around and we wrote a reggae number which will be on the next album, but I would like to have it out as a single," Robert Plant told Melody Maker of this contentious song in November 1972. Though promo 45s were issued in the UK (backed with 'Over The Hills And Far Away' as Atlantic K10296), it ended up on *Houses Of The Holy*, and was widely singled out for criticism in reviews. As Page told Sounds in April 1973, "It's not really reggae, is it? I personally see it as more like a 50s thing – it started off like that for a laugh." Jones and Bonham were unamused – according to Jones, Bonham "wouldn't play anything but the same shuffle beat all the way through it. He hated it, and so did I. It would have been all right if he had worked at the part – the whole point of reggae is that the drums and bass really have to be very strict about what they play. And he wouldn't, so it sounded dreadful." The title is based on an old pun on the word

'Jamaica' (which is how it should be pronounced), and appears nowhere in the lyrics. The drum sound, meanwhile, was modelled on Dee Dee Warwick's minor 1969 US hit 'Foolish Fool'. A US edition of the single reached #20 that December, but the band barely played it live, choosing only to incorporate snatches of it onstage during their 1975 US tour and subsequent Earl's Court shows in London.

Dylan, Bob
b. May 24th 1941
American singer-songwriter responsible for a notable piece of Led Zeppelin apocrypha. It's said that at a party in LA Peter Grant introduced himself with the words "I'm Peter Grant, manager of Led Zeppelin," to which came the reply: "I don't come to you with my problems, do I?" Cameron Crowe has since said it was the only time he saw Grant lost for words.

Jimmy Page went on to tell the NME on August 4th 1979 that "We met [Dylan's] mum once, actually. It was about the third tour and we were in Miami, and this typical Miami woman comes up with the spectacles and tinted hair bit, and she says 'Oh, I hear you're a group. My son's a singer. You've probably heard of him – Bobby Dylan. He's a good lad,' she said." Another link to the band came with their decision to record 'In My Time Of Dying' for *Physical Graffiti* – Dylan had featured a similar arrangement of the song on his debut album.

Earl's Court

West London arena in which the band played five concerts between May 17th and May 25th 1975. These were their first UK appearances in two years, and the demand for tickets was such that the number of performances was increased from three to five. A total of 85,000 people saw them there, though demand was still far from met. It was the first time a British audience had witnessed the dazzling stage show that had become a mainstay of their US appearances, and the band was very pleased with the shows – as Bonham told Melody Maker in June 1975: "I thought they were the best shows that we've ever put on in England. I always get tense before a show, and we were expecting trouble with such a huge audience. But everything went really well and although we couldn't have the laser beams at full power, I thought the video screen was well worth doing. It cost a lot of bread, but you could see close-ups you'd never be able to see normally at a concert. It was worth every penny."

Immediately after the dates the four band members went on holiday. Their next three concerts, scheduled for August 23rd and 24th (Oakland Stadium) and September 6th (Pasadena's Rose Bowl) were cancelled owing to Robert Plant's accident in Rhodes on August 4th, and they didn't appear onstage again until almost two years later, on April 1st 1977 (at Dallas's Memorial Auditorium).

Edgewater Inn

Seattle motel and setting for arguably the most infamous episode in Led Zeppelin's history: July 28th 1969's so-called 'shark incident'.

Electric Magic

Name given to two concerts given at Wembley Empire Pool, London on November 20th and 21st 1971, jointly promoted by Peter Grant and Rikki Farr (organiser of 1970's Isle Of Wight Festival). All 9000 tickets for each show cost 75p, and no one was allowed to buy more than five. Additionally, a special poster was designed by Steve Hardstaff, which is highly-prized by collectors today (they cost 30p at the gig). Support came from Home, Stone the Crows and Bronco (the latter featuring Plant's old friends Kevyn Gammond, Jess Roden and Robbie Blunt), as well as circus acts. As Farr told Melody Maker: "Wembley's an excellent opportunity for a highly original production incorporating all sorts of acts. There may be animals onstage, too." Ultimately only two performing pigs (complete with ruffs and police helmets) were located, but they evidently suffered from stage fright and failed to fulfil their duties, despite soiling the stage. Having been largely away from the UK in 1971, the band were received rapturously and gave performances that they were very pleased with.

Ellis, Royston

b. Feb 10th 1941

Leading UK beat poet and early acquaintance of the Beatles, behind whom Jimmy Page played guitar for a time in the early 1960s, including an appearance at London's Mermaid Theatre during the National Poetry Festival in July 1961.

Emerson, Keith

b. Nov. 2nd 1944

Progressive keyboard wizard who was reportedly considered for invitation to join the band after their first couple of US tours in 1969, in order to add full-time keyboards to their sound. Led Zeppelin later used Emerson, Lake & Palmer's Manticore studios to rehearse for their 1977 US tour.

England

The band's home country, though they were frequently ambivalent about its press and audiences. As early as April 1969 Jimmy Page was telling the NME that "In America the audiences get into their music more. They are more appreciative. They will listen to the sort of patterns you are playing. In Britain all they are interested in is the way to the bar." In the band's early days Peter Grant had the same problem finding them work, telling the NME in February 1975: "When the band started, British promoters weren't really interested… So you had to come over [to the US] to get to people." Early receipts from gigs were indeed dispiriting compared to the US – on their second series of UK one-nighters, starting on March 1st 1969, they earned fees between £60 and £140

a pop. As John Paul Jones told Melody Maker reporter Roy Hollingworth in New York in July 1972, "The scenes have possibly amazed you, but this has been happening for four years now. I think we all feel a bit annoyed that nobody really knows it back home." Nonetheless, Page expressed considerable patriotism in an interview with the NME on September 11th 1974, stating: "I wouldn't leave even if I had to live in a cottage. There's just the thing about England, the tradition of thousands of years and the beauty of the countryside… I wouldn't want to be without that."

By the following July the band was in tax exile in Switzerland, though they evidently felt nostalgic about it. As Plant told the NME in February 1976: "It's a very sad situation, you know, to have to leave one's own country for the sake of money. The government in England is almost saying, 'Well, never mind, they'll come back you know, they're English and they'll come home.' And they're damn right! The number of times we have come so close to getting on a plane and going home! The spirit of Albion is really embedded in everyone's soul." During their 1977 US tour in June 1977, he went on to tell Melody Maker that "if we did just an acoustic set back in England it would probably be our finest hour! But there's a kind of excitement in an American audience that belongs only to an American audience." Though the UK music press constantly criticised the band for their long absences from British stages, England continued to hold a unique place in the band's estimation. As Plant told Melody Maker in August

1973: "Playing in London always gets me nervy. London was always the place that I seemed to think had to be A-1."

Entwistle, John

Bassist with the Who, and possibly the person who came up with the name 'Lead Zeppelin', rather than the Who's drummer, Keith Moon (as is commonly believed). As Entwistle later stated: "Once, when we were in New York, I sat down with Keith and our chauffeur, a guy called Richard Cole, and tried to come up with possible new names for the band we were going to form. That's when I flashed on Led Zeppelin, and I also came up with an idea for a first album jacket with a Zeppelin going down in flames. Not long afterwards Richard Cole, the chauffeur, went to work for Jimmy Page and Peter Grant and he must have told them the idea. But I was definitely the one who thought of it. Later on Keith Moon claimed that he came up with it, which made me very angry. When I heard Jimmy was going to use it, I was a bit pissed off about it, but later on I didn't care that much." Page has queried this version of events, stating: "I don't know about that at all... to start with, the thing about the cover is completely wrong. We did that quite separately. The other – well, Keith Moon gave us the name. We've always credited him with that. Maybe John Entwistle did think of the name and told it to Keith Moon, in which case I suppose he might have cause to be a bit angry."

Epps, Stuart

b. 1951

UK engineer who worked with Jimmy Page on the *Coda* project in 1982. He'd been in the music business since 1967, and toured America as Elton John's personal assistant before focusing on engineering in the 1970s. By 1981 he was working at the Mill Studio in Cookham, Berkshire, which producer Gus Dudgeon then sold to Jimmy Page. Page kept him on as an engineer and producer there, and in April 2008 Epps told BBC Berkshire: "He's an amazing producer, quite a shy guy. He played the guitar with a bow and was very inventive with effects. He was very interesting for me to work with."

Equinox

Occult bookshop and publishing venture started by Jimmy Page in 1975, with help from a fellow Aleister Crowley enthusiast named Eric Hill. Based at 4, Holland Street in London's Kensington (not far from the guitarist's home), the venture was not intended to make money, but simply to assist the circulation of rare occult publications. "There was not one bookshop in London with a good collection of occult books, and I was so pissed off not being able to get the books I wanted," he told the NME in February 1975. The first two books it published were a facsimile of Aleister Crowley's translation of *The Book of Goetia* and *Astrology: A Cosmic Science* by Isabel Hickey. The shop stocked numerous signed works by Crowley, as well as a highly valuable first edition of Crowley's ten volume work *The Equinox*, from which the Zoso symbol is thought to have been extracted. The shop's lease expired in mid-1979, and Page conceded to the NME that August: "It obviously wasn't going to run the way it should without some drastic business changes, and I didn't really want to have to agree to all that. I basically just wanted the shop to be the nucleus, that's all."

Ertegun, Ahmet

b. July 31st 1923 / d. Dec 14th 2006

Turkish-born founder and president of Atlantic Records, to which Led Zeppelin signed in November 1968. As Peter Grant commented, "I think Ahmet is the best record executive in the business. He's had a great upbringing through the music business and has done a lot for all of the people he's recorded." Ertegun championed Led Zeppelin throughout their tenure on the label, and even approved their controversial decision to leave their name off their fourth LP. The band greatly admired him and his honourable business practices, and he in turn though very highly of them. "I can only say that I consider it a great honour and privilege having been able to work with them," he said after their dissolution. Jimmy Page told Mojo magazine in December 2007 that "Ahmet was a man of stories and adventures, a good guy to hang out with, a real party animal. You could relate to someone like that in the business in a way that you couldn't with, say, someone working in the legal department." The band's reunion that month was in Ertegun's honour – as Robert Plant commented: "During the Zeppelin years, Ahmet Ertegun was a major foundation of solidarity and accord. For us he WAS Atlantic Records, and remained a close friend and conspirator – this performance stands alone as our tribute to the work and the life of our longstanding friend."

Fallon, BP
b. 1946
Veteran Irish-born publicist who'd worked for the Beatles' Apple label and Island acts such as Free and King Crimson, as well as helping to foment 'T-Rextasy', before starting work for Led Zeppelin in October 1972. Nicknamed 'Beep', he was hired by Peter Grant specifically to counter negative press stemming from the fact that the Rolling Stones were touring the US at the same time as his charges. Having been flown to Montreux, Fallon's first encounter with the band proved memorable, as he told Melody Maker in January 1977: "I remember they were doing a soundcheck, and I went onto the stage, and I was sitting on an amp. Then I suddenly realised that I wasn't sitting on an amp, I'd fallen asleep and fallen off the amp. In the middle of this noise I'd passed out." He had a baptism of fire at a gig at Green's Playhouse, Glasgow in December that year, when three thugs beat him up when he suggested they had been counterfeiting tickets, and attended all Led Zeppelin concerts thereafter, as well as controlling press access to the band. He also became the butt of numerous practical jokes, such as having a pony and numerous chickens installed in his hotel room, and left the band's employ after about a year.

Fallon told Melody Maker in January 1977 that he'd written a book of memoirs about his time with the band entitled *Over The Top*, but had decided not to publish. "None of the band have seen it, and I won't show them," he said. "I daren't show it to them. There's friendships that have to be considered too... I could have said who was sleeping with who, and who's whacking what up their nose. But I wasn't interested, because I don't want to betray the confidence that people have in me." Following Bonham's death, he paid the following tribute in Melody Maker: "There's so much bullshit in the Fleet Street rags about Led Zeppelin's karma – Zeppelin have given more pleasure to more millions than possibly any other band in the world. Fragments of memories are burning through my mind... like being in a Lear jet with Zeppelin when Bonzo took it into his head to pilot this small executive rocket. Bits of chicken leg and bottles of champagne swizzling around the tiny cabin as Bonzo looped-the-loop. It was so exhilaratingly terrifying that all we could do was laugh and hang on to our seats, literally!"

Family Dogg
Studio aggregation headed by producer Steve Rowlands. Their October 1969 *A Way Of Life* LP (Bell SBLL 122) featured session contributions from Jimmy Page, John Paul Jones and John Bonham.

see *Proby, PJ*

Feliciano, Jose
b. Sept. 10th 1945

Blind Puerto Rican singer whose 1973 album *Compartments* served as inspiration for the cover of 1975's *Physical Graffiti*. Like the Led Zeppelin LP, Feliciano's showed a building with dirty brown brickwork, whose die-cut windows were filled with images on a removeable inner sleeve.

Felix, Julie
b. June 14th 1938

Folksinger and TV presenter on whose *Julie Felix Show* Jimmy Page appeared solo on Sunday April 26th 1970, playing 'White Summer'. That June, John Paul Jones travelled with her by helicopter to the Bath Festival, where she reportedly danced on the side of the stage. In 1972 Jones made a guest appearance on her *Clotho's Web* LP (RAK SRKA 6752).

Fijian Police Choir

After Led Zeppelin's concert at Brisbane's Festival Hall on February 29th 1972, John Paul Jones and John Bonham decided to stay up all night, as their flight was at dawn. They soon found themselves in the same bar as a group of burly individuals who introduced themselves as the Fijian Police Choir. After a few drinks, they proceeded to share their repertoire with the duo. When they'd finished, they insisted that the bassist and drummer should reciprocate. Their protests were in vain, and they ended up hollering out Everly Brothers classics together. Sadly, no bootleg recording is thought to exist.

Fillmore

Name of two prestigious live venues – East and West – owned by promoter Bill Graham in San Francisco and New York. The band played both on their first American tour, and were rapturously received, something that played an important part in establishing their reputation in the US. They were especially moved by their reception at the Fillmore West between January 9th – 11th 1969. As Jimmy Page told *Record Mirror* that April: "At places like the Fillmore, where you play encore after encore, you just have to stretch the numbers out – especially when we first went over, because we didn't have that much time to rehearse new numbers. We ended up adding whatever came into our heads – Beatles numbers, and at one show nearly a whole volume of *Elvis's Golden Records*." John Bonham, meanwhile, told Record Mirror in June 1970, "America gave us our chance. When we formed, we couldn't get a gig here worth playing. America wanted us because Jimmy came from the Yardbirds... it was the Fillmores that made us, and the kids have been great ever since." Plant agreed, telling Melody Maker in February 1976: "I remember when we played the Fillmore West in San Francisco, Bonzo and I looked at each other and thought, 'Christ, we've got something'. That was the first time we realised that Led Zeppelin might mean something." Page expressed almost the same thought in the NME in September 1973, stating "I can tell you when I knew when we'd broken through, which was in San Francisco."

Fingers

Travelling to London's Victoria railway station to rehearse for the band's forthcoming tenth US tour in December 1974, Jimmy Page managed to trap his finger in the door of a train at Haywards Heath, forcing him to develop a new three-digit technique until it healed. "I was at the front of the train, planning to rush off an grab a taxi, when the train stopped abruptly," he explained to the NME the following February. "I must have grabbed at something and the finger got caught in the hinge of the door. I was just totally numb – numb with shock. I just looked at it and said 'oh, no'. I mean, it's the most important finger for a guitarist: third finger, left hand." The incident had a precedent: he'd sprained another digit in some fencing while signing autographs at San Diego airport in 1973, and history repeated itself in November 2007, when the band's reunion was postponed owing to what was said to be yet another finger injury, this time caused by the guitarist falling over in his Holland Park garden.

Finn, Mickey

Born Mickey Waller, UK singer in whose band 'the Blue Men' Jimmy Page briefly featured. The two met at Club 59 in Hackney (in London's East End) in 1963. According to his website: "I couldn't believe someone was as good! Jimmy Page is the first guitar player I saw who used special effects with his guitar." Page may have played on their 'Pills' / 'Hush Your Mouth' 45 (Oriole CB 1927, May 1964), but had departed by July. The band released numerous other singles, and Page may have contributed guitar (in a session capacity) to one of them, the freakbeat masterpiece 'Garden Of My Mind' / 'Time To Start Loving You' (Direction 58-3086, December 1967). Finn should not be confused for his namesake, who collaborated with Marc Bolan in Tyrannosaurus Rex. Both took the name from the slang for a spiked drink.

Flock, the

Violin-driven US prog band who had the misfortune to precede Led Zeppelin at the Bath Festival on June 22nd 1970. Peter Grant was determined for his boys to play as the sun set, so when the Americans started to over-run he simply instructed his road crew to unplug their equipment as they played.

Flying

Though the band did not like flying, they spent much of their career on aeroplanes. In March 1969 a plane they were on had to make an emergency landing at Bremen airport – as Plant told International Times the following month, "The captain came on and told us there's going to be an emergency landing and then, from being way up in the blue one minute, we're suddenly going down, but very down. My Scotch went up in my face…" In June 1973 Page told Disc "I'm getting petrified of flying… in the past we've had lots of funny experiences. Like looking out of the windows and seeing fuel pouring out of the wings and all." John Bonham was also a bad flier – as his sister Debbie told Q magazine in 2003, "He had a genuine fear of flying, which is quite bizarre because I'd never known him to have a fear of anything. He'd be frightened of being on a jet that somebody else was driving quite safely, and yet he'd get into a Roadster or a Ferrari and not think twice when everybody that got in with him was bloody terrified." Their misgivings were consolidated by a bad experience of turbulence on a rented Falcon jet towards the end of their 1972 US tour, and as a result Peter Grant instructed road manager Richard Cole to find a larger aircraft for the band to use thenceforth. Tales of merry-making aboard 'the Starship' are legion, and the riotous atmosphere helped take the edge off the band's nerves. Bonham had another method of coping, too: "He flew us all the way from New York to LA once," Grant later claimed.

see *The Starship*

Fool In The Rain

This Latin-influenced song appears on 1979's *In Through The Out Door* and was the band's final single, climbing to #21 in early 1980 (backed with 'Hot Dog' as Swan Song SS 71003). One of several departures for the band on the album, it starts as a melodic pop number before unexpectedly breaking into a samba, supposedly inspired by TV coverage of the June 1978 football World Cup, held in Argentina a few months before the band recorded the album. They never performed it live.

Ford, Susan

b. July 6th 1957

The daughter of Gerald Ford, thirty-eighth President of the United States of America. She appeared on US TV's popular Dick Cavett Show early in 1975, and told the host that her favourite band was Led Zeppelin. As Plant put it in the March 13th 1975 issue of *Rolling Stone*: "I think it's really a mean deal that we haven't been invited around there for tea. Perhaps Gerry thought we'd wreck the joint… I was pleased to hear that they like our music around the White House. It's good to know they've got taste."

For Your Life

The bleak second track on 1976's *Presence*. Page told Rolling Stone's Cameron Crowe that it had been made up in the studio, though Plant's despondent lyrics were clearly put together with care. They apparently refer to an old friend (possibly even Jimmy Page) who'd become addicted to drugs. A snorting sound can be heard about five and a half minutes into the song, which was never performed live by the quartet. It was, however, the only track at their 2008 reunion never to have been performed before.

Foster, Perry

Leading exponent of the blues in the Midlands, and a notable early influence on Robert Plant, who sang in his Delta Blues Band for a time and who credits him with turning him onto the blues. "Perry was an incredible eight-string guitarist. Instead of playing it in the normal way, he used to play like Big Joe Williams with it half on his lap," he told Melody Maker on September 12th 1970. "He was a horrible bloke at times, but he was a real white bluesman, and when I was fifteen I fell immediately under his spell." As of 2008, Foster is still touring, and occasionally supports Plant at gigs.

'Four Seasons'

In an interview with Chris Welch published in Melody Maker in November 1977, Jimmy Page stated that his home studio at Plumpton Place had finally been finished, and excitedly spoke of a long piece he was at work on. It was "basically an instrumental. The original idea was to have four sections for the vocals, coming back to the same theme each time. But there would be four separate melody lines dealing with the four seasons. Robert would be doing the lyrics for it, but right now it's hard to tell if the lyrics would deal with the seasons." He went on to explain that it would definitely be a group effort, but that his efforts on it were being hampered by an assistant recently having lost two and a half years' worth of his cassettes while coming through customs. The untitled piece, which almost certainly evolved from the 'Swan Song' instrumental he'd mentioned earlier in the decade, was never recorded by the band.

Four Sticks

Built around an insistent riff reminiscent of 'Immigrant Song' from Led Zeppelin III, this complex number was recorded in December 1970 at Island Studios in London, and opened the second side of the band's untitled fourth LP. It took its title from the fact that John Bonham used two drumsticks in each hand to play its tribal rhythm, in apparent frustration at his difficulty in playing it with just two. As Jimmy Page later stated, "We tried that on numerous

occasions, and it didn't come off until the day Bonzo picked up two sets of sticks, so he had four sticks, and we did it. That was two takes, but that was because it was physically impossible for him to do another." The finished track also featured John Paul Jones on Moog synthesizer. Engineer Andy Johns later recalled: "It was a bastard to mix... I did five or six mixes." Page and Plant revisited the song in March 1972, when they taped some abortive sessions in India with the Bombay Orchestra. The band are thought only to have played it live once, in Copenhagen on May 3rd 1971.

Four Symbols

Informal name given to the band's untitled fourth album in 1971, inspired by the fact that each member was credited under an odd runic symbol in the artwork, rather than a name. According to Page, 'Four Symbols' was also what the band referred to the album as amongst themselves. Plant's symbol was an Egyptian-inspired feather feather in a circle (representing his role as writer), Page's was an odd self-designed rendering that looked like the word 'Zoso', Jones's was a circle containing three intersecting curves (culled from Rudolf Koch's Book Of Signs, at Page's suggestion) and Bonham's was three interlocking rings, which can be interpreted as a representation of man, woman and child, an aerial view of a drum kit, or the logo for Ballantine ale. Guest vocalist Sandy Denny also had a symbol (reproduced inside the sleeve), showing three triangles touching at their tips. As the drummer remarked at the time: "The runes are symbols which apply to each one of us. I wouldn't like to state what they mean. Each of us picked one." Plant added that "each of us decided to go away and choose a metaphorical-type symbol which somehow would represent each one of us individually – be it a state of mind, an opinion or something we felt strongly about, or whatever." Either way, the enigmatic concept meant that the press were obliged to represent the symbols in their coverage of the LP, something Page conceded had given the band 'a good laugh'.

Fox, Mitchell

US Swan Song employee who became an assistant to Richard Cole in 1977. According to Cole's memoirs, 'Mitchell spent most of his time trying to control the other assistants so I could have contact with the band members themselves.' He left the band's employ in 1978 in order to manage the Kentucky Headhunters, and is credited with being the first person to break the news of John Bonham's death on US radio, sharing his thoughts with a Philadelphia station – something Grant later said had 'angered' him.

Francis, Paul

Popular session drummer whom Beat Instrumental magazine reported was to join the New Yardbirds in the summer of 1968. According to his website, 'It was prior to a tour in Germany that Paul was called by Chris Dreja after being recommended for the job with the New Yardbirds. It was left that Chris would contact Jimmy Page to sort out a meeting, but on returning from Germany, Paul found that Chris Dreja had left the band and a meeting was never arranged.'

Friends

This eerie, Eastern-influenced ode to friendship was written at Bron-Yr-Aur and appears on Led Zeppelin III. It opens with some brief studio chatter before the repetitive acoustic riff comes in. After nine seconds, Page can be heard to exclaim 'Fuck!' As he told the NME in October 1974, "A lot of the songs we've done are just weird tunings, when I've altered the strings until they sounded right. 'Friends' is one – nobody would ever be able to work that out." The song features a memorable string arrangement by John Paul Jones, though he did not receive a songwriting credit, and ends with some Moog synthesizer, fading it into 'Celebration Day'. It was performed live only once, in Osaka, Japan on September 29th 1971, but was one of two tracks recorded by Page and Plant with the Bombay Symphony Orchestra in March of the following year (the other being 'Four Sticks').

81

Gallows Pole

This atmospheric song, which opens side two of *Led Zeppelin III*, has roots in numerous ancient folk ballads in which the female protagonist begs her executioner for a delay until her lover can bring the gold required to buy her reprieve. The band's rendition is similar to the 1939 arrangement by bluesman Huddie Ledbetter (or 'Lead Belly'), entitled 'Gallis Pole', though Jimmy Page learned it from a Folkways LP by US 12-string guitarist Fred Gerlach, and Plant adds an unorthodox ending in which she is in fact hanged. The recording features Page on banjo, 6 and 12-string guitar, and Jones on mandolin. It was only played live in 1971, but typified the band's ongoing interest in folk music.

Gates, Samantha & Stefan

The young brother and sister who can be seen clambering over the Giant's Causeway in County Antrim, Northern Ireland on the cover of *Houses Of The Holy*, shot over the course of several dawns in Ireland in October 1972. "It was wet and cold, and I've never been a Led Zeppelin fan," Samantha informed Q magazine in 2003. Still, the experience didn't deter her from working with Hipgnosis again: she can also be seen on the back of 1976's *Presence*.

Gerrard Street

It was in a basement below a record shop (or possible Ronnie Scott's jazz club) in this location in London's Soho that Led Zeppelin first played together one afternoon in August 1968, jamming on songs including 'Train Kept A-Rollin'' and 'As Long As I Have You'. According to Page, "The four of us just got together in this four-by-four room and started playing. Then we knew... we started laughing at each other." John Paul Jones had similarly happy memories: "There was just wall-to-wall amplifiers, Marshalls everywhere, a space for the door and that was it... The room just exploded. There were lots of silly grins..." Plant, meanwhile, said "All I can remember is that it was hot and it sounded good. Very, very exciting and very challenging, really... The power of it was remarkable." The success of the rehearsal was such that they immediately began preparing to record their debut album.

The Girl I Love She Got Long Black Wavy Hair

Blues classic performed only once by the band, during a BBC session on June 16th 1969 (for the Tasty Pop Sundae show). Their arrangement was based on the Sleepy John Estes original, entitled 'The Girl I Love She Got Long Curly Hair', and features a riff similar to that heard on 'Moby Dick' on *Led Zeppelin II*. It can be heard on the *BBC Sessions* boxed set, issued in 1997.

Gladsaxe Teen Club

Live venue just outside Copenhagen, Denmark, in which the band played their first ever gig, still billed as the Yardbirds, on Saturday, September 7th 1968. Audience member Jorgen Angel later stated: "They had this place in a school hall and they made an evening for young people every Saturday night. No alcohol. The hall could hold about one thousand people." The band arrived in the afternoon, set up and rehearsed as decorations were put up. Their performance that evening lasted about 45 minutes, and there was reportedly some displeasure in the audience when they found that Page had brought an entirely new line-up with him, though they apparently soon won them over. Also on the bill were local acts Fourways and Bodies.

Going To California

Similar in feel to 'That's The Way' on *Led Zeppelin III*, this optimistic ballad appears on the band's untitled fourth LP. It was written at Bron-Yr-Aur and is thought to have derived its inspiration from the work of Canadian singer-songwriter Joni Mitchell, whom all the band members admired. Plant confessed to *Spin* magazine in 2002 that it was "a bit embarrassing at times lyrically, but it did sum up a period of my life when I was 22." Page told Melody Maker in March 1971 that "the words relate to earthquakes, and right after we did the number the earthquake happened in California, which was a bit unnerving!" The band introduced the song to audiences on their March 1971 'Back To The Clubs' UK tour, and were still playing it in 1975, when they featured it at Earl's Court.

Goldberg, Danny

Well-known US rock journalist and publicist who served as US Vice-President of Led Zeppelin's Swan Song label from 1974. He upset Grant by signing female singer Mirabai in 1975, something Peter Grant later described as "a perfect example of people making decisions I wouldn't have made, and me having to support it." Grant sacked him in May 1976, reportedly over Goldberg's refusal to act in a manner he deemed unethical in arranging a Bad Company tour. Following Bonham's death, Goldberg told Rolling Stone: "He had this incredible talent. I don't think there's ever been anybody like him. As brilliant as Jimmy Page is, Led Zeppelin will never be the same without John. It may be better, it may be worse. But there's no one else in the world who can play drums like that." He also commented that the drummer "was a huge adult with the emotions of a six year-old child, and an artistic licence to indulge in any sort of infantile or destructive behaviour that amused him."

Golden God

At John Bonham's 25th birthday party in LA's Laurel Canyon on May 31st 1973, Robert Plant climbed a palm tree and proclaimed to anyone within earshot "I am a golden god!" The tongue-in-cheek utterance was duly immortalised by Rolling Stone writer Cameron Crowe in his *Almost Famous* film in 2000. "It was an unfortunate moment, because someone drove across the garden in a Cadillac and wedged it between two palm trees," Plant told Blender magazine in 2002. "And I was busy making sure everyone knew exactly who and what I was. I wanted to get it in perspective before the party really started. It was the night that George Harrison karate-chopped Bonzo's birthday cake, and therefore had to be flung into the swimming pool."

Good Times Bad Times

The first song on the band's debut, and a clear statement of their power and musicianship. "I remember there was a Hammond organ in [Olympic Studios]," Jones recalled, "which I used and I wrote the riff to 'Good Times Bad Times'." The memorable sound on Jimmy Page's guitar part was achieved by playing his Telecaster guitar through a Leslie speaker cabinet. John Bonham's drum part has been much admired, as he plays triplets on a bass drum using a single pedal, while most drummers require two pedals to achieve the same effect. As Page told Guitar World magazine in 1993: "The most stunning thing about the track, of course, is Bonzo's amazing kick drum. It's superhuman, when you realise he was not playing with double kick. That's one kick drum! That's when people started understanding what he was all about." The track was issued as a 45 in the US on January 12th 1969 (backed with 'Communication Breakdown'), and climbed to #80. Though parts of it were incorporated into 'Whole Lotta Love' and 'Communication Breakdown' onstage, the band never played it live in its entirety. To the surprise of many hardcore fans, however, they opened their December 2007 reunion gig with it.

Graham, Bill

b. Jan 8th 1931 / d. Oct. 25th 1991

Famed US promoter who did much to help Led Zeppelin break America in early 1969, by booking them at his Fillmore venues in New York and San Francisco. Perhaps the era's most influential individual in live music, he went on to assist the band on subsequent tours, though his relationship with them broke down after the notorious 'Oakland incident' of Saturday July 23rd 1977. After two of his employees had been seriously assaulted by Peter Grant, John Bonham, Richard Cole and John Bindon, he released a statement declaring: "There were ten years of ongoing respectful relationship between members of the Led Zeppelin organisation and myself. However, the incident in question that took place on Saturday afternoon encroached on moral boundaries." What also infuriated him was that "we weren't the only ones it happened to. We were just the *last* ones." Graham also stated that he would never book the group again, adding: "For these people to assume that might makes right takes me back to Nazi Germany, and I've blocked pretty much all of my childhood out." John Paul Jones was unmoved by such remarks, later commenting that "The first time we turned up at the Fillmore I remember him just screaming and shouting at everybody. He was quite an unpleasant person."

Graham, Bobby
b. 1940

Prolific session drummer with whom Jimmy Page worked as a double act on innumerable mid-60s sessions. They met in 1960, when Page was playing with Neil Christian and the Crusaders and Graham was backing Joe Brown, and became friends. When Graham moved into session and production work a couple of years later, he used Page as often as possible, and the two of them formed 'Jimbo Publishing' to cover the songs they wrote. Like Page, he also released some sides of his own on Fontana in 1965 – 'Skin Deep' / 'Zoom, Widge and Wag' (TF521, 1/65) and 'Teensville' / 'Grotty Drums' (TF667, 2/66). Page contributed to these, and Graham returned the favour by playing drums on the guitarist's 45. He also produced some records for the Pretty Things, and wrote 'You Don't Believe Me' with Page and singer Phil May for their *Get The Picture* LP (Fontana TL 5280, 1965). On his website, Graham comments: "Jimmy wasn't one of the most way out and weirdest characters

I ever met, he was very quiet, very shy. He had a slightly dirtier sound than Big Jim Sullivan, they used to alternate a lot."

Grant, Anthony
b. May 29th 1925

Long-serving MP and Parliamentary Secretary to the Board of Trade in 1970, in which capacity he presented the band with gold discs on October 16th for sales of a million copies of the 'Whole Lotta Love' 45 in the US and a million copies of *Led Zeppelin II* in Europe. Again, the band's contribution to the UK economy was being publicly acknowledged by the government, this time accompanied by what Sounds called 'a delightfully 'hooray' speech, full of cross-references between progressive pop and progressive government'.

see *Dunwoody, Gwyneth*

Grant, Gloria
Peter Grant's diminutive wife, whom he married in 1962 and went on to have two children with, Warren and Helen. A local ballet teacher who shunned the limelight, she looked after their house and children during his lengthy absences on tour, but left him for their farm manager in 1975, prompting him to suffer a major breakdown. According to film-maker Peter Clifton (director of *The Song Remains The Same*), "Gloria loved him… she really loved Peter. But she told me that Peter loved Jimmy more than her." Unusually, Grant took custody of their children following their divorce. The couple were never reconciled.

Grant, Peter

b. April 5th 1935 / d. Nov 21st 1995

Unquestionably the 'fifth member' of Led Zeppelin (who knew him as 'G'), this enormous, swashbuckling individual managed their career from its outset to its end. As Robert Plant told Melody Maker in September 1970: "Had we not had Peter behind us we could easily have gone to pieces. As much as the credit goes to us, it goes to old Peter as well."

Born illegitimate and raised in south London by his mother (who worked for the Church of England pensions board), Grant rarely referred to his impoverished childhood in later years. He was evacuated to Surrey during the war, and left school at 13 for work in a sheet-metal factory. Abandoning that after five weeks, he gained early insights into showbiz by working as a stagehand at the Croydon Empire. When that came to an end he earned a living as a waiter and a messenger for Reuters before doing National Service in the army. He enjoyed this, as he was put in charge of the dining hall and thus arranged entertainments for the other soldiers. Upon demob he worked as – amongst other things –a holiday camp entertainments officer (in Jersey), a doorman at the 2Is Coffee Bar in Soho ('the birthplace of British rock and roll'), a film extra (doubling for Robert Morley and Anthony Quinn), a wrestler ('Count Massimo') and a minibus driver (for artists).

An imposing six-footer who weighed in at a minimum of 18 stone, his talent for hustling made him a natural for the music world, which he entered as an agent for notorious promoter / manager Don Arden in 1963. As well as tour-managing for US artists visiting Britain, such as Little Eva, the Everly Brothers, Jerry Lee Lewis, Bo Diddley, Gene Vincent, Chuck Berry and Little Richard, he signed up acts such as the Nashville Teens and the Alan Price R&B Combo (later the Animals, with whom he first visited the US). He quickly earned a reputation for fiercely protecting his acts and taking no nonsense from promoters. As he told Melody Maker on June 22nd 1974: "All I know is that if I hadn't been a fucking stagehand at the Croydon Empire for 15 bob a show, and if I hadn't done all the things I have, like being a film extra and on the road with Gene Vincent and the rest, there's no way I could've coped with the events of the past five or six years."

By late 1966 he'd formed RAK Music Management with his old friend Mickie Most, occupying a shabby office at 155 Oxford Street which remained Grant's base until 1974. His early signings (the Flintstones, the She Trinity) had limited success, but he struck gold with novelty studio act the New Vaudeville Band, who'd had a UK #4 hit with Winchester Cathedral in September 1966. The single went to #1 in America that December, so he criss-crossed the States with a hastily cobbled-together version of the group, gaining important knowledge of life and work on the road. Having learnt valuable lessons such as the importance of radio play and the stranglehold promoters had on concert earnings, in May 1967 he took over management of the Yardbirds from Simon Napier-Bell, apparently at Jimmy Page's instigation (Page knew him from the sessions he'd done for Most). Grant was horrified to learn how little the Yardbirds themselves were earning, and swiftly shook up the approach groups usually took towards touring, insisting that the band and not the promoter should receive the lion's share of the proceeds from gigs. As he told *Sounds* on October 24th 1970: "I thought the musicians, who bring the people in, should be the people who get the wages. Now we take the risks. We pay the rent of the hall, we pay the local supporting groups, we pay the promoter to set it up for us. And that is the way big names are made these days. Not via the press or *Ready, Steady, Go!*, but by people seeing them and making up their own minds."

The Yardbirds had two guitarists when Grant took them on, but Jeff Beck soon departed, leaving Page to lead the band on innumerable tours and recording sessions. Grant was also overseeing the careers of Beck and singer Terry Reid, with all three being produced by Most. The frail, intense and brilliant Page appealed strongly both to Grant's protective and commercial instincts, and when the Yardbirds collapsed in mid-1968, the two agreed to set about putting a new band together. Grant later told Tight But Loose of an occasion when he was driving Page down Shaftesbury Avenue that summer: "We were in a traffic jam, and I said to Jimmy, 'What are you going to do? Do you want to go back to sessions, or what?' And he said, 'Well, I've got some ideas'.

He didn't mention anybody. I said, 'What about a producer?', and he said, 'I'd like to do that too, if you can get a deal'. So I thought, great, let's do it." At the recommendation of Terry Reid they went to see Robert Plant singing with Obbstweedle in Birmingham that July, but before they could finalise the nascent band's line-up Grant had to fly to America with the Jeff Beck Group. In his absence, Page and Plant got to know each other at Page's Pangbourne home, and Plant recommended John Bonham. John Paul Jones had independently contacted Page, and the quartet soon set about rehearsing.

Grant, meanwhile, was witnessing first-hand how desperate American audiences had become for heavy blues-rock. He stayed in touch with Page via long-distance telephone (later recalling the guitarist's excitement at Bonham), and on his return he flew to Scandinavia with them, where they were fulfilling outstanding Yardbirds dates as 'the New Yardbirds'. He saw them play for the first time at Copenhagen's Gladsaxe Teen Club on September 7th, and later told Tight But Loose: "I remember standing on the side of the stage and being amazed." They returned to England on September 18th and entered London's Olympic Studios to record their debut soon afterwards. The New Yardbirds was clearly not a good enough name for such a promising band, so Page suggested 'Lead Zeppelin', after a quip Keith Moon had made in 1966. Grant removed the 'a' from 'Led' in order to avoid mispronunciation, and began to scout about for a deal. At the end of October he and Page flew to New York, completed album tapes and artwork in hand. They duly signed a five-year contract with Ahmet Ertegun and Jerry Wexler at Atlantic, to the outrage of Columbia (who assumed that their efforts on behalf of the Yardbirds would earn them first refusal). The $200,000 advance Grant secured was described as a record at the time, and led to accusations that the group was a hype. In typically insouciant fashion, he and Page responded by naming the group's publishing wing 'Superhype'. By December Grant was busy organising the band's first US tour and, after some warm-up dates in the UK, the band departed for California on Christmas Eve, 1968.

Extraordinarily, Grant never had a contract with Led Zeppelin. Instead, it was all done on a handshake basis, with total trust on both sides. Over the next twelve years Grant subsumed much of his own life into the band, whom he treated as if they were his sons, and his blunt approach sent ripples through the industry. His immense bulk and intimidating presence was a vital part of their image from the start. Determined to avoid the naïve merchandising deals that had cost the Beatles so dear, he later commented: "I was paid to protect the boys' assets in every way. I was always fair, though, and went by my instincts." He used his close knowledge of the US live market to tailor the band's approach towards it, strategically building their profile in different areas. As Rolling Stone put it on March 4th 1971, 'Grant has it all mapped out. He gets in contact with local radio stations in America and finds out what are the most popular cuts in a particular area, and then gets the group to feature them at concerts. It's that sort of attention to detail that pays off.' Having befriended Bill Graham, he also oversaw the band's move from small clubs to larger venues – they became the first foreign band to play Graham's Fillmore Auditorium in San Francisco, for example.

A lover of the road, he insisted on attending almost every gig the band played, thereby making it clear that they were not to be ripped off. He was quite happy to do his own dirty work with crooked promoters and bootleggers, too. As he remarked to Sounds: "If I'm out at a concert and somebody is gonna do something that's snide to one of my artists, then I'll fucking tread on 'em without thinking about it. I mean, that's what they hire you for. I don't believe in pussyfooting around if it's my artist." A believer in what he called 'verbal violence', he preferred prodding people to punching them; he was even known to use his formidable gut to shove people away as an intimidation tactic. Arguably the only genuinely revealing moment in the ill-conceived *Song Remains The Same* film comes when Grant berates a promoter whom he believed had sanctioned the sale of unofficial merchandise inside Baltimore Civic Center on July 23rd 1973. For their part, the band were always mindful of the importance of Grant to their success. "Peter is ultra-important, the fifth member of the group," Plant told Melody Maker in February 1976. "He's never run us, he's always put things to us for joint decisions. I know what the alternatives in management can be, even nowadays, and they're far, far removed from our joyous little relationship."

He never participated in the band's musical decisions, recognising that their functions were very different, and that the days of managers interfering with band's musical policies had passed with the 1960s. "I wasn't a musician, and didn't profess to know much about music," he said after the band's demise. "My main contribution to Zeppelin was marketing and dealing with the business." He did, however, have input into their artwork, suggesting the paper strip that ran around copies of *Houses Of The Holy* and packaging *In Through The Out Door* in a brown paper bag. Grant never lost sight of the importance of Led Zeppelin's mystique, keeping a tight rein on the number of interviews they gave, declining all offers of TV work from 1970 onwards and blocking any 45 releases in the UK. He revelled in his disregard for such conventions, telling Melody Maker on June 22nd 1974: "I know some of the bigshots at the record company cringe when they're with me, because I don't even own a suit, just two pairs of jeans. But I know they have to do it because of what you represent. Which is great."

By all accounts Grant combined an ability to terrify those who transgressed with a distinctive sense of humour and personal flair. Once, for example, he offered a jaded American hotel manager the chance to hurl the contents of a room out the window, and picked up the $490 tab himself. He dressed scruffily, typically in jeans, huge satin shirts and jackets with elbow patches (often accessorising with a coonskin cap, a neckerchief and copious jewellery), and always had Country Life magazine delivered to him on tour. Like Page, Grant avidly collected Victorian and art nouveau pieces, and they would frequently comb antique shops for bargains, as well as buying art nouveau at auction. Having lived in Norwood and Shepherd's Bush, in 1971 Grant and his wife Gloria moved to a luxury estate in Purley, Surrey (opposite comedian Ronnie Corbett), which cost £36,000. His next move was to the imposing Horselunges Manor, near Hellingly in Sussex, bought for £100,000 in 1973. A moated Elizabethan mansion set in 65 acres of land, it perfectly complimented Grant's buccaneering image, and he filled it with his collection of antiques, including a four-poster bed that had once belonged to Sarah Bernhardt. When he was there he would usually refuse to speak to anyone other than the band members. According to ill-fated *Song Remains The Same* director Joe Massot, "At home in the country he was another person, playing with his children, who adored him. He was not at all pretentious in his home life, and he really was a warm family man." Mickie Most concurred, recalling: "He'd throw big parties with jousting on the lawn and people would dress up in Knights of the Round Table outfits, with jesters, drinking mead and all that. He had some fun there."

Grant's obsession with the band, to say nothing of the temptations that beset them on the road, led him to neglect his marriage, and in 1975 his wife announced she was leaving him. He was stunned. "The split-up with Gloria was like the nail in the coffin," said Mickie Most. "Then he was kind of morally broken and he wasn't the Peter Grant that we all knew and had a good time with." Always overweight and a heavy smoker, by 1977 he was using cocaine heavily, and his explosive temper had started to become more of a liability than an asset. Backstage at the Oakland Coliseum on July 24th, Grant went a step further, crossing the line into assault. The so-called 'Oakland incident' greatly damaged his reputation, and was one of the only things he would subsequently admit to regretting. "Oakland was a nightmare and very heavy," he later said. "It was a flashpoint situation that got out of hand. It could have got a lot worse. It was just a very regrettable incident." In early 1978 he suffered a minor heart attack. Increasing paranoia made him cover his home with security cameras, and when there alone between tours he would frequently call the police, fearing intruders. It was a long way from the swaggering super-confidence of the band's heyday. By the late 1970s the industry was changing, too. Accountants were playing an ever-larger role, and the rough and ready, cash-based approach that Grant was used to was fast being superseded.

John Bonham's death on Septeber 25th 1980 hit him very hard, and though he was theoretically still managing the other three band members, by his own account "by 1982 I just wasn't up to it – mentally and everything. I'd just had enough." He negotiated Plant's solo deal, and arranged Page's ill-fated soundtrack for Michael Winner's appalling *Death Wish 2*, but his activities on their behalf tailed off thereafter as his addictions took deeper hold and he ran through his earnings to feed them. His Range Rover (numberplate LZ1) was occasionally seen in the local supermarket car park, but he was a recluse for much of the decade, and eventually moved to a flat above the garage at Horselunges because the house had been so neglected. By 1990 he had lost weight, conquered his addictions and moved to a flat in Upper Carlisle Road, Eastbourne, where he enjoyed life as a grandfather and local celebrity. In a twist he loved, he was even approached to become a magistrate. Instead, he stuck to unofficial pursuits, guesting at music industry conferences, giving the occasional interview and even dressing up as a chauffeur to ferry couples about on their wedding day in one of his vintage cars.

He died of a heart attack whilst driving his son Warren on November 21st 1995, and was buried on December 4th. Alan Callan, the former UK head of Swan Song, gave the eulogy, saying: "His greatness was that he was a man of parts. He was as adept at the ominous glance as he was at the disarming remark... Wherever Peter is going now, I hope they've got their act together." Robert Plant, meanwhile, issued his own tribute in the form of a statement: "I owe so much of my confidence to they way he calmed and nurtured and cajoled all of us to be what we were. He was larger than life. A giant who turned the game upside down. Fierce, uncompromising, with great humour."

Greer, Germaine

b. Jan 29th 1939

Feminist, Big Brother contestant and self-described 'supergroupie' who can be seen flirting embarrassingly with Robert Plant in Sydney in the band's 2003 retrospective DVD, footage shot in February 1972. She also attended their famous Royal Albert Hall concert of January 9th 1970. 'The sound came up to me with a force that pummelled me breathless,' she panted in the Daily Telegraph on December 10th 2007. 'No other band ever managed to make a sound like that. It was certainly loud, but it was also driving, pushing along with incredible energy...' She evidently hadn't lost her predilection for the singer either, contending that 'the spring god

Dionysus had arisen and was shaking his streaming red-gold mane on stage'.

Groupies

Though three of the four members of Led Zeppelin were married from the band's earliest days (and Jimmy Page was in a steady relationship with Charlotte Martin), rumours of their sexual voracity on the road persisted. Many of the most salacious tales are contained in road manager Richard Cole's memoirs, *Stairway To Heaven*. 'I would often saunter down to the hotel lobbies where the young ladies would congregate and invite some of them up to our rooms,' he writes. 'They were looking for some fun – and so were we. There was no emotional involvement on either side.' Cole goes on to describe the infamous 'shark incident', as well as a lesser-known tale involving him and Page putting live octopi into a bathtub with a pair of groupies on their second US tour. 'As we watched them play, the octopuses somehow instinctively knew just where to congregate and just where to place their tentacles,' he observes. On another occasion, he says, the band took it in turn shaving the pubic hair off a girl named Candy. 'We saw no reason to show any self-restraint ourselves,' he continues. 'The flesh was out there for the taking, and it was easy to become a hedonist. There seemed to be no reason not to.'

On their 1973 US tour, the band were apparently impressed by a particularly eager (and wealthy) coterie of Texas groupies who'd hired their own plane to tail the Starship through airspace. Nonetheless, touring was by no means a non-stop orgy. "I was in Chicago with

Robert once," publicist BP Fallon told *Vox* in December 1994. "We were in his hotel room and these girls came and banged on the door, all ready for the third-leg boogie, and we're sitting there playing Monopoly." Indeed, the novelty of taking advantage of groupies wore off after their first few US tours. According to Cole, by the mid-70s 'Many of the old groupies had simply disappeared. Some had simply grown up. A few had gotten married. Too many had died of drug overdoses.'

see *Des Barres, Pamela / GTOs, the / Maddox, Lorri*

The GTOs

An acronym for 'Girls Together Outrageously', a five-strong collective of Los Angeles groupies assembled by Frank Zappa in 1968. "I was young when I first went to America," Robert Plant later remarked. "I was 19 years old, and I went crazy. I met The GTOs and my mind just snapped. I'm from a nowhere town in the Midlands and here were these girls with bare breasts blatantly coming on, and of course we went crazy." One of the GTOs was Pamela Ann Miller, known (as per the quintet's conceit) as 'Miss Pamela'. "When you saw Led Zeppelin play," she gushed in her *Let's Spend The Night Together* book, "it was all over bar the orgasm." In her case, that happened too, as she became Jimmy Page's lover from July 1969. The GTOs' sole album, *Permanent Damage* (Straight STS 1059, 1969), is an entertaining if self-indulgent mish-mash of spoken word and half-baked music (including a contribution from Jeff Beck), and contains a dedication to Page.

see *Des Barres, Pamela*

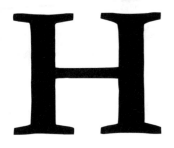

Hale, Norman

One-time member of the Tornados (from 1961-62) who was working as house pianist at Jersey's Behan's club in 1975. On December 3rd he was joined onstage by John Paul Jones and John Bonham, who promised to bring their bandmates along a week later. Sure enough, the whole of Led Zeppelin played a 45-minute set with him on December 10th, tearing through rock and roll standards and a handful of their own songs to the delight of the 350-strong crowd. Plant remained seated throughout, owing to injuries sustained in Rhodes that August, but was reported to have enjoyed the reunion greatly. The band were in tax exile on Jersey, and hadn't performed since their gigs at Earl's Court in May.

Hammer Of The Gods

Penned by US rock hack Stephen Davis, this controversial 1985 book – boasting considerable input from Richard Cole – focused on the more sensational aspects of Led Zeppelin's career, much to their disgust. "The worst thing about that book was that it had no humour in it," John Paul Jones told Blow By Blow magazine in 1992. "All that stuff was a hell of a lot of fun. All the stories, when told properly, were great fun." Jimmy Page, meanwhile, remarked: "I opened it up in the middle somewhere and started to read, and I just threw it out the window. I was living by a river then, so it actually found its way to the bottom of the sea." Plant, meanwhile, told Spin magazine in 2002 that "The guy who wrote that book knew nothing about the band. I think he'd hung around us once. He got all his information from a guy who had a heroin problem who happened to be associated with us."

Hammerwood Park

Grade I-listed 65-room mansion in East Grinstead, bought at auction by the band in 1973, with a view to creating a studio akin to Headley Grange or Mick Jagger's Stargroves. As Swan Song boss Alan Callan recalled, "they were going to turn it into Swan Song offices, residential apartments and a studio complex. They didn't have time to get more detailed planning because they were going off on tour. Peter Grant had this great idea they would lend the house to the local constabulary, so they could train their police dogs there." Unfortunately it proved too riddled with dry rot for anything much to be viable, though Grant filmed his 'fantasy' sequences for *The Song Remains The Same* there. Thereafter the band allegedly forgot they owned it. It was eventually sold in 1982.

Hampstead Country Club

Quaintly-named North London venue which Jimmy Page, Robert Plant and Peter Grant travelled to on July 31st 1968 to check out John Bonham performing with Tim Rose. Duly impressed, they set about persuading him to join their new band.

Hands

A prominent feature of John Bonham's drum solos onstage was his ability to play using his hands instead of sticks. "You just get a lovely little tone out of the drums that you don't get with sticks," he told Melody Maker in April 1970, adding to Disc that June: "You get the absolute true sound, there's no wood involved. It hurts at first, but the skin hardens and now I can hit a drum harder with my hands than with sticks."

Hardie, George

b. 1944

Designer of the sleeve to *Led Zeppelin I*, having been recommended to Peter Grant on the strength of work he'd done on Jeff Beck's *Truth* LP. "I was summoned to an office on Oxford Street," he told *Q* magazine of his first meeting with Grant in October 1968. "I sat waiting for him with the group. Robert Plant kept running off to the Marquee, where the band were playing that night, to see if a queue was forming outside." Hardie's original concept for "a multiple sequential image of a zeppelin with clouds and waves" was pooh-poohed by Page, who briefed him to manipulate the famous image of the Hindenburg airship crashing in 1937 instead. He was paid only £60 for his efforts, though the result helped him find design work for other bands including Pink Floyd and Black Sabbath. He is now Professor of Graphic Design at Brighton University.

Harper, Roy

b. June 12th 1941

Idiosyncratic British singer-songwriter who met and befriended Jimmy Page and Robert Plant at the 1969 Bath Festival. Both were already fans of his work, and acknowledged his influence on their own songs by naming the closing track on *Led Zeppelin III* 'Hats Off To (Roy) Harper'. "He's a really talented bloke who's had a lot of problems," Page told Disc in October 1970. Page played lead acoustic guitar on 'The Same Old Rock' on Harper's 1971 *Stormcock* LP, recorded between July and December 1970, under the pseudonym 'S Flavius Mercurius'. Harper toured America with Led Zeppelin in 1973, opening for them at certain gigs. According to UK tabloid journalist Bob Hart, Harper was "an extraordinary choice of opening act. The audience was bored shitless, half-asleep, stoned out of their minds, ready to rock... I don't know why Led Zeppelin had Roy Harper there – he's totally nuts. It was hard to tell just what San Francisco thought of this eccentric Englishman, sitting on a chair, playing acoustic guitar in front of 50,000 people and singing songs about cricket!" After the tour, Harper filmed a cameo (as a businessman) in Peter Grant's section of the *Song Remains The Same* movie.

On February 14th 1974 Plant, Page and Bonham joined him onstage at London's Rainbow Theatre to launch his *Valentine* album, which featured a dedication to the quartet. Bonham even wore ballet tights and played guitar. The album included another track with Page playing lead guitar, 'Male Chauvinist Pig Blues'.

They said I was leaving to join George Harrison. Well, I've never even met the guy. That's how much I know him. I'd like to meet him." His wish was granted on May 31st 1973, when the Beatle joined the band for the drummer's birthday celebrations in Laurel Canyon after the LA Forum gig later bootlegged as 'Bonzo's Birthday Party'. As Atlantic executive Phil Carson later recounted: "When the time came for Bonzo to cut this giant birthday cake they'd made for him, George rushed over, lifted off the top tier and tossed it at Bonzo. John wasn't having any of that of course, so he picked up the second tier and heaved it after a fast-disappearing Harrison. It caught him right between the shoulders, a beautiful shot. Not long afterwards, Bonzo heaved George into the pool and Patti Boyd followed. Everybody but Peter Grant ended up in the pool… When George and Patti left the party wrapped in blankets, George said he hadn't had so much fun in years."

The same year the band sought to sign Harper to Swan Song. In February 1975 Plant told French magazine Rock & Folk: "He is a strange man, you know. He doesn't want to make any concessions… it upsets us that he's not as well-known as he should be." The mutual respect went on well past the 1970s: Harper and Page collaborated on an LP (*Whatever Happened To Jugular?*) in 1985, and in February 1994 he described Plant as 'a massive talent' to Dirty Linen magazine, adding: "He knows how to take an old blues song that's been around for a hundred years and turn it into something that's immediately AM radio for 18 year-olds. That's a huge pop talent."

Harrison, George
b. Feb. 25th 1943 / d. Nov. 29th 2001
Beatles guitarist with whom it was rumoured in 1970 that John Bonham was planning to leave Led Zeppelin to play with Harrison, to which he responded the following November in Melody Maker, saying: "There was an unbelievable rumour about a year ago.

Harry, Bill
Veteran music journalist and press agent hired by Peter Grant in 1969 to handle the band's media enquiries. "My job basically as a PR was to keep the press away," he commented of his unorthodox brief. "In those days pop stars would do anything for publicity. Peter just wasn't interested. He'd say 'no' to everything." He toured the US with them in 1969 and attended the chaotic Newport Festival on July 6th, as well as the party afterwards ("one of the boys went to say something to one of the girls and he was sick all over her"). He later recalled: "We went to all these clubs in America and

the places were flooded with groupies. It was always booze, and mainly lager. Everybody had hangovers. But most of that was caused by sitting around in rooms for 15 hours of tension before a gig." He resigned in 1972 (after John Bonham drunkenly ripped his shirt and trousers in the Coach and Horses pub in London's Soho), and was replaced by BP Fallon.

Harwood, Keith

Engineer who worked on *Houses Of The Holy*, *Physical Graffiti* and *Presence*. Speaking of the November 1976 *Presence* sessions, Jimmy Page told Guitar World magazine in 1998: "Me and the engineer, Keith Harwood, just started mixing until we would fall asleep. Then whoever would wake up first would call the other and we'd go back in and continue to work until we passed out again." Harwood tragically died in a car accident on his way home from a mixing session for the Rolling Stones' *Love You Live* in London's Olympic Studios in September 1976. His death was later tastelessly linked to the supposed 'curse of Led Zeppelin'.

Hats Off To (Roy) Harper

The closing track on *Led Zeppelin III*, and an eccentric tribute to their friend Roy Harper. According to Plant, "Me and Pagey just sat in the studio at Headley Grange and played through some distortion machines and said 'Hats off to Harper', along with all the roadies up the back singing 'yeah' and banging tambourines. When we played it for old Harper he didn't know what to say... Despite the subsequent confusion of critics, who somehow misconstrued the meaning and thought that it was some kind of putdown, it's just an acknowledgement of a friendship." Credited as arranger is one 'Charles Obscure' (thought to be a flippant pseudonym for Page), and indeed the arrangement is obscure, incorporating snatches of 'Shake Em On Down' by Bukka White and 'Lone Wolf Blues' by Oscar Woods, as well as heavily treated vocals by Plant. The song was edited from a longer version on which the band jammed around numerous other songs, and they never performed it live.

see *Harper, Roy*

Haymarket

English pub in LA where Robert Plant riotously celebrated his 21st birthday after a gig in Indianapolis on August 20th 1969. Now that he was old enough to drink in the US, Watney's Red Barrel beer was on tap, and he was given a cassette recorder as a present.

Headley Grange

18th Century manor house in Headley, East Hampshire, where numerous Led Zeppelin classics were recorded. Built as a workhouse ('Headley Poor') in 1795, it was the scene of a famous riot in 1830 and was converted into a private residence by one Thomas Kemp in 1870. It remained thus until the 1960s, when it became a hostel for students from nearby Farnham School of Art. In 1970 or thereabouts it was converted into a studio, which it remained for much of the decade. Jimmy Page heard of it from Fleetwood Mac, who'd been rehearsing in the village, and Led Zeppelin first used it for the *Led Zeppelin III* sessions in May 1970, shortly after Page and Plant had left Bron-Yr-Aur. Page later told the BBC that "It was a sort of three-storey house with a huge open hall with a staircase going up… It was a pretty austere place, I loved the atmosphere of it. I really did, personally. The others got a bit spooked out by it… You didn't have anything like a snooker table or anything like that. No recreational purists at all. It was really good for discipline and getting on with the job." He went on to tell Guitar World magazine in January 2002 that it was "very Charles Dickens, dank and spooky." Though Peter Grant had some nostalgia for the area, having been evacuated there in the Second World War, Jones later remembered the house as a "horrible place, dripping with damp", adding that "we all ran in when we arrived in a mad scramble to get the driest rooms."

Its atmosphere proved no barrier to creativity, however: they went on to tape large chunks of *Led Zeppelin III*, their untitled fourth LP and *Physical Graffiti* there. While there the band used the Rolling Stones' mobile recording truck, which considerably reduced the pressure they faced in formal studios. "You really do need the sort of facilities where you can take a break for a cup of tea and a wander around the garden, and then go back in and do whatever you have to do," Page commented in 1970. "Instead of that feeling of walking into a studio, down a flight of steps and into fluorescent lights… and opening up the big soundproof door

and being surrounded by acoustic tiles." Plant concurred, remarking during the sessions for the band's fourth album that "a recording studio is an immediate imposition on you. It's rather a limiting factor as opposed to sitting around a fire, playing away. You can also do quite a lot of experimenting when you've got a mobile truck. Most of the mood for this album was brought about in settings that we hadn't come across before. We were living and recording in this old falling-apart mansion way out in the country… the mood was incredible."

Heartbreaker

Featuring one of Jimmy Page's most celebrated riffs, this hard rock staple starts side two of *Led Zeppelin II* and featured the debut of the guitarist's celebrated Gibson Les Paul / Marshall speaker stack combination. The frenetic stand-alone solo was in fact recorded separately, and spliced in almost as an afterthought. It was one of only two songs the band played live every year that they toured (the other being 'Communication Breakdown'). Page would often incorporate elements of other songs and tunes during his solo onstage, including folk standard 'Greensleeves' and Simon & Garfunkel's '59th Street Bridge Song'.

Hendrix, Jimi

b. Nov. 27th 1942 / d. Sept. 18th 1970
Arguably the foremost electric guitarist of his generation. Jimmy Page told Mojo in August 2004 that Hendrix "was like a volcano at the time," though he never saw him live. "Being in the Yardbirds and then Zeppelin, it was always, 'Oh

well, I'll see him next time'. And then there wasn't a next time." He also told Guitar World magazine in 1993 that "I did actually go into a club in New York called Salvation, and he was there, but he was totally out of it. He didn't really know who anybody was – he was barely conscious. Somebody was just kind of holding him up." Plant, meanwhile, commented on Swiss radio in 2002 that "I saw Hendrix when I was 19, in the middle of English candy pop. There was, as there is today, a lot of very shallow music, and in the middle of it, all just when you were about to plunge your head in the gas oven and say goodbye because you couldn't stand it anymore, you saw those three guys playing. The power and intensity it was unbelievable." John Paul Jones, meanwhile, told Mojo magazine in December 1997 that "I never used to listen to rock at all apart from Jimi Hendrix – about the only rock record I had, I think."

Hey Hey What Can I Do?

The only non-LP track to be released by the band during its lifetime, this folk-pop tune tells the tale of a wronged lover and was taped at London's Island Studios in July 1970. It appeared as the B-side to their November 1970 'Immigrant Song' 45, and was also included on the March 1972 compilation *The New Age Of Atlantic* (Atlantic K20024). Melody Maker's review of the album called the song 'a pleasant group composition, with Zeppelin swinging in their best non-heavy groove'.

Hinton, Mick

John Bonham's long-term (and long-suffering) drum roadie. His brave attempts to salvage Bonham's kit during the riot at Milan's Vigorelli Velodrome on July 5th 1971 landed him in hospital with severe head cuts from a hurled bottle. One famous tale has a drunk Bonham wetting himself in first class on a transatlantic flight in 1975, only to make his way to economy and offer a delighted Hinton an exchange of seats. As well as setting up and tuning Bonham's kit, Hinton's responsibilities included the nerve-wracking task of covering the drummer's gong with lighter fuel and setting it alight at the right moment at gigs. His work evidently proved exhausting: during one gig at the LA Forum he reportedly fell asleep inside Bonham's bass drum.

Hipgnosis

Graphic design agency founded by Storm Thorgerson and Aubrey 'Po' Powell in 1969, and responsible for many underground rock LP sleeves, as well as the mystical artwork for *Houses Of The Holy* and *Presence*. Their relationship with the band got off to a shaky start, according to Page, who told Guitar Player magazine in 1998 that "This guy Storm came in carrying this picture of an electric green tennis court with a tennis racquet on it. I said, 'What the hell does that have to do with anything?' And he said, 'Racket – don't you get it?' I said, 'Are you trying to imply our music is a 'racket'? Get out!'" Though realising the sleeve for *Houses Of The Holy* ultimately proved complicated and frustrating, the agency was used again in 1976 for *Presence*. The concept for the artwork was that of placing an alien, futuristic object into everyday situations from the recent past, in order to create an unsettling effect. Thorgeson later explained that the idea was "to tamper with nostalgic pictures of the 30s and 40s with an object from the future, which was basically a funny shaped black hole. To me it represented Zeppelin power, which people at home, or school, would have to have a blast of every few hours, like the ultimate drug." The design duo wanted the album to be named 'Obelisk' (after the black object in question), but Page was resolute. They were, however, commissioned to manufacture a thousand obelisks to be used a promotional tools, which helped fuel confusion and debate about the artwork. Hipgnosis went on to design the publicity material for the band's monumental Knebworth gigs in August 1979, as well as the six different sleeves (each concealed in a brown paper bag) for *In Through The Out Door* (released the same month), and the starker cover for 1982's *Coda* LP.

Hobbs, Rick

Jimmy Page's personal assistant and chauffeur at the time of John Bonham's death. On the night of September 24th 1980 he put the drunk Bonham to bed at Page's home in Windsor, the Old Mill House, and was therefore the last person to have seen him alive.

Hobbstweedle

see *Obstweedle*

Hoch, Abe

American promo man who was appointed head of Swan Song in the UK in 1976, but only lasted six months before he was succeeded by Alan Callan. His surname is pronounced 'hock'.

Holmes, Jake

b. Dec 28th 1939

US singer-songwriter who wrote the original version of 'Dazed and Confused', which appeared on his US-only 1967 debut LP *The Above Ground Sound Of Jake Holmes* (Tower T 5079). Jimmy Page and Yardbirds drummer Jim McCarty heard the song when Holmes (and the Youngbloods) played on the same bill as the Yardbirds at New York's Village Theatre on August 25th 1967. McCarty rushed to buy the LP the next day, and the song was swiftly incorporated into the Yardbirds' repertoire. Holmes was blissfully unaware at the time, but he has commented subsequently: "In the early 1980s, I did write them a letter and I said basically 'I understand it's a collaborative effort, but I think you should give me some credit at least and some remuneration'. But they never contacted me." In February 2005 he told Record Collector magazine "I wasn't a fan of the band, as I was a bit of a rock snob. I hadn,t even heard them, except for 'Stairway to Heaven', which I actually rather liked. Later when I actually found out, I thought I didn't have a case. But the cachet of rock victim has stood me in good stead over the years!" Holmes released one further collection of psychedelic folk for Tower (1968's *A Letter To Katherine December*, ST 5127) before moving in a more mainstream direction with three albums on Columbia. In an odd twist, he toured the UK in August 1970 with Stone The

Crows, another band managed by Peter Grant. He later became a well-known author of advertising jingles.

Homer

Obscure 1969 American B-movie about a Wisconsin farmboy who rebels against his parents by riding a motorcycle, growing long hair and starting a rock band. Its soundtrack (released as Cotillion SD 9037 in the US and Atlantic 2400 137 in the UK) features 'How Many More Times' from Led Zeppelin's debut. The soundtrack also contains songs by some of the leading US West Coast acts of the time, such as Buffalo Springfield, the Byrds and Country Joe McDonald. The film was directed by John Trent and stars Mia Farrow's sister Tisa, who was apparently bitten by a rabid cat during the shoot. It has yet to appear on DVD.

Horselunges Manor

Peter Grant's 15th Century home near Hellingly in Sussex, bought for £100,000 in 1973. A moated Elizabethan manor set in 65 acres of land, it perfectly complimented his buccaneering image, and was filled with his collection of antiques, many acquired on tour with Jimmy Page. According to ill-fated *Song Remains The Same* director Joe Massot, "It's really an ancient place and incredibly gorgeous. It has a beautiful feeling to it, probably because so many different people had lived in it through the ages." Mickie Most concurred, recalling: "He'd throw big parties with jousting on the lawn and people would dress up in Knights of the Round Table outfits, with jesters, drinking mead and all that. He

had some fun there." When its running costs spiralled to £800 a week in the late 1980s, he moved to a detached home in nearby Eastbourne, before settling in a flat in the town, where he remained until his death.

Hot Dog

Upbeat rockabilly pastiche that closes side one of 1979's *In Through The Out Door* and served as the B-side to their 'Fool In The Rain' 45. Robert Plant was a confirmed rockabilly fan and collector, and the impetus behind this slight effort. The band would often play 1950s classics in rehearsal and during live jams, and the song evolved from there. They played it at Knebworth in August 1979, though the singer forgot some of the words, causing it to be omitted from their retrospective DVD in 2003. The song also featured on their 1980 'Led Zeppelin Over Europe' tour.

Hots On For Nowhere

Upbeat song included on 1976's *Presence*, with lyrics in which Plant allegedly takes swipes at Jimmy Page and Peter Grant. The song also features the band's only use of the word 'fuck' in a song ('I've got friends who will give me fuck all…'). They never performed it live.

Houses Of The Holy (album)

The band's fifth album, released in March 1973. It was recorded between January and August 1972 at Stargroves and Headley Grange (using the Rolling Stones' mobile studio), as well as at Island Studios in London. It was mixed at Olympic Studios in London and Electric Lady Studios in New York, with engineer Eddie Kramer later recalling that the sessions were "Great, inspiring, wonderful. They were so confident, and so happy with what was going on. The general feeling was excellent."

The material spans the anthemic 'Song Remains The Same', contemplative mini-epics 'The Rain Song' and 'Over The Hills and Far Away', Eastern-tinged 'Dancing Days', eerie 'No Quarter' and more conventional rock of 'The Ocean'. More controversial were two light-hearted pastiches, 'The Crunge' (tackling funk) and 'D'Yer Mak'er' (touching on reggae). The LP's appearance was delayed from the proposed December 1972 date owing to problems with its striking sleeve – the first to be designed for the band by Hipgnosis. The cover photo was taken by Hipgnosis' Aubrey Powell at the Giant's Causeway in County Antrim, Northern Ireland, drawing inspiration from the ending of Arthur C Clarke's novel *Childhood's End*. The children were originally meant to be silver, not purple, but it proved near-impossible to get the colours right. As Page explained to Sounds the following April: "They just couldn't do it. The colours are just so different. It was a photograph in a collage. Then it was hand-painted, took a long, long time. In the end we just had to settle for a compromise... because the sky started to look like an ad for Max Factor lipstick and the children looked like they'd turned purple from the cold." It was the only Led Zeppelin sleeve to include lyrics (printed on an inner sleeve), and instead of having the band's name emblazoned on it, the package came with a paper

'obi' band wrapped around it (an idea of Peter Grant's), partially intended to obscure the children's bottoms.

Plant has stated that he "much prefers" *Houses Of The Holy* to the band's fourth album, but the critical response was mixed. Nonetheless, it knocked Elvis Presley's *Aloha From Hawaii: Via Satellite* off the US #1 spot in May 1973 – another symbolic milestone for the band, having toppled the Beatles' *Abbey Road* in December 1969.

Houses Of The Holy (song)

This taut, melodic rock tune was recorded for the album that bears its name, but wasn't released until 1975's *Physical Graffiti*. Plant has stated that the band were "quite smug that we'd done 'Houses Of The Holy' as a song, but didn't release it until *Physical Graffiti*." The version on the album was unchanged from the final mix prepared in June 1972 by Eddie Kramer in New York's Electric Ladyland Studios. It has been speculated that its title refers to concert venues, but the band never played it live.

How Late It Is

Short-lived UK TV show, presented by Michael Wale, on which Led Zeppelin appeared on March 21st 1969 (as replacements for the Flying Burrito Brothers), a week before their debut was finally released in the UK. They played 'Communication Breakdown', and reportedly found the results underwhelming, hardening their resolve to avoid television appearances. Transmission was at 10:50 pm, and no footage or sound recording survives.

How Many More Times

Built around a classic Page riff, this crunching, multi-sectioned, semi-improvised hard rock epic closes the band's debut LP. It incorporates elements of Albert King's 'The Hunter', as well as Howlin' Wolf's 'How Many More Years?', leading to co-writing credits being added for both in latter years. In 1993 Page told Guitar World magazine that the song "was made up of little pieces I developed when I was with the Yardbirds, as were other numbers such as 'Dazed and Confused'. It was played live in the studio with cues and nods." The original sleeve timing was given as only 3:30, though the song in fact lasts 8:28. This has been said to be a ruse to persuade radio stations to play the track, though when queried about it by ZigZag magazine in November 1972 Page commented: "I don't know – maybe it's a misprint." The song was a regular feature of their live performances until 1970, but occasionally returned to thereafter.

Hudson, Joan

The band's long-term accountant, who announced to them in 1975 that they had to go into tax exile. After Bonham's death she became a trustee of his estate.

Huston, Chris

b. June 25th 1943

Welsh-born recording engineer, and former guitarist for Merseybeat also-rans the Undertakers. His first engineering success came with the Young Rascals (a cover of whose 'You Better Run' was released by Robert Plant and Listen in November 1966). He went on to engineer 'The Lemon Song' and 'Moby Dick', included on *Led Zeppelin II,* and is now a leading expert on acoustics, based in Nashville, Tennessee.

see *Mystic Studios*

Hyatt House

see *Continental Hyatt House*

I

I Can't Quit You Baby

Slow blues penned by Willie Dixon, popularised by Otis Rush, played live by the Yardbirds and included in a powerful, semi-improvised arrangement on Led Zeppelin's debut. Another rendition was taped by engineer Vic Maile at London's Royal Albert Hall on January 9th 1970, and appeared on 1982's *Coda* compilation. The song was regularly performed live until 1970, and occasionally revived thereafter until 1973.

Iceland

Northern European island that the band flew to on June 22nd 1970 as part of a cultural exchange initiative organised by British agent Jasper Parrott. Unusually, Peter Grant did not accompany them, as he was busy making arrangements for the Bath Festival on the 28th. Fans presented them with flowers at the airports there, and the enthusiasm of audiences at the gigs greatly impressed them. Newsreel footage of the visit exists, including a brief interview with Robert Plant, in which he states: "It's extremely friendly – the reception we've had is incredible. We haven't played for about a month, since we came back from America, and it's very strange to play this far north. I've never been here

before, and it's all rather exciting." Plant's interest in Nordic mythology at this time is well-documented, and the lyrics to 'Immigrant Song' are thought to have been inspired by the trip.

I'm Gonna Crawl

The soulful, bluesy closing track on 1979's *In Through The Out Door*. Largely composed by John Paul Jones, it features a smooth synthesized string arrangement and a guitar solo from Jimmy Page that harks back to the band's early-70s heyday, but they never performed it live.

Immigrant Song

The first track on *Led Zeppelin III*, and something of a tongue-in-cheek mission statement for the band, exemplified by Plant's declaration: 'We are your overlords'. As he told the NME, the song "really typifies my approach to things. I mean, I just wrote the lyrics, but how much better could I have gotten it if I had written the music? Who else could have taken it into the reaches it went to? I really love that song." It was written in the summer of 1970, with especial inspiration being derived from their visit to Iceland in June. It opens with echoed feedback and a brisk count-in from Bonham, before an insistent riff kicks in, over which Plant wails like a frenzied Viking. The song was perhaps inspired by the band's trip to Iceland in June 1970, though Plant had a long-standing interest in Nordic lore. He told *Disc* in April 1973, "History has a big pull on me, so in 'Immigrant Song' I was wondering about the ancient characters from whom we stemmed, and what they were like, and what they thought about and how they sang their songs". Against the band's wishes, it was issued as a single in the US in November 1970, coupled with the non-LP 'Hey Hey What Can I Do?', and climbed to #16. The songs was a regular opener of their live sets from 1970-72, after which it was relegated to an encore in 1973, then left out altogether.

In Concert

BBC radio programme that allowed bands the chance to perform at greater length than a standard session permitted. Led Zeppelin played on its pilot (aired as *One Night Stand* during John Peel's *Top Gear* show on August 10th 1969), and were finally able to fulfil a long-standing promise to return on April 1st 1971 (aired April 4th), during their 'Return To The Clubs' tour. An earlier date, March 25th, had to be cancelled at the last minute, owing to Plant losing his voice, so the disappointed audience returned to Lower Regent Street's Paris Theatre a week later for the hastily-rearranged show. The band gave a stunning performance, including the broadcast debuts of 'Black Dog', 'Stairway To Heaven' and 'Going To California' (as part of their acoustic set, a feature of their gigs at the time), an 18-minute 'Dazed and Confused' and a 'Whole Lotta Love' that incorporated numerous blues and R&B standards. The programme was personally remixed and edited by Page on May 11th for release as a transcription disc to BBC outposts around the world, perhaps accounting for the voluminous bootlegs that subsequently appeared, and is widely regarded as one of their finest-ever recordings.

In My Time Of Dying

This 11-minute epic closes side one of *Physical Graffiti*, and is based on the blues standard 'Jesus Gonna Make Up My Dyin' Bed', concerning the desperate attempts of a dying man to justify his life. The original was taped by Blind Willie Johnson in 1927, with a different arrangement being recorded by Josh White in 1933. A folk version appeared on Bob Dylan's 1962 debut under its new title, which Led Zeppelin retained for their rendition, while rearranging it into a blues rock tour-de-force. Unusually, Bonham takes the lead songwriting credit, an acknowledgement of his often-overlooked work as an arranger, and the song was often played live.

Insurance

As the band grew more and more famous, and the touring industry around them grew in value, so did their insurance premiums soar. As Alan Callan, head of Swan Song in the UK from 1977, commented: "If one of them is injured, then the tour is cancelled and everyone has to get their money back. That's why the insurance companies started imposing conditions. So when the band went on the road they'd find themselves being locked into hotel rooms for months on end. This is where the room trashing came from... People thought that when Led Zeppelin had six limousines and police motorcycle outriders that they were just being flash. What they didn't understand is that the insurance companies wouldn't let them all travel in the same car together."

In The Evening

The first track on 1979's *In Through the Out Door* is closest the album comes to hard rock, and the only song jointly credited to all four band members. It opens with some distorted, droning guitar (reportedly adapted from the music Jimmy Page had prepared for the soundtrack to Kenneth Anger's *Lucifer Rising* earlier in the decade) before a crunching riff breaks in, underpinned by synthesizer. The song's basic structure was devised by John Paul Jones, though it features Page's most notable contribution to the album, playing his blue 1960 Fender Stratocaster. The band quickly incorporated the song into their live performances, featuring it at Knebworth in August 1979 and on their 'Led Zeppelin Over Europe' tour in June and July 1980.

In The Light

This lengthy, Eastern-influenced song started life as 'In The Morning' (or 'Take Me Home') during jams in 1973, but eventually appeared on *Physical Graffiti* in 1975. It was largely devised by John Paul Jones on a synthesizer. "That was played in a guitar tuning very close to the standard Indian sitar tuning, but then again it's like a mish-mash, really, because it's sort of pseudo-Indian and pseudo-Arabic as well, so that what comes out still has some sort of Western feel," Jimmy Page explained. It's said to be one of only three Led Zeppelin songs that feature Page on bowed guitar (the others being 'Dazed and Confused' and 'How Many More Times', both on the band's debut), though it's not easily discernable. The guitarist has named it his favourite track on the album, but the band never played it live (despite Robert Plant's eagerness to), as Jones deemed it too hard to reproduce onstage .

In Through The Out Door

The band's final album, recorded in Abba's Polar Studios in Stockholm in November and December 1978 and released on August 22nd 1979. Though they were preceded by six weeks of rehearsal, the sessions were marked by a lessening of control from Page, meaning that Plant and Jones largely defined its sound. As Jones told Tight But Loose in 1997: "For much of the time only Robert and I were turning up. There were two distinct camps by then, and we were in the relatively clean one. We'd turn up first, Bonzo would turn up later, and Page might turn up a couple of days later." Or, as Richard Cole put it, 'the truth of the matter was, we never turned up until the middle of the night until we had scored. The other two got there when they were supposed to and just messed around doing stuff'.

In the absence of their guitarist and drummer, Plant and Jones began to work up material, as well as drinking large quantities of Pimms. There are far more keyboard parts than on previous albums, especially on the epic 'Carouselambra', as well as uncharacteristic songs like the rockabilly throwaway 'Hot Dog' and unabashedly sentimental 'All My Love'. "It was actually a slog to do it," Grant told Tight But Loose in 1993. "We used to get the noon flight out on Monday and then return on Friday for the weekend. It was cold and dark all the time." The sessions were engineered by two Swedes,

Leif Masses and Lennart Ostlund, and were completed by December. Page then took the tapes to his home studio at Plumpton Place, where he worked on them over Christmas. A final mix was carried out back in Sweden at the start of 1979. The album title was a sly reference to how hard the band might find it returning to the musical fray after the punk revolution.

Though the album features some uncharacteristic bum notes from him, Page seemed bullish about the LP when interviewed in the NME in August 1979, telling Chris Salewicz: "When we'd finished our album I knew that it didn't matter if it didn't come out for nine months afterwards, because I knew I could rely on the fact that Led Zeppelin hadn't dated... I think some of the numbers are the most immediate we've done, anyway." The lavish packaging by Hipgnosis involved a bar being photographed from six vantage points, then each shot being used as a front cover variant (lettered from A-F on the spine), enclosed in a brown paper bag – an idea of Peter Grant's. The inner sleeve was also notable for featuring an effect whereby water made it change colour (something Page had noticed in one of his young daughter Scarlet's books).

Despite mixed reviews, the album swiftly rose to #1 on both sides of the Atlantic, and had sold 3 million copies by the end of the year. Even more impressively, it propelled each and every one of their previous LPs back into the Billboard Top 200 in October (*Led Zeppelin I* – #174, *Led Zeppelin II* – #150, *Led Zeppelin III*

– #189, the untitled fourth LP – #101, *Houses of the Holy* – #91, *Physical Graffiti* – #130, *Presence* – #183, *The Song Remains The Same* – #164). Nonetheless, Plant remarked in Australia's Juke magazine the following August: "I don't think it's a particularly bad album. On reflection, there may be a couple of numbers that aren't so hot, but there are some pretty good ones."

Iron Butterfly
Heavy US band who were often compared to Led Zeppelin in their early days, a comparison assisted by the fact that they shared numerous dates on the latter's first US tour. "We started off not even on the bill in Denver," Plant told *Creem* magazine in September 1973, "and by the time we got to New York we were second to Iron Butterfly and they didn't want to go on!"

It's Been A Long Time
Early title used by Robert Plant to announce 'Rock and Roll' at gigs in 1971.

Ivor Novello Awards
The UK's most prestigious songwriting honour. On May 12th 1977 Led Zeppelin was presented with an 'Outstanding Contribution To British Music' award at a ceremony attended by Page, Jones, Plant and Peter Grant at London's Grosvenor Hotel (during a two-week break in their eleventh US tour). The awards were handed over by comic actor John Inman, of *Are You Being Served?*. Twenty years later, in May 1997, the band was honoured with a Lifetime Achievement bauble at the 42nd annual handout.

than all the money he made, because we really had fun then, we were young and I had the same kind of rebellious spirit that he had. It really was the fun side of his character that made him what he was."

Jack and the Beanstalk
Children's storybook John Paul Jones is seen reading to his two daughters in the *Song Remains The Same* movie.

James, Nicky
b.1943 / d. Oct 15th 2007
Born Michael Nicholls and nicknamed 'Thunderthroat', this Birmingham-based singer led 1960s band the Nicky James Movement, which featured John Bonham in 1965, as well as – at different times – Mike Pinder (the Moody Blues) and Roy Wood (the Move). As the drummer told Melody Maker in June 1975: "I had a group with Nicky James, an incredible lead singer. But we had so much of the equipment on hire purchase, we'd get stopped at night on the way back from a gig and they'd take back all the PA. Nicky had a big following then, and he could sing any style, but he couldn't write his own material." James went on to record several singles and LPs. On his website, he commented: "John Bonham came along and forgot his sticks and had to play with his hands and I thought, that's the geezer I want. So, John and me had great fun... He always talked about those days with fondness, about when we had the PA taken away by the HP company. It was more important to him

Jammer, Joe
b. 1951
Born Joseph Wright, this US guitarist befriended the band on their first US tour, meeting them backstage at Chicago's Kinetic Playground on February 7th 1969. Having already been a guitar tech for the Who and Jimi Hendrix, he was employed by the club to oversee its weekly Tuesday jam session, which Plant, Page and Bonham attended after their gig. A shared interest in guitars with Page earned Jammer the job of roadie for the band on their third US tour that summer, when he also customised some of Page's guitars. "It was then that I started jamming with the group and that's how I got my nickname," he told Sounds newspaper on November 7th 1970. "It was kind of a joke, you know, a roadie playing guitar, and Jimmy started calling me Joe Jammer. By this time I knew the group very well, and the people associated with them like Peter Grant, and so I came over to England in December." Shortly afterwards he formed a band and began recording an album in London, under Grant's management and with Mickie Most producing. "The album's almost completed and Robert and Jimmy are writing some songs and they're going to give us one of them for a single," he went on to enthuse to Sounds, though that proved fanciful.

The nascent band was booed offstage at the Bath Festival on June 28th 1970 (headlined by Led Zeppelin), with their performances described by Melody Maker as 'untogether and tedious'. Jammer went on to join prog rockers Paladin in April 1972, before finally releasing a power trio LP in 1973, *Bad News* (Regal Zonophone SLRZ 8515), which sold poorly. He is still active on the music scene in Chicago.

Jansch, Bert
b. Nov. 3rd 1943
Scottish-born acoustic guitarist and a major influence on Jimmy Page, whose guitar parts on 'Black Mountain Side' and 'Bron Y Aur Stomp' are reminiscent of Jansch's 'Blackwaterside' and 'The Waggoner's Lad', both included on his 1966 *Jack Orion* LP (Transatlantic TRA 143). "Probably my greatest influence on acoustic guitar is Bert Jansch, who was a real dream weaver," Page told the NME in April 1973. "He was incredibly original when he first appeared… His first album had a great effect on me." The same month he told Sounds that "at one period I was absolutely obsessed with Bert Jansch. When I first heard his first LP, I couldn't believe it. It was so far ahead of what anyone else was doing. I mean, there was just nothing anybody else was doing – no one in America could touch that… That was what got me into playing acoustic." In an NME interview in October of the following year he added: "Bert Jansch just turned my head right around with acoustic. Oh yeah, far more than John Renbourn or Davy Graham – Jansch was definitely the one."

Japan
The band first visited the world's fastest-growing rock market in September 1971, playing a five-date tour taking in Tokyo, Osaka and Hiroshima. They donated the proceeds of their show at Hiroshima's Municipal Gymnasium on the 27th to a charity for the victims of the atomic bombing, and were awarded medals by the mayor in return. They were less popular in Tokyo, where Bonham and Cole's vigorous deployment of samurai swords in their rooms (and a comatose John Paul Jones's) in the Hilton hotel earned them a life ban, consolidated by a fruit fight in a corridor. Osaka, meanwhile, saw the band stricken with severe diarrhoea, after a raucous train journey involving a sake binge and further food fighting, to the despair of promoter Tats Nagashima.

Nonetheless, they loved the country. Bonham enthused to Melody Maker in

November: "It was a fantastic place to play… the people were so friendly and we had the best rock promoter in the world looking after us. It turned out that 'Immigrant Song' is one of our biggest songs in Japan, and it's the number with which we always open the act, so the audiences went potty!" Plant also found their responses bracing, telling Melody Maker in November that "the kids there show their appreciation in the most basic manner, which is what it used to be like over here." The band's second and final tour of the country was in October 1972, when they played seven gigs in Tokyo, Osaka, Nagoya and Kyoto. The visit was notable for an especially vicious row between Plant and Bonham – according to Peter Grant, "Robert came offstage with a split lip. It was a dispute over money. He still owed Bonzo £70 petrol money from some tour years before. But that's how it was." The band was due to return in December 1975, but Plant's car accident on Rhodes that August prevented it.

Jasani, Viram

Tabla player who appeared on 'Black Mountain Side', thereby becoming one of the few people to have guested on a Led Zeppelin recording. John Paul Jones later recalled that his contribution was recorded one evening in September 1968, with only Page present.

Jasta division

Luftwaffe division charged with using zeppelins against English military and civilian targets in World War One. In 1969 artist David Juniper doctored a photograph of them for the sleeve of *Led Zeppelin II*, adding the band members' faces as well as those of Peter Grant, Richard Cole, Blind Willie Johnson and Glynis Johns. Left in from the original were airmen Sebastian Festner and Karl-Emil Schäfer (both of whom were given beards, and the latter dark glasses) and Wihelm Reinhardt. Removed, however, was Manfred Von Richtofen – better known as 'the Red Baron'.

Jennings Farm

Located in Blakeshall, Wolverley, near Kidderminster, Worcestershire, this 18th Century farmhouse was the Plant family homestead as of November 1969, when the singer reportedly bought it for £20,000 and lovingly set about restoring the ruined Georgian farm buildings. As he told Disc on January 17th 1970: "I wake up in the morning and there are no buses, no traffic. Just tractors and the odd pheasant hooting in the next field." He told the same paper on June 13th that "when I'm away onstage I'm so into it that if I didn't have the farm I'd go mad. The farm is the other end of the scale for me." His holding included three acres, with an option to buy another 300. He also had six goats, which Disc revealed his wife Maureen milked.

Jennings Farm Blues

An early electric-guitar version of what later became 'Bron-Y-Aur Stomp', recorded in Olympic studios, London at the start of work on *Led Zeppelin III* in November 1969. It has appeared on bootlegs but has never been officially released.

Jersey

Tax haven off the coast of Normandy where the band was based for several months in late 1975. After his car accident in Rhodes during August 1975, Plant couldn't recuperate at home in the UK as he had already used up his allowance of days there, and would therefore be liable for a full year's tax. Instead he flew to Jersey, with his leg in plaster, and stayed at the home of lawyer Dick Christian. He had to be removed from the aeroplane in a forklift truck, organised by Richard Cole. The following day he, Page and Bonham gave a press conference on the island to announce the cancellation of their proposed world tour. The guitarist and drummer stayed in the Atlantic Hotel on the North of the island, though Bonham spent much of his time in the Victoria pub in St. Peters. He and Page flew back to the UK in September to attend the Melody Maker Awards, but otherwise they remained on the island. By October Plant was ready to travel again, so they flew to Malibu to rehearse for the *Presence* sessions. Having recorded the album, the band returned to Jersey in December, and even performed an impromptu gig at a club called Behan's West Park, accompanied by the house pianist, Norman Hale.

see *Behan's / Christian, Dick*

Jesus Christ Superstar

Hit musical penned by Andrew Lloyd-Webber and Tim Rice in 1969. In 1972 Rice told interviewer Michael Wale, for the book *Vox Pop*, that when searching for a singer to perform the title role on the LP (which preceded the stage version) "We were trying to get hold of Robert Plant. We had about three appointments with Peter Grant, and he broke every one. We kept turning up at his office and 'Oh, Mr. Grant's in America', and this, that and the other. And, despite the fact he said he was interested and wanted to see us, I doubt if Robert Plant ever knew we were after him. After about four broken interviews, we thought 'Well, stuff that for a lark'." The duo ended up using Deep Purple's Ian Gillan, described by Rice as "a phenomenally talented singer".

JG's Skiffle Group

Skiffle band that the young Jimmy Page played in. They were founded by one Joe Gardiner, though he'd left by the time they appeared on TV talent show 'All Your Own' in April 1958. Their rehearsals took place at Page's home in Miles Road, Epsom, but the band broke up soon after the broadcast. A photograph of them can be seen in Bourne Hall Museum in Ewell, Surrey.

Joans, John Paul

Born John Davidge, this Manchester cabaret artiste caused consternation in the Led Zeppelin camp in January 1971 by using a similar name to the band's bassist for his January 1971 #25 UK hit 'Man From Nazareth' / 'Got To Get Together Now' (RAK 107). Jones had been approached in 1966 by Davidge's and his shared manager, Harvey Lisberg (who also handled Herman's Hermits), with a request for the comic to use the name. This he granted, on the basis that it wasn't employed for musical endeavours.

Peter Grant stated in Melody Maker on January 30th: "So the position remained until Joans's recent record success. We have now advised his new manager – Miss Maureen Press – that under present circumstances John Paul Jones has no option but to take whatever steps may be necessary to protect his name." It is thought that Davidge agreed to stop using the name soon afterwards.

Jobriath
b. Dec. 14th 1946 / d. Aug. 3rd 1983

Born Bruce Wayne Campbell, this androgynous US pop hype's second LP, 1974's *Creatures Of The Street* (Elektra 7E-1010), featured a guest appearance from John Paul Jones, presumably as a favour to producer Eddie Kramer. Elektra label boss Jac Holzman later commented: "It was an awful album…. It's an embarrassment, something that's come back to haunt me."

Johns, Andy

Youthful studio wiz (and brother of Glyn) who engineered *Led Zeppelin II*, *Led Zeppelin III* and the band's untitled fourth LP, as well as assisting in the mixing of the latter. This was not a painless procedure, as Page later explained. "There were so many foul-ups, basically by engineers. Andy Johns said he knew a place where we could mix the album, Sunset Sound in LA. He convinced us it was the best place to do it, the best missing room… we wasted a week wanking around. From that point on Andy crapped himself and he disappeared." Plant was no more charitable, adding: "We were just disgusted at the amount of time it had taken to get the album finished.

The sound of the mixing room that Andy Johns had taken Jimmy to was really duff." Nonetheless, Johns is also credited with work on *Physical Graffiti* and *Coda*.

Johns, Glyn
b. Feb. 15th 1942

Veteran engineer whose credits include work for the Beatles and the Rolling Stones, as well as *Led Zeppelin I*. Though Jimmy Page told ZigZag magazine in November 1972 that "Glyn Johns is, and always has been, an ace engineer", he refused him a co-production credit, commenting to Guitar World magazine in 1993 that "He tried to hustle in on a producer's credit. I said, 'No way, I put this band together, I brought them in and directed the whole recording process, I got my own guitar sound – I'll tell you, you haven't got a hope in hell'. And then we went to Eddie Kramer for the second album, and Andy Johns after that." In the same interview, Page remarked that "He just couldn't accept that someone knew something that he didn't know – especially a musician! The pompous git!"

Johns, Glynis
b. Oct 5th 1923

Actress best-known for playing Winifred Banks in 1964's *Mary Poppins*. She also put in a surprise cameo on the sleeve for *Led Zeppelin II*, her inclusion presumably a play on the name of engineer Glyn Johns.

Johnson, Robert
b. May 8th 1911 / d. Aug. 16th 1938

US bluesman and a major influence

on Robert Plant and Jimmy Page. The singer told Melody Maker on March 19th 1977 that "the liaison between the guitar playing and his voice was so sympathetic, it almost seemed as if the guitar *was* his vocal cords. There was a tremendous amount of emotional content in the guitar and the vocals. It was the most amazing thing I'd ever heard... I never consciously had the idea of mirroring the guitar with my voice, but I remembered Robert Johnson had done it, and when I started singing with Jimmy it just seemed natural."

Jones, John Paul
b. Jan 3rd 1946
Led Zeppelin's bassist, keyboards player and principal arranger, described by Jimmy Page in an April 1972 Disc interview as "the best musician of us all. He had a proper training and he has quite brilliant ideas."

Born John Baldwin in Sidcup, Kent to parents who performed as a musical comedy duo, he was exposed to a wide range of music – from jazz to pop and classical – from early childhood. Vaudeville was waning, but he toured with his parents and was exposed to exotic music from foreign acts on the same bills. He boarded at Christ College in Blackheath from the age of five (as his parents were on tour so much), and dabbled with piano and guitar. Inspired by Phil Upchurch's 1961 hit 'You Can't Sit Down' and Johnny Kidd & the Pirates' 'Shaking All Over', he bought his first bass guitar aged 15, with the proceeds of his part-time job as the local choirmaster. His academic performance

was unimpressive, as he was too preoccupied with playing in his band, the Deltas, who were regulars at local dances and air force bases. By 1962 he'd absorbed enough to find employment backing singer Chris Wayne. Though Wayne had no hits, Jones decided not to attend the Royal College of Music when he turned 17, and to pursue a pop career instead.

He took to hanging around in Archer Street, Soho, where many musicians congregated in search of work. One afternoon he approached Jet Harris and Tony Meehan, formerly of the Shadows. They had no immediate use for him, but suggested he join a jazzy outfit named the Jett Blacks. After he'd played a few gigs with them, Harris and Meehan got back in touch in January 1963: they had hit #1 with 'Diamonds' (the first chart-topper to feature Jimmy Page) and agreed to give the teenager an audition for an upcoming tour. After a try-out in the Roebuck pub in Tottenham Court Road, Jones became their bassist and was launched into a hectic round of gigs alongside rhythm guitarist John McLaughlin. As he told Guitar Player magazine in July 1977, "Those were the days when they used to scream all the way through the show. It was just like now, really, where you have to make a dash for the limos at the end of the night." Working with Meehan and Harris also served as his introduction to the lucrative, hectic life of the session man, and his musical talents were soon recognised by producers. When Harris and Meehan's partnership ended in 1964, the 18 year-old shifted his focus towards arranging and playing on records by Rod Stewart, the Rolling Stones, Nico, Tom Jones, Wayne Fontana, the Walker Brothers. Cat Stevens, Dusty Springfield, Lulu and others. Many of these were under the aegis of Mickie Most, and Jones was greatly influenced by the bass playing on Motown discs. He also issued a rare instrumental solo 45, 'Baja' / 'Foggy Day In Vietnam' (Pye 7N 15637) in April 1964 (see *Baja*). Having worked extensively for Andrew Oldham, in 1966 he signed up as musical director for another hit producer, Mickie Most, leading to work with Herman's Hermits, Donovan, Jeff Beck and many others.

He certainly encountered Jimmy Page frequently at this time (and even contributed cello and arrangements to latter-day Yardbirds tracks 'Ha Ha Said The Clown', 'Ten Little Indians' and 'Little Games'), though the two didn't meet properly until the session for Donovan's *Hurdy Gurdy Man* album in 1967. Page and Jones were both credited on Ian Whitcomb's *You Turn Me On* LP (Ember NR 5065), and he told Ritchie Yorke for the NME in April 1970 that "I've rated Jimmy for years and years. I'd heard of him before I heard of Clapton or Beck. I've always thought he was far superior to any of them." By 1968, as Page contemplated forming a new band, Jones was not only exhausted by the demands of session work, but also bored of it, telling Disc in December 1969: "It just turns you into a vegetable." When his wife, Mo, saw a piece in the same paper stating that Page was putting a new band together, she suggested he give the guitarist a call. Page was about to go to

Birmingham to see Plant perform, and was happy to involve Jones – not only was he an experienced arranger and bassist, but he could also play keyboards to a high standard.

Once Page had secured the services of Plant (and hence Bonham), he arranged an inaugural rehearsal for the quartet in London's Gerrard Street in August 1968. "Robert had heard I was a session man," Jones told Guitar World in July 1977, "and he was wondering what was going to turn up – some old bloke with a pipe?" In fact they hit it off musically and personally at once, though Jones has since admitted to not having known the songs they played, Garnett Mimms' 'As Long As I Have You' and Johnny Burnette's 'Train Kept A-Rollin''. In fact, Jones has stated that he listened almost exclusively to soul at the time. "I'd never heard of Robert Johnson or Willie Dixon before I joined Zeppelin," he told Mojo magazine in December 1997. "I used to like jazz – I listened to it for relaxation, recreation. When starting Zeppelin, I was listening exclusively to soul music… I never used to listen to rock at all apart from Jimi Hendrix – about the only rock record I had, I think."

He played an important role as arranger from the start, as well as bringing with him the basic ideas for 'Good Times Bad Times' and 'Your Time Is Gonna Come' (both recorded for their debut that September and October). Jones went on to make vital contributions to 'Black Dog' (whose riff he devised), 'No Quarter' and much of *In Through The Out Door*. His interest in other instruments greatly helped to diversify the band's sound: his love of the mandolin led to its inclusion on tracks on *Led Zeppelin II* and *IV*, and he played the recorder parts on 'Stairway To Heaven', for example. His ongoing interest in keyboards, including Hammond organs, Mellotrons and Moog synthesizers, culminated in their central role on numerous tracks on *In Through The Out Door*. "I'd get bored playing bass all the time," he said in 1972. Despite his obvious versatility and creativity in the studio, Jones has since stated that his contributions as a songwriter weren't always credited. "Looking back now, there were some major contributions that seemed to get lost in the final credits," he told Tight But Loose in November 1997. Jimmy Page, however, told the BBC that: "We were always trying to encourage him to come up with bits and pieces, so to speak,

because that's usually what they were – he never came up with a complete whole song until *In Through The Out Door*." As a musician, Jones was aware of the pitfalls of trying to steal the limelight. "I try to never forget my role as a bass player," he explained in 1970 "to play the bass and not mess around too much up at the top all the time, and that's the most important thing."

A fundamentally retiring character, as early as December 1969 he was telling *Disc* that "one can get fed up with touring… it's all a mass of hotels, that's all you ever see." Home was a wood-panelled manor house in Chorleywood, Hertfordshire, bought that year for £45,000. A family man, he was largely detached from the debauchery surrounding him on tour. According to UK journalist Bob Hart, on the band's 1973 US visit "Jones had a deal where he didn't even stay on the same floor as the rest of the band. There had to be at least two floors between them. He'd sit up in his room playing little medieval reed instruments." By late 1973 he was so sick of being away from his wife and three daughters that he told Grant he wanted to leave the band, allegedly to become choirmaster of Winchester Cathedral (he has since stated that this was a joke made to a reporter). Grant persuaded him to think again, but the incident highlighted the increasingly stressful and hectic life the band was obliged to lead on the road, and thereafter their live schedule significantly diminished. Nonetheless, Jones was more than capable of enjoying himself – at least according to former security man Don

Murfet, whose autobiography, *Leave It To Me*, describes Jones as 'gifted – both at laying down the deep, throbbing basslines that melded the Zep sound together and at laying the countless women that fell willingly at his feet.' His dry sense of humour occasionally found an outlet on stage – when a delegation from the Russian embassy in Washington DC attended a gig as Grant's guests in May 1977, Jones amazed them by extemporising variations on Rachmaninov during 'No Quarter'. He would also throw in a humorous section of 'Amazing Grace' or B. Bumble and the Stingers' 1962 novelty hit 'Nut Rocker' for good measure.

By and large, however, he kept a lower profile than his bandmates, onstage, on tour and in the media. "I always had a sanity plan on the road, " he told the Daily Telegraph in September 1999. "I was never one to wake up at 4pm and have room service for the rest of the day. I used to get out, walk a lot and meet people. I had a great time, but a lot of it was apart from everything else that was going on." Typical of this attitude was his response to the so-called 'Oakland incident' on July 24th 1977. As the police entered San Francisco's Hyatt Hotel to arrest Peter Grant, Richard Cole and John Bonham, "Me and my family got into the service elevator, went down to the street and jumped into this motor-home, which I had never driven before. I just headed for the freeway."

The quartet barely saw each other again until 1978, and when they travelled to Stockholm to record *In Through The Out Door* that November, Jones found himself taking over from Page as musical director. "Robert and I moved in the daylight, while Bonzo and Page tended to move at night," he said later, adding: "I suppose you could say that *In Through The Out Door* is my album, the way *Presence* was Jimmy's album." In September 1980, during rehearsals for the forthcoming US tour, Jones and roadie Benji Le Fevre found Bonham's dead body in a guest suite at Jimmy Page's Windsor home. As he told Tight But Loose in 1997: "It was just so tragic. I remember after we found him I came out and Jimmy and Robert were in the front room laughing about something. I had to go in and say 'hold it', and tell them what happened. It was such a shock." Following the break-up of the band he moved to Devon, and kept as low a profile as ever. As he told an interviewer at the height of the band's fame: "I don't care if people recognise me or say 'Oh, you're not Jimmy Page'. I'm quite happy – I'd rather be in the background, anyway. It's just my way."

Jones, Maureen

John Paul Jones's wife since 1966, and mother of their three daughters, Jacinda ('Cindy'), Tamara ('Tammy') and Kiera. Nicknamed 'Mo', she can take the credit for her husband joining Led Zeppelin in mid-1968 – as Jones told Tight But Loose in 1997: "After a few years of non-stop sessions it got too much. I was making a fortune, but I wasn't enjoying it any more. It was my wife, Mo, who noticed an item in Disc saying that Jimmy was forming a new band out of the old Yardbirds. She prompted me to phone him up. It was the chance to do something different at last."

Juniper, David

A fan of Led Zeppelin's debut album, this young art director was bored of his job and decided to mock-up a cover design for their follow-up and present it to their management. Peter Grant was impressed, and gave him the commission for *Led Zeppelin II*. Briefed only to come up with something 'interesting', he decided to doctor an image of the Luftwaffe's Jasta division, which had used zeppelins against English military and civilian targets in World War One. The band's faces were removed from a familiar publicity still and superimposed. Also included were Peter Grant, Richard Cole, bluesman Blind Willie Johnson and actress Glynis Johns. Left in from the original photo were airmen Sebastian Festner and Karl-Emil Schäfer (both of whom were given beards, and the latter dark glasses) and Wihelm Reinhardt. Removed, however, was Manfred Von Richtofen – better known as 'the Red Baron'. Juniper was subsequently invited by Grant to create album covers for artists including Donovan and Lulu, and is still a busy graphic designer today.

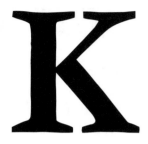

Kaleidoscope

Though Robert Plant was usually Led Zeppelin's champion of US West Coast music, Jimmy Page saw this multi-instrumental San Francisco-based psychedelic fusion band at San Francisco's Avalon Ballroom in 1967 (when he was on tour with the Yardbirds) and told ZigZag magazine in November 1972: "They're my favourite band of all time – my ideal band – absolutely brilliant." He went on to tell the NME in October 1974: "I thought a lot of what was coming out of San Francisco was laughable. Yet there was this one group called Kaleidoscope who were the best band I've ever seen." Led by David Lindley, they made three albums in their first incarnation – *Side Trips* (Epic BN 26304, 4/67), *A Beacon From Mars* (Epic BN 26333, 11/67) and *Incredible Kaleidoscope* (Epic BN 26467, 6/68).

Kashmir

Originally titled 'Driving To Kashmir', this epic was included on 1975's *Physical Graffiti* and has been named by Page, Plant and Jones as the single track that best embodies the band's quintessence. Its powerful riff had been devised by Page while practising at home, and

was shaped when he and Bonham played around with it in the studio. In the final mix, Bonham's drums were phased, greatly adding to the song's mystical atmosphere. Jones added the Eastern-influenced strings, while Plant's evocative lyrics were inspired by the long drive from Goulimine to Tan-tan in Southern Morocco (the area once called Spanish Sahara), which he had undertaken in 1973. "The whole inspiration came from the fact that the road went on and on and on," Plant explained to Rolling Stone in 1975. "It was a single track road which cut neatly through the desert. Two miles to the East and West were ridges of sandrock. It basically looked like you were driving down a channel, this dilapidated road, and there was seemingly no end to it." It is unclear why the song was named after a North Indian province, rather than somewhere in Morocco. "None of us have been to Kashmir," Page told Crawdaddy magazine in June 1975. "It's just that we've all been very involved in that sort of music. I'm very involved in ethnic music from all over the world." Page, in fact, hadn't even visited Morocco at the time of the song's recording. Though the finished piece was universally praised upon the LP's release, Peter Grant recalled that the demo was less impressive. "The funny thing is, when it was first finished it was decided it was a bit of a dirge. We were in Paris and we played it to Atlantic and we all thought it was a dirge, so Richard Cole was dispatched to Southall in West London to find a Pakistani orchestra. We put the strings on and the end result was just exactly what was needed. He was a master arranger." After its 1975 debut, the song was played live at every Led Zeppelin concert.

Kezar Stadium

San Francisco venue the band played on June 2nd 1973. Promoted by Bill Graham, the show lasted two hours and forty-seven minutes and broke their own record (set at Tampa Stadium on May 5th) for the highest gross for a single gig, raking in $325,000. Support came from Lee Michaels, the Tubes and Roy Harper. They would shatter their record again at the Silverdome in Pontiac, Michigan on April 30th 1977, grossing $792,361.50.

see *Tampa Stadium / Pontiac Silverdome*

King, Rex

Roadie employed by the band in 1977 to act as what Peter Grant later described as John Bonham's 'whipping boy'. King also was Bonham's companion on his way to Jimmy Page's Windsor home on the last day of his life. He later worked as tour manager for Rod Stewart.

Kirke, Simon

b. July 28th 1949

Drummer for Bad Company, and one of the few musicians to have jammed with Led Zeppelin onstage (for an encore of 'Whole Lotta Love' at Munich's Olympiahalle on July 5th 1980). As he later recalled, "Bonzo and I did a duet. We had two kits set up. He had phoned all the instrument dealers in Munich and said, 'I want a drum kit sent down right away... it was all [rehearsed] on the knees in the hotel room before we went

onstage. I dunno how, but I got through to the end..." As such he was much-touted as a successor for John Bonham in the days following his death. Peter Grant told Tight But Loose in 1993: "I remember John joking with him about how the job was his type of thing after they'd done the jam in Munich... and I reckon he thought he was going to get the job."

Knebworth

Hertfordshire stately home and venue for two of the band's most celebrated gigs, on August 4th and 11th 1979. These would also be their last-ever UK performances.

The band was originally associated with the site when it was reported in Melody Maker on May 25th 1974 that they'd be playing the 'Bucolic Frolic' festival that summer. An estimated 100,000 tickets had been sold before it was announced that they would not in fact be appearing, as Peter Grant did not feel it was suitable at the time. Five years on, the band was in a very different position. The loss of Plant's young son, combined with Page's drug use and Bonham's alcoholism, meant that they hadn't toured or even rehearsed much since 1977. Grant knew they would need to make a suitably flamboyant comeback gesture. In 1975 they'd played the UK's largest indoor venue – Earl's Court Arena – so he decided to mount the largest outdoor rock show the UK had ever seen. A date was booked with promoter Freddie Bannister, but demand for tickets was such that another was added for a week later.

The band played two warm-up shows in Copenhagen's 2000-capacity Falkonertheatre on the 23rd and 24th July, the choice of city perhaps reflecting a nostalgia for their earliest days together (they'd played the city in September 1968, shortly after forming). Reviews for these were lukewarm ('they appeared sloppy and under-rehearsed, bewildered and lost', said the NME), and nerves began to set in. On July 20th Page told the NME that "People can buy the album and we won't see how they're reacting to it. But I will at Knebworth. The LP's a frozen statement... but Knebworth's going to be different." Support at the gigs came from Commander Cody & His Lost Planet Airmen, Chas & Dave, Southside Johnny & the Asbury Jukes and Utopia, with Fairport Convention appearing on the 4th and the New Barbarians (featuring Keith Richards and Ron Wood) on the 11th.

The band checked into the nearby Roebuck Inn on August 2nd (though Plant soon moved to the Blakemore Hotel to avoid fans), and sound-checked at the venue the following day. When they finally came onstage for the first show, they played a cross-section of material from their 1973 and 1977 tour setlists, introducing only two songs from the forthcoming *In Through The Out Door* ('Hot Dog' and 'In The Evening'). Plant was on talkative form, jokily acknowledging the band's lengthy absence from UK stages by referring to the gig as a 'blind date' between them and the audience. Their performances are generally considered to have been little better than mediocre, accounted for by nerves and lack of adequate rehearsal time. Reviews for the first show were tepid ('they have a lot to do to surpass their own past work, and much more if they want to be properly innovative', said the NME), and Plant couldn't help commenting on the fact from the stage at the second performance a week later. His carping achieved little, though – Sounds described it as 'a passable Led Zeppelin concert' and called the band 'a living fossil'. Even Peter Grant acknowledged that they were 'rusty'. Nonetheless, the audience received them rapturously, though they would never again play in the UK.

The singer told Mojo magazine in June 2004 that "I was watching it on the DVD and thinking, Christ, that was crap. That was a shit gig. I know how good we had been, and we were so nervous." Page begged to differ, however. "The reality of Knebworth was that it was fantastic," he stated. "I mean, we had to come in by helicopter and you could see this huge sea of people. It was fantastic."

see *Bannister, Freddie*

Knight, Ian

English-born designer, of Showco Productions, Dallas, Texas, who designed many of the lighting effects used by the band on tour as of the release of *Houses Of The Holy*. Until then the band had not placed much emphasis on stage lighting. Along with a team of twenty, 'Iggy' commandeered what the San Diego Union described in 1975 as '184 loudspeakers, 172 lights, a dry-ice smoke machine, laser apparatus, mirror-balls and all the rest of the equipment that adds up to one of today's most flamboyant rock n'roll shows'.

Korner, Alexis
b. April 19th 1928 / d. Jan. 1st 1984

Known as 'the Godfather' to British rock, this blues musician was held in high regard by all the members of Led Zeppelin. As early as 1961, he had reportedly offered Page a place in his band, Blues Incorporated, though the guitarist turned it down in favour of his art studies. In 1968 Korner gave especial encouragement and employment to Robert Plant immediately before he joined Led Zeppelin, having seen him sing with the Band Of Joy at London's Speakeasy club. "I used to sleep at his place in Queensway," Plant told Q magazine in March 1988. "'Goodnight, Robert', he'd say; 'you'll have to sleep on the couch tonight – oh, by the way, it's the same couch that Muddy used to sleep on when he stayed here'." They did some gigs together around the Birmingham area, but the only track they recorded was 'Operator', later included on a double compilation LP entitled *Bootleg Him!* (Rak SRAK SP51, 1971). Korner later said: "I always thought Robert had the makings of a very strong singer and harmonica player. I didn't think the rest of the Band Of Joy were up to his talents. I always knew it would happen to Robert – I mean, it *had* to happen to him."

On October 11th 1968, shortly before Led Zeppelin taped their debut, Plant honoured a booking he'd made with Korner (and pianist Steve Miller) for a BBC session, which was broadcast on Korner's BBC World Service show, *Rhythm & Blues*, on November 5th. The following April Led Zeppelin appeared as guests on the show, performing 'I Can't Quit You Baby', 'You Shook Me' and the otherwise unknown 'Sunshine Woman'. It was broadcast on Monday April 14th 1969, though sadly, the master recording is no longer in existence. An acetate has apparently survived, however. In 1970 Korner formed a pop big band entitled CCS ('Collective Consciousness Society'), which recorded a version of 'Whole Lotta Love' that rose to #13 in the UK chart that October. Produced by Mickie Most, it was later adopted as the theme tune for the BBC's Top Of The Pops TV show (which, ironically, Led Zeppelin had vowed never to appear on).

Kramer, Eddie

The director of engineering at Electric Ladyland Studios in New York, Edwin Kramer worked with Led Zeppelin from 1969-76, assisting with *Led Zeppelin II*, *Led Zeppelin III*, *Houses Of The Holy*, *Physical Graffiti* and *The Song Remains The Same*. Already well-known for his extensive work with Jimi Hendrix, the South African first worked with Page in 1969. "It was a wild time," he told Stephen Davis in *Hammer Of The Gods*. "We mixed the album in two days on the most primitive console you could imagine." Though there was apparently a subsequent disagreement involving one of the band's roadies spilling some curry on a valuable rug in the studio, Karmer has stated: "The thing I want to emphasise more than anything else, is that we had so much fun making those records. I rejoice in the memories of those Led Zeppelin days." Jimmy Page was barely less ecstatic, remarking to Guitar World magazine in 1993 that "Eddie was always very, very good. I got along well with him, and I must say, when I went through all the old recordings for the boxed sets, all of his work held up very well, very well."

Larke, Johnny

Led Zeppelin roadie (and one-time member of beat groups the Gladiators and Peter Jay & the Jaywalkers) whose function, according to Richard Cole's autobiography, was 'keeping our room refrigerators fully stocked'. According to Robert Plant at a 2005 press conference, however, "We had a guy called Johnny Larke… whose only job was to run down the corridors of these huge stadiums – you'd hear his feet go clap clap clap clap – and he'd come through the door and go, 'sticks, chaps', which meant that Bonzo had finally left his hand work on the drum, so 'Moby Dick' was going to end any week now. And then we'd have to finish whatever we were doing, you know, get dressed and leg it back to the stage."

Lead Zeppelin

The band's original name, coined by Who drummer Keith Moon to describe the likely prospects of the impromptu band (consisting of himself, Jimmy Page, John Paul Jones, Jeff Beck and Nicky Hopkins) that had recorded 'Beck's Bolero' in May 1966. The name stuck in Page's memory, though Peter Grant later removed the 'a' to avoid pronunciation errors.

Leander, Mike

b. June 30th 1941 / d. April 18th 1996

Born Michael Farr, this youthful producer / arranger for Decca Records spotted the young Jimmy Page at the Marquee in 1962 and offered him his first session, contributing guitar to Carter-Lewis's Your Momma's Out Of Town. Leander went on to achieve the double distinction of arranging for both the Rolling Stones ('As Tears Go By') and the Beatles ('She's Leaving Home'), as well as Van Morrison, Marc Bolan and others, but found his greatest success with Gary Glitter in the 1970s.

Led Wallet

Nickname for Jimmy Page, on account of his alleged reluctance to part with money. As Peter Grant explained to the Sunday Mirror on October 10th 1970: "Jimmy is known as Led Wallet because he's always got a heavy wallet and it stays in his pocket." Plant wasn't immune to charges of thrift, either: according to Richard Cole, 'Robert used to ring Atlantic, tell them to send him four boxes of Led Zeppelin records, and then he'd go round to the garage and use them to pay for his petrol'.

Led Zeppelin I

The band's debut was recorded in Olympic Studios in Barnes, London between September 20th and October 10th 1968, shortly after they returned from their brief engagement in Scandinavia as The New Yardbirds. Much of it comprised odds and ends Page had been storing up from the latter days of the Yardbirds, and it has often been described as his album rather than the fuller collaborations that followed. As Jones later commented, "The first album was pretty much a recording of [a Scandinavian gig]… That's all we had ready to play at that time, but the sound and the performance was fantastic. It was old-style recording. We just sat there in Olympic with a few screens to cover the amps up. It was a big 'live' room, so everything leaked into everything else, which was part of the sound."

The sessions took a mere 36 hours (at most), so energised was the quartet, and the total studio bill (paid by Page) is said to have been a mere £1782. "They had rehearsed themselves very healthily before they got into the studio," engineer Glyn Johns has commented. "I had never heard arrangements of that ilk and certainly never heard a band play in that way before." Page would tell Record Mirror in April 1969: "I wish we'd recorded it now instead of when we did – we hadn't been together too long and it could have been a lot better." For all that, he is on superb form throughout, while Bonham and Jones had already formed a rhythm section of superhuman intuition and power. Plant's lyrics were perhaps not as confident as they'd become (and quote various songs by others), but his vocal range is deployed to remarkable effect throughout. Though he contributed significantly to the arrangements, he received no credits as he was still under contract to CBS at the time. Indeed, he went on to tell Uncut magazine in May 2008 that "During *Led Zep I*, as far as I was concerned, I thought that I was going to go… I didn't feel that

comfortable, because there were a lot of demands on me vocally… And I was quite nervous." In the same magazine, however, Page stated: "I don't think he'd ever sung like that before the first Led Zeppelin album. I don't think John Paul Jones had ever played like that before. Nobody had played like that before. I certainly hadn't."

The aim was to make an album aimed at the US market, as Peter Grant confirmed to Sounds on October 24th 1970: "There was a very important thing about those early days. Jimmy had first-hand experience of much of the US musically, so we knew the sort of LP to get together for America." Page went on to tell Uncut magazine in May 2008 that "I'd been touring America with the Yardbirds, and something that was apparent was that there were two streams of radio. One was the Top 40 AM stations, which were playing the singles, and the other was the FM stations, which put on whole albums. I thought this was magnificent, because you'd hear what a band was really up to. That registered with me. Those FM listeners were the sort of people I wanted to reach." With advance orders of 50,000, the album was released in the US on January 17th 1969 and charted at #99. It peaked at #10 in May 1969, during a 73-week chart run there, and had turned gold by August. The UK release wasn't until March 28th, accompanied by the slogan 'Led Zeppelin – the only way to fly'. It made its chart debut in April, eventually peaking at #6.

see *Hardie, George* / *Zeppelin, Eva Von*

Led Zeppelin II

The band's second album, which swiftly cemented their status as the word's premier hard rock act. Though it was largely written on the road as they frenetically toured earlier in the year ("We'd put down a rhythm track in London, add the voice in New York, put in harmonica in Vancouver, then come back to New York to do the mixing," Page told Disc in April 1972), it's remarkably coherent. Painstakingly produced by Page, its songs draw on pop ('Thank You'), blues ('The Lemon Song', 'Bring It On Home'), folk ('Ramble On') and even jazz ('What Is And What Should Never Be'), but the finished work remains first and foremost a rock and roll record. Its opening track, 'Whole Lotta Love', would come to define both them and the entire hard rock genre for the remainder of their career. The bulk of the songs were band originals, though they leaned heavily on the blues, with Howlin' Wolf and Willie Dixon later being acknowledged for their influence on 'The Lemon Song', 'Bring It On Home' and 'Whole Lotta Love'. The album did, however, feature Robert Plant's first writing credits. Page would later applaud the singer's emergence as a lyricist on 'Thank You'. When mixing the album, Page was especially aware of the fact that fans were likely to listen on headphones, so he used a range of stereo effects to maximise its impact.

Led Zeppelin II appeared in the US on October 22nd 1969 and in the UK on October 31st, a mere nine months after their debut. Before its release Page wasn't sure how it would be received, telling Record Mirror on February 21st 1970: "I think maybe we got too close to it, so that we knew every track backwards. I was far less confident about that album, although I was pleased with the variation we got into the songs." He needn't have worried; with advance orders of 500,000, it was certified gold on November 10th, and knocked the Beatles' Abbey Road off the top spot in the US on December 27th 1969, symbolising Led Zeppelin's ascendancy at the dawn of the new decade.

see *Juniper, David / Jasta division*

Led Zeppelin III

The band's third album, released in October 1970 and recorded in the brand-new Island Studio that July. Following the ecstatic response to the predominantly hard-rock sound of *Led Zeppelin II*, the band decided to develop the acoustic influences in earlier songs such as 'Babe I'm Gonna Leave You' and 'Ramble On'. Page and Plant wrote songs intensively at Bron-Yr-Aur, a small cottage in Snowdonia, before the band convened at Headley Grange (in Hampshire) and Olympic (in London) in May and June 1970, and at Island (also in London) in July. The results were mixed by Terry Manning that August at Ardent Studios in Memphis, and considerably diversified their sound. It opens with the thunderous, anthemic 'Immigrant Song', but thereafter only the demented 'Celebration Day', intense, bluesy 'Since I've Been Loving You' and hard-rocking 'Out On The Tiles' bore the hallmarks of their previous records. The remaining tracks were predominantly folk-influenced, straying close to pop on 'Tangerine' and 'That's The Way', with Eastern influences on 'Friends', traditional flourishes on 'Gallows Pole' and 'Bron-Y-Aur Stomp' and an odd tribute to their friend Roy Harper closing proceedings.

The LP's release was delayed, partially owing to complications with its elaborate sleeve (incorporating a rotating wheel), and got a mixed critical reception. Sales were initially strong, but tailed off sooner than those of *Led Zeppelin II*, something that stung the band. Soon after its release Page told Allan Rinde of LA's Rock Magazine that "a lot of good things had to be left off because of it being a single album. Had it been a double album, we'd have been in better shape, but we'd already scheduled it as a single and the cover was already done, so it was too late to change it into a double, which was really a shame."

see *Drew, Richard*

Led Zeppelin IV
see *untitled*

Le Fevre, Benji
Roadie, vocal sound engineer and assistant to Robert Plant, whom he got to know much better after his car accident on Rhodes. He served as the singer's companion in Malibu, where they flew in late August 1975, and later shared the melancholy experience of discovering John Bonham's body with John Paul Jones on September 25th 1980. Having taken the drummer's pulse, he summoned the doctor who pronounced him dead. According to Bonham's brother Mick, the drummer's wake in the Chequers pub on October 10th 1980 'wasn't the best time for Benji Le Fevre to start winding me up. I put him on his arse and legged it out the door… [Matthew Maloney] just looked at me through tearful eyes and said 'John would be proud of you. He would have enjoyed that'.' After the band split up there were rumours that Le Fevre might become Plant's manager, which Peter Grant later admitted had 'disappointed and hurt' him.

The Lemon Song
Recorded in Hollywood's tiny Mystic Studios in May 1969, this heavy blend of the band's blues influences appears on *Led Zeppelin II*, and borrows heavily from Howlin' Wolf's 'Killing Floor', which the band often played during their first US tour before it evolved into this shape. Indeed, the song was listed as 'Killing Floor' on early pressings of the LP. Led Zeppelin were later sued by the bluesman's estate, and his name was duly added to the songwriting credits. The words 'squeeze my lemon till the juice runs down my leg', meanwhile, are borrowed from Robert Johnson's 'Traveling Riverside Blues' (though Johnson himself is unlikely to have coined the expression), and it has been pointed out that the song also echoes Albert King's 'Cross-Cut Saw'. The band ceased to perform it live from the end of 1969, though Plant's invitation to squeeze his lemon continued to be made during renditions of 'Whole Lotta Love'.

Listen

Short-lived Birmingham combo featuring Robert Plant on lead vocals, as well as John Crutchley (guitar), Roger Beamer (bass) and Geoff Thompson (drums). Their sole 45, 'You'd Better Run' / 'Everybody's Gonna Say' (CBS 202456) was released in the UK on November 25th 1966, and in the United States (as Columbia 443967) shortly afterwards. It sold in neither territory.

The A-side was a spirited cover of a Young Rascals tune (by Felix Cavaliere and Eddy Brigati), while the B-side was a groovy organ-led number written by the whole band. "Coming out of that studio at the end of that session, I've never ever been so relieved in my life," Plant told journalist Barney Hoskyns in 2003. "It was like, 'Christ, I did it!'"

Little Roger and the Goosebumps

Humorous 1970s pop act from San Francisco, led by Roger Clark and Dick Bright. In May 1978 they released a parody of 'Stairway to Heaven' entitled 'Gilligan's Island (Stairway)', combining Led Zeppelin's music with the lyrics to the theme song of children's TV show *Gilligan's Island*, on their own Splash Records label (Splash SPL-901). Peter Grant did not see the funny side, and - though it was never likely to become a hit – he had the band's lawyers threaten to sue, and demanded that all remaining copies be destroyed. The fiasco was commemorated in a Trivial Pursuit question, and Robert Plant has apparently subsequently named it as his favourite cover of the song.

Live On Blueberry Hill

Famed early Led Zeppelin bootleg, capturing their superb show at LA's Inglewood Forum on September 4th 1970 and released by Blimp Records (later reissued by TMOQ, or 'Trade Mark Of Quality'). Though to have been recorded on a portable reel-to-reel tape machine near the stage, it came pressed on double coloured vinyl, with an insert, and featured material from their yet-to-be-released third album. It was sold through specialist shops as well as classified ads. Peter Grant was greatly frustrated by its appearance, and those of similar releases over which he had no control.

Liverpool University

Venue for the final appearance by 'the New Yardbirds', on October 19th 1968 (as quoted in Melody Maker). Thereafter they were billed as Led Zeppelin.

Livewire

Theatre in Ealing, West London, where Led Zeppelin rehearsed for their 1975 US tour as of November 26th 1974. On that day they reportedly played from 3pm until 10pm, covering Elvis standards like 'Hound Dog' and 'Don't Be Cruel' and old favourites such as 'When The Levee Breaks', as well as material from the forthcoming *Physical Graffiti* including 'Custard Pie', 'Trampled Underfoot', 'In My Time Of Dying' and 'Sick Again'.

Livin' Lovin' Maid (She's Just A Woman)

Short, snappy hard rock number on *Led Zeppelin II*. "It's all about a degenerate old woman trying to be young again,"

Page explained in 1969. It was used as the B-side of their 'Whole Lotta Love' single, and later charted in its own at #65. Early pressings of the album have the song incorrectly titled as 'Living Loving Wreck' on the label. Though it plays to several of the band's greatest strengths (memorable riff, powerful rhythm, soaring vocals and a taut solo), it has often been cited as one of their least favourite compositions and they never played it live.

London All-Stars

Mid-60s studio aggregation put together by session drummer Bobby Graham, and featuring Jimmy Page and John McLaughlin. They were formed on behalf of French label Barclay, in order to provide backing to French singers recording in London, such as Sylvie Vartan, Michel Polnareff and Eddie Barclay. In addition, a rare French LP was made by them entitled *British Percussion* (Barclay BB86, 1965), also released in Italy (Barclay SIBS 1004, 1966). Three of its songs were co-written by Page and Barclay ('Stop The Drums', 'Drum Stomp' and 'Lord Byron Blues'), and the whole album features prominent guitar-playing from Page. It has yet to appear on CD.

London and the Southeast

UK local TV news programme hosted by Bob Wellings, on which Robert Plant and John Bonham gave a rare interview on September 16th 1970, just after Led Zeppelin had replaced the Beatles at the top of the Melody Maker Readers' Poll. "I think these days at concerts the kids are coming to listen to what you're playing, not just to look at you," opines Bonham in a clipped English accent. Plant, meanwhile (sporting full Viking moustache), adds: "We've spent years and years on the road, playing in little church halls and being beaten up and having bricks thrown through the van windows and everything, and to have money at last is just another figment in my mind of mass acceptance, which is what we all work for." Wellings concludes the brief piece by wishing them well for their shows at Madison Square Garden on the 19th and stating (incorrectly) that it's their first appearance on British TV, before turning his attention to "a matter of concern for South-East anglers".

London, Mark

Canadian-born songwriter, producer and engineer who was Peter Grant's partner in a number of ventures from 1969, under the umbrella name of 'Colour Me Gone Ltd'. They met in 1965 when London visited the Oxford Street office Grant shared with Mickie Most, in order to play demos of some songs he'd written. He went on to have a smash in 1967 with Lulu's 'To Sir With Love' (produced by Most), and discovered Stone The Crows, whom Grant co-managed.

He later commented that "Peter Grant is exceptionally good in business dealings... What I most admire about Peter is his tremendous loyalty to his acts. He always puts the act first, no matter what." London also discovered and managed Scottish pop-rockers Cartoone, on whose 1969 debut LP Jimmy Page guested on guitar.

Look
Reportedly the working title for 1979's *In Through The Out Door* LP.

Lovelace, Linda
b. Jan. 10th 1949 / d. April 22nd 2002
Troubled US porn icon and star of *Deep Throat*, whom Peter Grant invited to announce the band on the last night of their stint at the LA Forum on March 27th 1975.

Lucifer Rising
Occult-themed underground movie directed by Kenneth Anger, for which Jimmy Page composed about 23 minutes of electronically-treated synthesizer instrumentals (with one contribution on electric guitar) before the two fell out. The music, recorded over about a year from mid-1973, was first heard at an LA screening of the incomplete film in September 1976, and shoddily bootlegged as 'Solo Performances' soon afterwards. In the mid-1980s Anger sold a print of the still-unfinished film to one Christopher Dietler (who also called himself 'Frater Zardoz'), of Carmichael, California. Having somehow copyrighted the music in the US, Dietler released it on a label called 'Boleskine House' in January 1987 as *Kenneth Anger's Lucifer Rising / Jimmy Page Soundtrack*. It was a numbered, limited edition of 1000 12" 45 rpm records, pressed on blue vinyl, housed in a thick card sleeve and accompanied by two inserts. It was only available briefly before an injunction from Anger prevented its proliferation. The film has still never been officially released, and nor has Page's music.
see *Anger, Kenneth*

Luton Technical College
Though Peter Grant told Dave Lewis in an interview for Tight But Loose in June 1993 that 'as I recall, we never played a gig after that American tour', this was the glamorous location for the Yardbirds' final gig, on Sunday, July 7th 1968. Jimmy Page formed the nascent Led Zeppelin shortly afterwards.

Lynn, Vera
b. March 20th 1917
Forces' sweetheart who (according to the website of photographer Ross Halfin) 'tried to get Jimmy evicted from Plumpton when he lived there, claiming he was bad for the village'. Any such effort was unsuccessful, and there seems to be no lasting enmity between the pair: Halfin also described the former neighbours lunching together at London's Savoy Hotel in March 2004, along with TV magician Paul Daniels. And, rather than any Led Zeppelin classic, it was Lynn's 'We'll Meet Again' that was played at Peter Grant's funeral.

Mclean, Unity
Carol Browne's successor as manager of Swan Song's London office between 1975 and 1981, and the individual charged with the unenviable job of manning the band's telephones at the most turbulent time of their history. She later moved to Boston, in the US.

Maddox, Lori
b. 1958
LA groupie who became closely associated with Jimmy Page in 1972, when she was 14. According to Richard

Cole in *Stairway To Heaven*, 'She was a sweet, still somewhat innocent kid who spent half her time dying to embrace Jimmy and the other half dying to kill him'. Page was introduced to her by BP Fallon, and is said to have left Pamela Des Barres for her, causing lasting enmity between the women. The relationship was conducted discreetly, for obvious reasons, and largely ended in 1973 when Page moved on to Bebe Buell.

Mad Dogs

Name thought to have been considered by Jimmy Page to replace the Ne   was settled upon. John Paul Jones, however, told Blow By Blow magazine in 1992 that "The Mad Dogs was the name that we were going to call ourselves on Danish TV, when Countess Von Zeppelin had an injunction out against us."

Madison Square Garden

Legendary New York venue with a capacity of 20,000, which Led Zeppelin first played on September 19th 1970 (two shows), returning on September 3rd 1971 and then for three consecutive nights in 1973 (July 27th – 29th), which were filmed and recorded for their subsequent live film and album *The Song Remains The Same*. They returned on February 3rd 1975, and then for six further shows between June 7th and June 14th 1977. The latter were not advertised, but sold out via word of mouth and one local radio announcement, with enough demand to cover an extra two shows, had it been possible.

Malibu

Exclusive beachfront area in California in which Led Zeppelin gathered in the autumn of 1975 to work on the album that became *Presence*. In June 1976 Robert Plant, who had suffered a severe car accident on Rhodes in August 1975, told Hit Parader of "being carted out to Malibu... lying on my back for 13 hours in first class." Tax exiles, they occupied houses in exclusive Malibu Colony Drive that they didn't feel at home in (Bonham and Plant eventually moved into LA's Hyatt hotel), and looked back on the period as depressing and tense. A Swan Song spokesman was quoted in Circus magazine of May 13th 1976 remarking: "Robert's very much into spiritual things, unexplainable forces and powers, and he was spending time sifting through his thoughts and being very introspective. He'd say, 'I never should have sung 'In My Time of Dying'.' Later, when some unusually high tides came up and virtually demolished the porch of the house he was staying at – so much so that he had to rent another one – he started thinking that he shouldn't have written 'The Ocean', and that he'd have to be very careful about his lyrics from now on."

Jones told *Tight But Loose* in 1997, "it became apparent that Robert and I seemed to keep a different time sequence to Jimmy. We just couldn't find him... There wasn't a lot of continuous rehearsal, and it was easy to lose interest." Adding insult to injury, while they were in Malibu Page's London home was occupied by squatters.

Maloney, Matt

Born Matthew Stanisewsky, this childhood friend of John Bonham's worked for him as a driver, roadie, personal assistant and farmhand as of March 1970. It was with Maloney at the wheel that Bonham memorably blundered into Belfast's battle-torn Falls Road area after a gig in the city's Usher Hall on 5th March 1971. "The street was covered in glass and there were armoured cars and kids chucking things," Bonham told Melody Maker. "We just kept our heads down and drove right through."

Manning, Terry

Legendary Memphis recording engineer who mixed *Led Zeppelin III*, and later acclaimed Page's effort in 'Since I've Been Loving You' as "the best rock guitar solo of all time". He was responsible for etching numerous phrases into the run-off grooves of the album plates. "I inscribed the sayings into the lead-out groove spaces (very carefully)," he wrote later. "Jimmy was a huge fan of Aleister Crowley, 'the first hippy', and Crowley's philosophies. He had given me the books, which I read, and was interested in, but I found it a little too free and unrestricted, that one could do anything one wanted. I remember asking Jimmy at mastering if it was OK to kill someone if you 'felt like it'. He wasn't amused. But I wrote 'Do What Thou Wilt' on one side of one set, and 'Shall Be The Whole Of The Law' on the other side of the same set. I remember writing 'So Mote It Be' on one side of another set, but I've forgotten the rest. We joked that with different things written on different lacquers, real fans would have

to buy two or more records to complete the set! This was absurdly funny to us, as we couldn't imagine anything like that might really happen." Page told ZigZag magazine in November 1972 that "it was intended as an esoteric little touch, and it was hoped that nobody would see it… I was the only one in the group who knew about it."

Manticore

London rehearsal space owned by Emerson, Lake & Palmer, in which Led Zeppelin rehearsed for their eleventh US tour in January and February 1977.

Marquee

Legendary London club in which Jimmy Page had played numerous times with the Yardbirds, Cyril Davies and others. One of Led Zeppelin's first-ever UK gigs was played there (as the Yardbirds) for a fee of £150 on Friday, October 18th 1968, supported by a band called Sleepy. "The group was very loud," remembered the club's manager John Gee. "I thought they were overpoweringly loud for the size of the Marquee. Anyway, the lads received an enthusiastic, but not overwhelming, response from the audience." By Tuesday December 10th they were back, with a new name and support from the Bakerloo Blues Line. Melody Maker reviewed the concert on December 21st, calling them 'Led Zepplin' and commenting that 'there seemed to be a tendency for too much volume, which inevitably defeats musical definition', and that Bonham 'is forceful, perhaps too much so'. It wasn't all bad, though: praise was reserved for a number the paper named as 'Days Of Confusion'.

Marriott, Steve

b. Jan 30th 1947 / d. April 20th 1991
Singer with the Small Faces and Humble Pie. Plant had been an ardent fan of the former as a teenager, and the arrangement of 'Whole Lotta Love' owes a good deal to 'You Need Lovin'' on the Small Faces' debut LP. It has been said that Marriott was Jimmy Page's idea of a model singer when he was forming Led Zeppelin, and Plant told Melody Maker on June 25th 1977: "I could never be compared with Steve Marriott, unfortunately, because he's too good! He has got the best white voice, for sheer bravado and balls... he is the master of white contemporary blues." Marriott had attended some Led Zeppelin rehearsals at London's Manticore studios that January, prompting Plant to remark that "To me, the two of us singing Muddy Waters songs was almost as hair-raising as our first gig."

Martin, Charlotte

Jimmy Page's French-born partner for much of the band's lifetime. The blonde model had been Eric Clapton's girlfriend during his tenure with Cream, and he wrote of her in his 2007 autobiography: "Charlotte was an incredible girl, more interested in films, art and literature than in modelling, and we had a great time together." Page met her after Led Zeppelin's celebrated gig at the Royal Albert Hall on January 9th 1970 (also his 26th birthday), through Roger Daltrey of the Who and his girlfriend Heather. According to Richard Cole's memoirs, 'Charlotte was the type of girl who you couldn't look at just once. Tall. Thin. Blonde. Perfect features. You had to glance a second time.' Nonetheless, he didn't like her, describing her as 'aloof, unfriendly and indifferent'. Page and Martin had one child together, Scarlet (born in March 1971 and now a successful rock photographer), and split up in the early 1980s.

Masses, Leif

Swedish engineer who worked with the band on *In Through The Out Door* at Stockholm's Polar Music studios in late 1978, assisted by Lennart Ostlund. Three of the tracks he engineered were left off that album, but appeared on 1982's *Coda* compilation – 'Ozone Baby', 'Darlene' and 'Wearing and Tearing'.

Massot, Joe

Described by Richard Cole as 'in his forties, tall, dark and smoking Havana-sized cigars', this US-born film-maker was the first to collaborate with the band on the Song Remains The Same. He'd already worked on documentaries and pop-friendly films including Wonderwall and Zachariah, so his credentials for working with pop musicians were reasonable, and he was a friend of Jimmy Page's partner Charlotte Martin (his home in Wallingford was only 10 miles from the Pangbourne Boathouse, where the couple lived). Page already knew his wife Penny, and he and Page got along well. In 1972 he contacted the guitarist at his new home, Plumpton Place, to pitch the idea for a Led Zeppelin movie, combining live performances with documentary footage. Peter Grant was initially unconvinced, but changed his mind halfway through the band's ninth US tour in July 1973, with the stipulation that Massot was to have no rights in the finished product. The director was given 48 hours to assemble a crew and get to Boston with cameraman Ernie Day, where they met Grant and explained that the budget for the live filming would be around $100,000. This was approved, but it didn't prove easy to extract his crew's wages in the months ahead.

Having finished filming in the US (culminating in the theft of $203,000 from the band at New York's Drake Hotel on July 29th), Massot returned to the UK, where it emerged that there were gaping holes in the concert sequences. A decision was thus taken to shoot individual 'fantasy' sequences with each band member. As he later contended, "We didn't just want a concert film, we wanted to show them as individuals, but not in the traditional way with interviews. They wanted more symbolic representations of themselves." The results – including Page blundering about a mountainside as Old Father Time, Plant posing as an Arthurian knight, Jones togging up as a highwayman and Bonham supping a pint in the pub – were not critically acclaimed. With them in the can, Massot began the unenviable task of editing the enormous amount of footage he'd shot. Grant was impatient for results, so a rough cut was screened early in 1974. The band were dismayed, and soon afterwards the director, already on the edge of a breakdown, was sacked by letter.

His subsequent attempts to contact the band were unsuccessful, though Plant eventually called to request another screening. On that occasion Bonham laughed uproariously at the sight of Page in a false beard, which apparently infuriated the guitarist. After another week of silence, the axe fell for good in March. Soon afterwards Peter Clifton took over the project. Massot had no legal recourse, as he had no contract, so he resorted to hiding the rushes and wrangling with the band (and its representatives, legal and otherwise) until he had been paid. The final insult came when he had to buy a ticket to the New York premiere from a tout, though Page later conceded: "Maybe we were just too impatient, certainly in the early days, and we became very annoyed at the screw-ups." Massot died in 2002.

see *Clifton, Peter* / *The Song Remains The Same* (film)

McCallum, David Sr.
b. March 26th / d. March 21st 1972
Distinguished violinist (and father of his namesake, the star of *Man From U.N.C.L.E.*) who first suggested the idea of playing a guitar's strings with a bow to Jimmy Page, during a mid-1960s session.

Mellotron
Developed in the early 1960s, this unconventional and unwieldy instrument consists of two keyboards that mimic the sounds of strings, flute, brass, percussion and more, through the use of pre-recorded tapes contained inside it. Mellotrons were used by Led Zeppelin on 'The Rain Song' and 'Kashmir'. The recorders on 'Stairway to Heaven' were

played by John Paul Jones, though he did use a mellotron to recreate their sound onstage. He later remarked: "We used the wretched mellotron for string pads and flute stuff… it used a system of tape loops and it was totally mechanical, with plumbing inside it and everything. As the gig would heat up, the tapes would start stretching and the motors would slip. I spent my entire technical career trying to replace the mellotron." He eventually settled on the Yamaha GX1 in 1978, and took a Fairlight CMI synthesizer on their 1980 European tour.

Melody Maker Poll

The most respected readers' poll in the UK music press, dominated by the Beatles throughout the 1960s. In 1969 Led Zeppelin were named third-brightest hope, but they swept the board in the 1970 poll (announced on September 19th), something that made headlines around the world.

The quartet took the top British and international group prizes – the first time the Beatles had been toppled since the days of Beatlemania eight years earlier – while *Led Zeppelin II* was named best British album and Plant best British male singer. He was also third best international male singer, while Page was second top international guitarist (after Eric Clapton), Jones was second top international bassist (after Jack Bruce) and Bonham was fifth best international drummer. 'Whole Lotta Love' was voted sixth best international single, and *Led Zeppelin II* second best international album (after Frank Zappa's *Hot Rats*).

Melvin Giganticus and the Turd Burglars

Led by Melvin Gittus, this Midlands group played with Robert Plant during Led Zeppelin's hiatus in late 1977 and 1978, including a gig at the Wolverley Memorial Hall, near his home, in July 1978. "During quiet times with Zep I used to record with chums," the singer told Q magazine in May 1990. "Every Christmas this chap from my village pub would get pissed and sing doo-wop carols in the bar – so well, in fact, that we rented a studio in Worcester and cut 'Three Months To Kill' by Heulyn Duvall on Challenge and 'Buzz Buzz A Diddly' by Freddy Cannon, for Bird's Nest Records. Melvin Giganticus and The Turd Burglars was the name of our group, because he had a huge penis." The band was also known as Melvin's Marauders, and later became Billy Bowel and The Movements.

Memphis Minnie

b. June 3rd 1887 / d. Aug 6th 1973
Born Lizzie Douglas in Algiers, Louisiana, this prolific blues singer / guitarist wrote the original version of 'When The Levee Breaks', recorded with her husband Kansas Joe McCoy in 1929, in response to the cataclysmic Great Mississippi Flood of 1927. She received a co-credit with Led Zeppelin for their version, which closes the band's untitled fourth LP.

Memphis, Tennessee

Elvis Presley's hometown. In April 1970 Led Zeppelin were made honorary citizens and presented with scrolls and keys to the city, an honour only previously accorded to Presley and Carl Perkins.

Mendelssohn, John

Rolling Stone hack whose negative review of *Led Zeppelin I* in March 1969 ('offers little that its twin, the Jeff Beck Group, didn't say as well or better three months ago') and clumsily sarcastic review of *Led Zeppelin II* in December ('who can deny that Jimmy Page is the absolute number one heaviest white blues guitarist between 5'4" and 5'8" in the world?' etc) did much to harden the band against the magazine.

Mercurius, S. Flavius

Pseudonym under which Jimmy Page played lead acoustic guitar on 'The Same Old Rock' on Roy Harper's 1971 *Stormcock* LP, recorded between July and December 1970. His real identity was only officially revealed on the album's 2007 reissue, though it had always been an open secret.

Miles Road

Street in Epsom, Surrey, where Jimmy Page lived (at number 34) from the age of eight, and where much of his formative musical explorations took place in the late 1950s. "The Page family had a typically small suburban London house, two rooms up and two down," his childhood friend John Gibb later recalled. "The best part of the house was devoted to Jimmy and his music — there was no doubt about that. In most homes the front room is usually a family room, but Pagey's parents had turned it over to Jimmy. There were records everywhere, a tape recorder, a couple of

amps and guitars and other instruments. Plus a really good hi-fi system. Jimmy's mum usually stayed in the kitchen, brewing tea for everybody." Jeff Beck remembered the Pages' music room too, telling Mojo magazine in August 2004 that "there wasn't even room to swing your knob."

Mimms, Garnett

b. Nov 16th 1933

US soul / R&B singer whose classic 'As Long As I Have You', beloved of Robert Plant, was one of the first two songs played by the nascent Led Zeppelin in the autumn of 1968, along with 'Train Kept A-Rollin''. The band frequently incorporated the song into live medleys.

see *Gerrard Street*

Misty Mountain Hop

Built around a catchy electric piano riff devised by John Paul Jones at Headley Grange one morning while his bandmates slept, this relatively simple number features some of the most powerful drumming John Bonham ever recorded. Its lyrics apparently describe a hippy being hassled by the police in a park, and deciding to head for 'the misty mountains' – a likely Tolkien reference. The earliest UK pressing incorrectly lists the song as 'Misty Mountain Top'. The song appeared in the US and Australia as the B-side to the 'Black Dog' 45, and was a regular feature at gigs in 1972 and 1973.

Mitchell, Joni

b. Nov. 7th 1943

Canadian singer-songwriter admired by

all four members of Led Zeppelin. She served as the inspiration for 'Going To California' (included on the band's untitled fourth LP). "When you're in love with Joni Mitchell, you've really got to write about it now and then," Plant confessed in 1974.

Moby Dick

Originally titled 'Pat's Delight' in honour of John Bonham's wife, this instrumental served as the drummer's showcase throughout the band's live career and was given its new title by his young son Jason in 1969. It starts with a suitably lumbering Page riff (appropriated from Bobby Parker's 1961 single 'Watch Your Step' and later adopted as the theme to the BBC's *Disco 2* TV show), before the drum solo, played with sticks and bare hands, kicks in. Pieced together from various recordings, it's relatively concise on disc, but onstage it typically lasted twenty minutes or more. As Bonham told Melody Maker in June 1975: "Not everybody likes or understands a drum solo, so I like to bring in effects and sounds to keep their interest."

Monty Python

British comedy troupe whose film *Monty Python and the Holy Grail* was partially financed by Led Zeppelin in 1974. In his *Diaries 1969-1979*, published in 2006, Michael Palin records in his entry of Thursday April 3rd 1975: 'Today our second film opens [in London]… afterwards a party had been laid on in the Marquee Club. Messrs Page and Plant are standing, almost shyly, together. They are great fans of the show – they liked 'The Bicycle Tour' especially –

and apparently many pop groups now carry video cassettes of Python, as an obligatory part of their equipment.' The duo also attended the New York opening on April 27th.

Moon, Keith

b. Aug 23rd 1946 / d. Sept 7th 1978
Hard-living drummer with the Who, and the person who coined the name 'Lead Zeppelin' in 1966 (though the Who's bassist John Entwistle also claimed credit for it). He was also one of the few outside musicians ever to join the band onstage – a bearded Moon played along with John Bonham on 'Moby Dick', as well as joining in the encores of 'C'Mon Everybody' and 'Rock and Roll' at the LA Forum on June 23rd 1977.

"Bonzo loved Keith Moon, and Keith Moon certainly loved him," Jimmy Page later told *Guitar Player* magazine. "He let Keith Moon come up and play during his solo, which I don't think he would let any other drummer do. There was great respect between the two of them." In fact, Simon Kirke did just that at Munich's Olympiahalle on July 5th 1980. Moon died in his sleep after taking thirty-two Heminevrin tablets, prescribed to help him beat his alcoholism.

Morocco

North African kingdom that gave inspiration to Robert Plant and Jimmy Page during Led Zeppelin's heyday, though the singer told Circus magazine in January 1976: "I don't think Morocco is the most inspiring place that I shall ever go to. It's my ambition to go to Kashmir, and I'm saving that as the last trek." That February he told the NME: "On the Monday morning after the last gig at Earl's Court I was on my way to Agadir with Maureen, and three weeks later Jimmy flew out to meet me in Marrakech, where we spent several nights at the folk festival. That gave us a little peep into the colour of Moroccan music and the music of the hill tribes." The duo then set off in a rented Range Rover, driving south for a few days and having numerous adventures en route, often at the hands of the local militia. In July they reluctantly returned via Spain to Montreux, where they were based in tax exile before moving to Jersey in August. As Plant continued: "It was devastating leaving behind Morocco and suddenly finding ourselves in Europe." He elaborated to the Independent On Sunday in November 2003, adding: "After two months in southern Morocco with Jimmy Page, we awoke one morning in Goulimine, a small desert town near

the Atlantic coast, with a compulsion for Europe and cold beer. Three days later, after agitating northward hour after hour, we found ourselves under flashing lights on a disco dancefloor in Torremolinos clutching pints of Watney's Red Barrel. Sad, really, isn't it? But this is what the desert can do."

In fact, so unsatisfactory did he find his return that he decided to take his family on holiday to Rhodes, where they suffered a serious car accident on August 4th. The heady atmosphere in Morocco seemed to have affected Page deeply – the following March he told Sounds: "There's a man in Morocco, in fact a holy man, but he'll invite you for mint tea, and while he's standing there mint grows up around his feet and he picks it, makes tea and a small animal eats the stalks and it's gone. I haven't seen that, but the person who had and told me has no reason to lie."

Most, Mickie

b. June 20th 1938 / d. May 30th 2003
Born Michael Hayes, this hit-making record producer met Peter Grant in 1957, when they were both employed in Soho's 2Is coffee bar ('the birthplace of British rock and roll'), and they went on to become business partners in the 1960s. He gave plenty of employment to Page and Jones in their session days and, having acquired Simon Napier-Bell's interest in producing the Yardbirds, he introduced them to Grant, thereby setting the wheels in motion for the formation of Led Zeppelin. Jones had a high opinion of him ("I loved working with him, he was a clever man... it was

great fun and a lot of laughs," he told Guitar World magazine in July 1977), though Page expressed less fulsome sentiments in the same magazine, stating: "[With the Yardbirds] it was chaotic in recording… we'd just finished the take, and without even hearing it Mickie Most said 'next'… it was all done very quickly, as it sounds. It was things like that that really led to the general state of mind and depression of Keith Relf and Jim McCarty."

Motival

Anti-anxiety drug that John Bonham is thought to have been taking at the time of his death in September 1980. It has been suggested that it contributed to his death, but his sister Debbie has stated: "It's not on the death certificate. There were no drugs found in his body whatsoever. He died from vomiting in his sleep after a bottle of vodka, three pizzas, a curry and a few other things. He'd eaten an awful lot that day. He'd fallen asleep. It's not anybody's fault. It happened, but it certainly wasn't drugs."

Musicland

Popular recording studio owned by disco supremo Giorgio Moroder and located in the basement of the Arabella Hotel in Munich, Germany, where *Presence* was recorded over 18 days in November 1975. Part of the reason for the speed of the sessions was that the Rolling Stones were booked in to record *Black and Blue* three weeks later.

Mystic Studios

Small Hollywood recording facility owned by UK expats Doug Moody and Chris Huston, in which Screaming Lord Sutch's *And Heavy Friends* album was recorded in the autumn of 1969, with help from Page and Bonham. Page was impressed by its compactness and the energetic sound it captured, and Led Zeppelin returned soon afterwards to tape 'The Lemon Song'.

Nagashima, Tatsuji

Known as 'Tats', this legendary Japanese rock promoter oversaw visits to his country by acts including the Beatles, Frank Sinatra and Led Zeppelin. According to Richard Cole, Nagashima was 'startled' by the latter's conduct on their first visit in September 1971. By his account, upon arriving in Tokyo the band got some geisha girls drunk, Cole insulted the waitresses in a restaurant, Bonham urinated on a nightclub DJ, and he and Cole proceeded to destroy several hotel rooms with samurai swords. By the time they ran riot on a bullet train to Osaka on the 27th, Nagasaki was apparently 'on the brink of hysteria', and had to telephone Ahmet Ertegun for reassurance. Nonetheless, the band greatly respected him.

Napier-Bell, Simon

b. April 22nd 1939

Flamboyant pop entrepreneur who'd earned notoriety by managing John's Children and the young Marc Bolan. He briefly oversaw the Yardbirds in 1966, and was managing them when Jimmy Page joined. He produced their 'Happenings Ten Years Time Ago' 45 (featuring both Page and Jeff Beck), but in mid-1966 he sold his interest in the band to Mickie Most (recording) and Peter Grant (management). He never had a contract with Page, and advised Grant to get rid of him, as he considered him troublesome to work with. Grant, however, was of the opinion that decent wages were all that was required to cheer the guitarist up. Napier-Bell found greater success with Wham! in the 1980s.

Nevison, Ron

Philadelphia-born engineer who worked on several of the tracks on 1975's *Physical Graffiti*. He came to the band's notice after assembling a mobile studio for Ronnie Lane, of the Faces, and set up shop with them at Headley Grange early in 1974, though he didn't see the project through to completion. "I never knew that *Physical Graffiti* was going to be a double album," he told Classic Rock magazine in December 2007. "When we started out we were just cutting tracks for a new record. I left the project before they started pulling in songs from *Houses Of The Holy* and getting them up to scratch. So I didn't know it was a double until it came out."

Newport Festival

Led Zeppelin headlined this Rhode Island event (properly known as 'The 16th USA Newport Jazz and Blues Festival') on Sunday July 6th 1969, on a bill also featuring Jeff Beck, Jethro Tull, Ten Years After, James Brown, BB King and others. They closed the festival, and didn't start playing till 1 am, following organisational chaos. They weren't happy about the timing, but considered the gig too important to pull out of.

New Victoria Theatre

Venue in London where the band rehearsed in May 1980 for their forthcoming European tour, having moved from the Rainbow Theatre after a week.

New Yardbirds, the

The name under which Led Zeppelin supposedly performed in September and October 1968, though no hard evidence has ever surfaced to prove that they ever ceased to trade simply as 'the Yardbirds' before changing to Led Zeppelin. The only poster ever to have surfaced advertising them as 'the New Yardbirds' (for an appearance at Surrey University's Great Hall on Friday, October 25th 1968) may well be a fake. Following the collapse of the former incarnation of the band in July 1968, Jimmy Page and bassist Chris Dreja agreed to stay together and honour a Scandinavian tour that autumn. In order to do so, however, they urgently required other musicians. For a drummer, Page sounded out fellow session player Clem Cattini as well as Aynsley Dunbar and Procol Harum's Barrie 'BJ' Wilson, while Beat Instrumental erroneously reported that September that Paul Francis (late of Tony Jackson and the Vibrations) was on board. The names of Steve Winwood and Steve Marriott were bandied about as vocalists, but Page was more interested in Terry Reid. Reid was busy building a solo career with Mickie Most, but recommended a singer he knew from the clubs, one Robert Plant, currently appearing with a West Coast-influenced outfit named Obstweedle.

Page (accompanied by Grant and Dreja) duly slogged up to a gig at a teacher training college in Birmingham, and was most impressed. "I immediately thought there must be something wrong with him personality-wise, or that he had to be impossible to work with, because I just could not understand why, after he told me he'd been singing for a few years already, he hadn't become a big name yet," he remarked later. Even more gratifyingly, Plant had a recommendation for the drumming vacancy: his friend and former bandmate John Bonham. Bonham, however, was earning what he considered to be excellent money ($40 a week) backing US singer-songwriter Tim Rose, and took considerable persuasion. Grant was away on tour in the US with Jeff Beck when Page saw Bonham, and on his return he waged a campaign involving sending over 30 telegrams to Bonham's local pub, the Three Men In A Boat, in Walsall. Page and John Paul Jones, meanwhile, had reconnected at a session for Donovan's *Hurdy Gurdy Man* LP that summer, and in August Jones volunteered to take the place of Dreja, who'd decided to start a new career in photography.

The quartet finally got together for a preliminary jam in a tiny basement below a record shop in London's Gerrard Street (don't look for it, it's not there anymore). This was the first time Plant and Bonham had met Jones, but they gelled at once, playing 'Train Kept A-Rollin'' and Garnett Mimms' 'As Long As I Have You'. They set off for Scandinavia in the first week of September in an optimistic frame of mind, in order to fulfil the last existing Yardbirds commitments. "We started under the name the New Yardbirds because nobody would book us under anything else," Jones told Guitar Player magazine in July 1977. The riotous success of their shows there convinced Page that he had far more than a short-term prospect on his hands. On October 12th Melody Maker reported Page describing the music of his new band as "blues, basically, but not Fleetwood Mac-style. I hate that phrase 'progressive blues'. It sounds like a hype". Recalling Keith Moon's joke at a May 1966 Jeff Beck session that the assembled company would 'go down like a lead zeppelin', the band – and manager Peter Grant, who altered the spelling so it wouldn't be pronounced 'leed' – renamed themselves Led Zeppelin and played their first gig as such at Surrey University on October 15th (though it has been suggested that their debut may have been at Newcastle's Mayfair Ballroom on October 4th).

Night Flight

Bludgeoning rock song recorded during the sessions for the band's untitled fourth LP at Headley Grange in 1971, but ultimately included on 1975's *Physical Graffiti* (a fate that also befell 'Boogie With Stu' and 'Down By The Seaside'). The confusing lyrics have been interpreted as being about nuclear war and draft-dodging, and the song was never performed live by the band (though there is a bootleg of them cantering through it during a soundcheck at the Chicago Stadium on July 6th 1973).

The 1980s – Part One

Title given to the band's planned 1980 North American tour, due to start in Montreal on October 17th and finish in Chicago on November 13th. The tour had been hard to arrange owing to Plant's reluctance to leave his family, but he finally came around after their 14-date European jaunt that June and July, agreeing to a two days-on, one day-off strategy. Peter Grant cancelled the 21 dates announced on September 15th when John Bonham died ten days later, on September 25th.

Nobody's Fault But Mine

The lengthy cut that opens side two of 1976's *Presence*. It is based on a 1927 original by bluesman Blind Willie Johnson, possibly via an interpretation included on UK folk guitarist John Renbourn's 1966 *Another Monday* LP (Transatlantic TRA 149). Led Zeppelin's version features some furious interplay from the band, as well as a harmonica solo from Plant, and was included in practically every concert they played from 1977 onwards.

Nobs, The

Pseudonym under which the band played a Danish TV show on February 28th 1970, and a subsequent gig in Copenhagen's K.B. Hallen, following a threat of legal action from Eva Von Zeppelin. The name was inspired by Swiss promoter Claude Nobs, and has also been quoted as 'The Four Knobs'. John Paul Jones, however, told Blow By Blow magazine in 1992 that the name they eventually played under was 'The Wanking Dogs'.

Nobs, Claude

b. Feb 4th 1936

Legendary Swiss promoter and Atlantic Records consultant for whom the band always had respect and affection. Nobs, who founded the Montreux Jazz Festival, is also thought to have served as inspiration for the band's one-off pseudonym for a Danish gig in February 1970. The band made a considerable effort to play two gigs in Montreux on November 27th and 28th 1972, which were thought to have been a favour for Nobs, and in the spring of 1975 Peter Grant rented his house in Switzerland as a base for the band in tax exile.

No Quarter

Ominous epic included on *Houses Of The Holy*, showcasing John Paul Jones's keyboard wizardry and a classic Page riff. Though the final version was recorded at Island Studios in 1972, an earlier and faster take had been taped at Headley Grange the previous year. The song was slowed down during the mastering process (at London's Olympic Studios), apparently to make its atmosphere eerier, with Plant's voice being manipulated for the same reason. The song quickly became a live staple, and was played at virtually every Led Zeppelin concert until they toured Europe in 1980. Live renditions offered Jones an opportunity to play extensive solos, during which he would extemporise on classical themes, which often lasted up to twenty minutes. The song was also used to soundtrack Jones's 'fantasy' sequence in the 1976 *Song Remains The Same* movie.

Northover, Dave

Assistant to John Paul Jones on the band's 1977 US tour, and – according to Richard Cole's memoirs – 'a pharmacist and a rugby player' too.

141

O

Oakland Incident

Name given to an outbreak of violence after a Led Zeppelin gig at San Francisco's Oakland Coliseum on Saturday July 23rd 1977. Promoter Bill Graham was already on edge after being asked to deliver an advance of $25,000 to the band's hotel the day before, only to realise it was to pay for drugs. The show was a success, but the atmosphere backstage was charged, with tension simmering between members of Led Zeppelin's entourage and employees of Graham. As the band left the stage violence flared up, with the band's security boss John Bindon taking exception to a remark made by roadie Jim Downey, "It's a long way up that ramp". This was interpreted as a slur on Peter Grant's size, and Bindon promptly smashed Downey's head against some concrete, leaving him unconscious.

Shortly afterwards things turned even nastier when Grant's son Warren asked one of Graham's security operatives, Jim Matzorkis, if he could remove a wooden plaque with the band's name on it. As lighting man Jack Calmes later recalled: "Peter Grant's kid, kind of spoiled, walked into a secure area and one of Bill Graham's guards kind of moved him aside; he didn't hurt him or

anything. Bindon and Peter grabbed this guy, took him into one of the trailers, and beat the crap out of him. From what I understand, they tried to pull out one of his eyes, really bad shit."

Graham was especially furious as Grant had assured him that no physical violence would be employed in defusing the situation. Bonham was also involved, and is thought to have kicked Matzorkis in the balls. After the assault, Grant insisted that Graham sign a form promising that no charges would be brought, on pain of the band cancelling their performance the following day. This was done, but Graham knew the document was unenforceable. The band played their scheduled show at the venue on the 24th, but the enraged Graham vowed never to book them again and refused to speak to Plant, who wanted to make amends. Richard Cole later described his part in the episode: 'I was outside the caravan with an iron bar, making sure no one could get in… The next day, the four of us got arrested… They handcuffed us, took us off to jail, and then they let us out after an hour or so. And off we went.' Bindon returned to the UK and the band moved on to New Orleans, where Robert Plant received the dreadful news of his son's death. The tour was over.

In February 1978 Grant, Bonham, Cole and Bindon pleased *nolo contendere* (in absentia) to charges relating to the incident, and were given light fines, to Graham's disgust. According to Cole's memoirs, 'The chips usually fell Led Zeppelin's way; this time, they did again'.

But for many, the incident represented the band's nadir. As Page told Q magazine in 2003, "It was a scandal, just abhorrent."

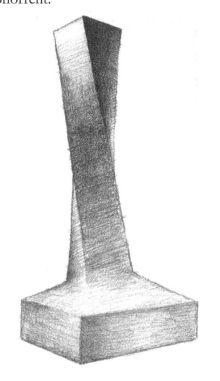

Obelisk

Rumoured title for *Presence*, as reported in Melody Maker on January 7th 1976. To promote the album Atlantic manufactured a run of 1000 individually numbered obelisks like the one on the album cover. They were sent to reviewers and radio stations, and are now prized by collectors.

Obstweedle

Walsall-based band Robert Plant was briefly fronting in July 1968, when Peter Grant, Jimmy Page and Chris Deja ventured to a teacher-training college outside Birmingham to watch him in action. Playing with him were John Bonham's cousin Bill Bonham (keyboards), Richard Brown (guitar), Mac Bailey (bass) and Barry Sargeant (drums).

Their name is usually given as 'Hobbstweedle', which is inaccurate, and they largely played covers of US West Coast material. Plant told Blender magazine in 2002 that "The only reason I got the job in Obstweedle, which always gets spelled wrong, is because the original singer got food poisoning. They were a rock band playing Moby Grape and Buffalo Springfield stuff. I stood in for the stricken singer, and wasn't there for long... it's a dreadful name, but it was at the last Obstweedle gig that Jimmy Page came along and waved his wand at me. He said 'Are you the roadie?' I said 'We can't afford roadies.' He said 'I'm looking for Robert Plant'. I said, 'So am I'."

Page informed ZigZag magazine in November 1972 that it was "a typical student set-up, where drinking is the prime consideration and the group is only of secondary importance." In 1982 the singer told the late radio presenter Chris Tetley that "there were about ten people in the whole place, so it wasn't a particularly atmospheric night to watch me or listen to me sing". Plant went on to tell Uncut magazine in May 2008: "I remember it very clearly. [Jimmy] was very reserved, very polite, slightly withdrawn, and it was evident to me that he didn't have the common touch and probably didn't need it." Nonetheless, Page was impressed and about a fortnight later he invited Plant to stay with him at his Pangbourne home.

The Ocean

Inspired by the sea of fans the band could see from onstage, this hard rock number closes *Houses Of The Holy*. It's counted in by John Bonham with the words "We've done four already, but now we're steady, and then they went, one, two, three, four!" This is a reference to the number of takes the band had already attempted. Bonham's squeaky bass drum pedal is also audible in the song, as is the faint ringing of a telephone (at approximately 1:37 and again at 1:41).

It ends with a change of tempo, with a light-hearted guitar solo and a doo-wop style chorus featuring rare vocal contributions from Jones and Bonham. The lyrical reference to a 'girl who won my heart' who 'is only three years old' concerns Plant's daughter Carmen, and as of November 1972 he updated her age to four when performing the song live. It was included in their set from 1972 to 1973, but abandoned thereafter.

The song made an unwelcome return to Plant's consciousness when he was languishing in a Greek hospital bed in August 1975 after his car smash on Rhodes. "I had to share a room with a drunken soldier who had fallen over and banged his head, and as he was coming around he kept focusing on me, uttering my name," the singer told Melody Maker in February 1976. "I was lying there in some pain, trying to get cockroaches off the bed, and he started singing 'The Ocean' from *Houses Of The Holy*."

Ocheltree, Jeff

John Bonham's drum roadie in 1977 and 1979. The American had been talent-spotted by Bonham at a Mahavishnu Orchestra gig at London's Crystal Palace Bowl, when he was working for Billy Cobham. He didn't enjoy touring with Led Zeppelin, however, largely because Peter Grant treated him so badly. "He was always bad-vibing people and he was just not a very nice person to be around," he later recalled. "That's why it was not really a comfortable situation to be involved in, because you never had faith in the consistency of his behaviour." Ocheltree also commented of Bonham's later years: "He was a little slower... It makes me sad to say that, but it's what I saw. He gained weight and didn't feel well. But still he never did a gig where he didn't play well."

The Old Grey Whistle Test

Long-running weekly BBC TV music show, which started in 1971. Following their policy of never playing on television, Led Zeppelin never performed live for it, but they did contribute in other ways. Their first appearance came on March 20th 1973, when presenter Bob Harris introduced an exclusive preview of 'No Quarter' from the forthcoming *Houses Of The Holy* LP, set to odd visuals. On January 17th 1975 an interview between Harris and Robert Plant was screened, having been taped backstage at Voorst National, Brussels, Belgium on January 12th. It finds Plant in a sunny mood, and largely concerns the forthcoming *Physical Graffiti* LP, the Swan Song label and the band's plans to play in the UK. On February 21st the show previewed two songs from *Physical Graffiti*, 'Houses Of The Holy' and 'Trampled Underfoot', set to further odd visuals. A similar ploy was undertaken on April 6th 1976, when the whole of 'Achilles Last Stand' (from the forthcoming *Presence* LP) was played, set to vintage black and white film footage. October 5th saw the show screening 'Black Dog', taken from the forthcoming *Song Remains The Same* movie, and on November 2nd 1976 Plant and Peter Grant were interviewed by Michael Appleton on a boat ('Swanage Queen') sailing up the Thames. They largely focus on the making of the film, and the violin bow segment of 'Dazed And Confused' is also shown. Whilst none of these appearances were especially revelatory, they gave starved UK fans practically the only chances they ever had to see Led Zeppelin on television.

The Old Hyde

This Cutnall Green, Worcestershire farm served as the Bonham family homestead from 1972. Over the following two years the drummer had the majority of the property knocked down and rebuilt, and restored the farm to working order. The architect for the project was Grace Plant, the wife of Robert Plant's cousin Malcolm — an insurance salesman who oversaw that side of things. As Chris Welch wrote in Melody Maker in June 1975, "A ranch style nameboard appears around a bend in a B-road, and twin white fences accompany a long, straight driveway to the modern brick farmhouse." Part of Bonham's dream was to raise a herd of pedigree Hereford cattle (serviced by Bruno the bull), and

to that end a farm manager named Brian Treble was appointed in late 1972. The herd flourished under his stewardship, but he was tragically killed in a road accident in 1974. The property had 100 acres with it, as well as a barn that Bonham converted into a car workshop. He told Welch that the house "used to be just a three-bedroomed house. My father did all the wood panelling, and I did a lot of the work with my brother and sub-contractors." The Bonham family still live there.

Old Mill House

Jimmy Page's home in Mill Lane, Windsor, in which John Bonham was found dead on September 25th 1980. Page had bought the place from actor Michael Caine for £900,000 only a month earlier, and is thought to have sold it in 2004.

Olympic Studios

Thameside recording facility located at 117 Church Road, Barnes, London, where Led Zeppelin taped their debut album in just 30 hours between September and October 1968. They subsequently used the facility to record songs featured on *Houses Of The Holy* and *Physical Graffiti*.

Ostlund, Lennart

Swedish engineer who worked with the band on *In Through The Out Door* at Stockholm's Polar Music studios in late 1978, as assistant to Leif Masses. Three of the tracks they worked on were left off that album, but appeared on 1982's *Coda* compilation — 'Ozone Baby', 'Darlene' and 'Wearing and Tearing'.

Out On The Tiles

Taking its name from an English idiom meaning to go out and have a good time, this heavy rock number closes side one of 1970's *Led Zeppelin III*. Its genesis lay in a risqué ditty John Bonham would sing en route to gigs, and he is given a co-writing credit, acknowledging that he came up with the riff as well. It wasn't often played live in its entirety, though its introduction was frequently employed just before the band played 'Black Dog' onstage, as well as Bonham's 'Over The Top' solo on the 1977 US tour.

Over Europe

'Led Zeppelin Over Europe' was the title of the band's brief, 14-date European tour in 1980, which began at Dortmund's Westfalenhalle on June 17th and finished at Berlin's Eissporthalle on July 7th. In between were dates in Brussels, Holland, Belgium and Switzerland. The intention was to cut back on the excesses of their 1970s stage show and present what Grant later described as 'a back-to-basics sort of thing'. As Plant told Q magazine in March 1988, the band wanted to prove it had "learned a hell of a lot from XTC and people like that. I was really keen to stop the self-importance and the guitar solos that lasted an hour. We cut everything down and we didn't play any song for more than four and a half minutes." Their performances were variable, with Plant acknowledging how much the music scene – and attitudes towards them – had changed since their glory days a decade earlier when he bade farewell to the audience after the first show with the words "Goodnight

– dinosaurs rule!".

The setlist was significantly changed from their 1977 tour and Knebworth dates of August 1979, with 'All My Loving' and 'The Rain Song' added, as well as a much shorter 'No Quarter' and the unexpected addition of opener 'Train Kept A-Rollin''. The tour also saw the reinstatement of Page's interminable 'White Summer' / 'Black Mountain Side' solo showcase. Guitarist Carlos Santana and Atlantic boss Ahmet Ertegun attended the show at Frankfurt's Festhalle on June 30th, with executive and friend Phil Carson joining the band onstage for an encore of Barrett Strong's 'Money'. After the show Grant and Ertegun discussed the possibility of signing the band to Atlantic for a further five years, but Bonham's untimely death on September 25th scotched the possibility. At their penultimate show in Munich's Olympiahalle on July 5th, Bad Company's drummer Simon Kirke joined the band on a second drum kit for the epic encore of 'Whole Lotta Love', before they repaired to a local nightspot. The next day they would travel to Berlin for their last ever performance.

see *Berlin Eissporthalle*

Over The Hills And Far Away

The third song on 1973's *Houses Of The Holy*, and a perfect example of the band's ability to move between delicate and heavy sounds within a composition. It was originally conceived at Bron-Yr-Aur in 1970, with an early version apparently being called 'Many, Many Times'. An excellent example of Jones and Bonham's tight interplay, it was released as a 45 in the US in May 1973, backed with Dancing Days (Atlantic 2970), but only reached #51 on the Billboard chart. The band debuted it onstage in the US in 1972 (well before its release on record) and consistently played it live thereafter, dropping it only for their European tour in 1980.

Over The Top

Preceded by the riff from 'Out On The Tiles', this was the title given to John Bonham's onstage drum solo on the band's 1977 US tour, when it took over from 'Moby Dick', whose riff typically concluded it. The phrase was coined by Jimmy Page – as the band's publicist BP Fallon told Melody Maker in January 1977: "Jimmy used to sit there sometimes, looking pretty whacked, and he's really a fragile geezer, and suddenly he'd be on his feet shouting 'Right! Over the top!'" In the same interview Fallon announced that he'd written a book of memoirs about his time with the band also called *Over The Top*, but had decided not to publish. "None of the band have seen it, and I won't show them," he said. "I daren't show it to them. There's friendships that have to be considered too… I could have said who was sleeping with who, and who's whacking what up their nose. But I wasn't interested, because I don't want to betray the confidence that people have in me."

Ozone Baby

Up-tempo rocker taped on November 14th 1978, during the *In Through The Out Door* sessions in Stockholm, but not released until 1982's *Coda* compilation. The song showcases Plant's harmonised vocal effect, often used onstage as of 1977, but rarely on record. It was never performed live.

Pace, Charles

b. 1920

Scottish-born undertaker and self-professed Satanist whom Jimmy Page hired to paint murals at Boleskine House in mid-1971. Page's intention was to recreate the ambience and look of the property at the time of Aleister Crowley's occupation. The work can't have been especially long-lasting or remunerative, however: by September 19th 1976 Pace was the main contributor to a News Of The World splash about the dark arts ('We expose Satanism, black magic and sex orgies in the respectable suburbs of Britain').

Page, Jimmy

b. Jan 9th 1944

Born in Heston, Middlesex to an industrial personnel manager and a doctor's secretary, James Patrick Page went on to become one of London's most prolific session guitarists before forming Led Zeppelin, for whom he played guitar and produced every album.

An only child, he spent idyllic childhood days on his uncle's Northampton farm, collecting stamps and visiting stately homes. Aged 8 he and his parents moved from Feltham (when Heathrow Airport was built) to 34 Miles Road, Epsom, Surrey. He told Q magazine in 2003 that he was "an only child who was totally obsessed with the guitar... My entire childhood was spent devouring records". He also described his childhood to Mojo magazine in August 2004 as "those sombre post-war days of rationing... Then this explosion came through your radio speaker when you were 11 or 12." The first song to make a major impact on him was Elvis Presley's 'Baby Let's Play House', and other early influences included James Burton and Scotty Moore (Presley's guitarists), Cliff Gallup (Gene Vincent's), Chet Atkins and Little Richard. Page's parents were not musical, but they indulged his passion , buying him a Spanish guitar, arranging for him to have basic lessons in Kingston and even allowing their front room to be dominated by his records and musical equipment.

Jeff Beck later remarked, "Jimmy was a freak for the [electric] guitar, but he didn't play one. He just used to draw strip cartoons of rock bands." An early interest in blues was encouraged by a collector who lived on the same road, and at the age of fourteen he finally got his first electric guitar, a 1949 Gibson Les Paul, for £200 (on hire purchase), which he helped to pay for by taking a paper round. He soon became inseparable from it, taking it to Ewell County Secondary School every day, only to have it confiscated and returned after classes.

Having joined his first bands, Red E Lewis and the Red Caps and JG's Skiffle Group (who appeared on TV talent show *All Your Own* in 1958), his reputation reached the ears of Neil Christian, a local singer who persuaded Page's parents to allow their boy to leave school and join his band, the Crusaders, in 1960. Page toured the UK with them for 18 months, but the long hours and poor diet enfeebled him. Nonetheless, his reputation as an innovative player was beginning to spread. In mid-1961 he left the band, convalesced, played briefly behind poet Royston Ellis, then enrolled at Sutton College of Art in Surrey that autumn (moving from a decent wage to a student grant in the process). As an art student Page was able to indulge his musical interests freely, and spent the vacations travelling around Europe. During term-time he began to hang out at London's Marquee Club and participate in jams on Thursday evenings, where he was soon noticed by leading R&B musicians Cyril Davies and Alexis Korner.

Both offered Page a slot in their bands, but were turned down as the guitarist wanted to continue at art school. Page did occasionally join Davies onstage for a couple of tunes, however, causing him to be talent-spotted by the young arranger / producer Mike Leander in 1962. Leander offered him his first session engagement, playing on Jet Harris's 'Diamonds' / 'Footstomp' (Decca F11563, 1/63), which reached number one, and Carter-Lewis and the Southerners' 'Your Momma's Out Of Town' / 'Somebody Told My Girl' (Oriole CB 1868, 1/63), which was a minor hit. For a short time Page continued to study by day and play sessions at night, but the former was soon abandoned in favour of the lucrative and never-ending studio work. He went on to play on major hits by Brian Poole and the Tremeloes ('Twist and Shout', 7/63), Heinz ('Just Like Eddie', 8/63), Lulu ('Shout', 5/64), the Rolling Stones ('Heart Of Stone', 6/64), the Nashville Teens ('Tobacco Road', 7/64), Marianne Faithfull ('As Tears Go By', 8/64), Dave Berry ('The Crying Game', 8/64), Them ('Baby Please Don't Go', 1/65), Tom Jones ('It's Not Unusual', 2/65) and many others. Controversy has long dogged his rumoured contribution to the Kinks' 'You Really Got Me' (8/64), and he is known to have been on hand (but largely surplus to requirements) for the Who's debut 45, 'I Can't Explain' (2/65). He also played on innumerable flops, including one of his own, 'She Just Satisfies' / 'Keep Moving' (2/65). Much of his subsequent session work was undertaken for the Rolling Stones' young manager, Andrew Oldham, who'd launched Immediate Records in August 1965. Page briefly served as an A&R man for the label, taping 'I'm Your Witchdoctor' and 'Telephone Blues' with John Mayall and jamming with Eric Clapton for a possible album, but he found the work frustrating. When he was asked to join the Yardbirds as bassist in June 1966, he accepted.

"Jimmy was so professional, and very fresh, as he hadn't been out on the road," recalled Yardbirds bassist Chris Dreja in 2001. "He was a very astute guy, too, and knew the business… as a businessman he had quite a tough edge to him because he'd spent a long time around producers". Page's stint with the band lasted for two years, upon which they splintered after a fractious US tour. Page and Dreja initially planned to form a new band together, in order to fulfil existing Scandinavian dates that September. When Dreja chose to pursue photography instead, however, he found John Paul Jones, Robert Plant and John Bonham. He already knew Jones from session work, while singer Terry Reid had recommended Plant, who was in turn an old friend of Bonham's. By the time the quartet was assembled, Page had a clear idea of what he wished to achieve. "I had a long-term plan that it wasn't just going to be a band that made singles and trite music," he told Uncut magazine in May 2008. "It was going to have longevity, and it was going to make profound music." He dominated the group musically and lyrically in its early days, telling Oz magazine in March 1969: "I know that I influenced pretty heavily the contents and arrangements on the first album, but that was only because we didn't have the time to discuss everything between us."

Future albums were indeed more democratic, with all four members contributing ideas, though Page produced them all, taking especial care over microphone positioning. As a producer he was something of a perfectionist, though he worked with the very best engineers in the business. "I lived every second of the albums, whereas the others didn't," he told

Trouser Press in October 1977. "John Paul and Bonzo would do the tracks and they wouldn't come in until needed, and Robert would do the vocals. But I'd be there all the time, and I'd live and cringe to every mistake."

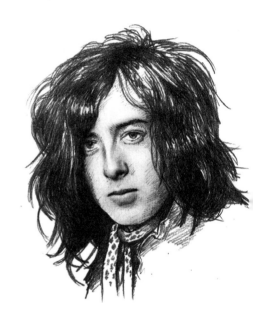

Journalist Ritchie Yorke attended a mixing session for *Led Zeppelin II* in 1969, and later wrote that 'We sat enthralled as Page issued simple, clear-cut instructions, quietly but forcefully. No ifs, buts or maybes. He knew what he was after and he would endure and inquire until he found it.' As Page told the Sunday Times in November 1990: "Before I formed Led Zeppelin, I'd played in a lot of bands and been on plenty of really good sessions. Everyone would be giving their all, but by the time it came to the playback the drummers sounded like they were hitting cardboard boxes, the guitars might as well have been rubber bands. And I determined that with Zeppelin we were going to make the instruments sound like real instruments, give them ambience, let them breathe." This thoroughness extended to his own solos ('Stairway To Heaven' being a case in point). "I get terrible studio nerves," he admitted in 1970. "Even when I've worked out the whole thing at home beforehand at home... When it comes to playing it again in the studio, my bottle goes. It's the studio nerves – you never lose them." He told Guitar World magazine in July 1977: "I don't like anybody else in the studio when I'm putting on the guitar parts. I usually just limber up for a while, and then maybe do three solos and take the best of the three."

Though he had a serious girlfriend named Charlotte Martin from January 1970 (and had a daughter named Scarlet with her in 1971), Page was not married during the band's lifetime. Always an enthusiastic traveller, he visited countries such as Morocco, Egypt and India when the band wasn't on the road, occasionally with Plant as his companion, soaking up local musical influences wherever he went. He was also an inveterate collector of antiques, specialising in the Pre-Raphaelite period. Other interests were gardening ("this summer we grew all the vegetables we needed and also enough to freeze for the winter," he told the NME in August 1973), vintage cars (though he couldn't drive) and occult literature (he funded a bookshop along those lines named Equinox). He was especially interested in the life and work of Aleister Crowley, whose former home, Boleskine Lodge, he bought and

set about restoring in 1971. This gave rise to the tabloid myth of 'the curse of Led Zeppelin', which greatly frustrated him over the years. As Plant told Q magazine in March 1988, "all that crap came from Page collecting all the Crowley stuff. Page had a kind of fascination with the absurd, and Page could afford to invest in his fascination with the absurd, and that was it." According to road manager Richard Cole's autobiography, 'He never talked about it much with the band, and he never tried to get any of us to become believers in a particular metaphysical concept. So, even though it all seemed a little weird to us, none of us ever interfered with whatever wavelength Jimmy might be on at the moment.' The guitarist confirmed this in an interview with Rolling Stone in March 1975, stating: "I'm not interested in turning anybody on to anybody that I'm turned onto...if people want to find things, they find them themselves. I'm a firm believer in that."

Despite his flamboyance during gigs, Page's personality was fundamentally retiring and quiet, something that fuelled his enigmatic image. "I guess I am pretty shy," he told Canadian newspaper the Kitchener Record in November 1969. "Nobody ever gets to really know me... It doesn't bother the rest of the group. I just sit back and try not to be noticed." It was onstage that his extroverted side would come out – as he explained to the NME that December, "most people are very calm at work and half-hysterical at home. People are more themselves at their house, where they spend most of their time. For me, the place I am most often is really in concert halls." Unfortunately, touring (and its attendant temptations) took a major toll on Page's health. By his own account he largely subsisted on banana daiquiri cocktails while on tour, and he told Disc in June 1972 (while on tour in the US): "I still get very ill being in the road. It's probably called malnutrition... I haven't eaten for about three days. You know, when you're fasting, after about three or four days you get these pains, and I had one onstage last night – bang." Looking back on the 1973 US tour, Page told Mojo magazine in December 2007 that "You couldn't just get off the plane and click back into real life. We'd had months and months of being bombarded, if you like, with intense images and sensations. I can remember coming back and suddenly the dimensions of the room you're in seem different from how they'd been before. It took time to settle down."

As the decade drew on, his reticence and frailty only served to fuel his mystique, and tales of his enigmatic behaviour and predilection for young girls (according to Richard Cole in *Stairway To Heaven*, he 'had a weakness for girls who were struggling with their first set of false eyelashes and wobbling on their first pair of high heels') became rife. Though he played occasional sessions outside the band (appearing on recordings by artists including Roy Harper, Al Stewart, Screaming Lord Sutch and Maggie Bell), Led Zeppelin consumed almost all of his energy. By 1976, emotionally and physically drained by ten straight years of touring and recording, he had started to take heroin and his live guitar playing was

beginning to suffer. As such, the *Presence* sessions in November and December 1975 marked a severe test not only for the band, but also for his capabilities. As he told the NME in February 1977, "there's absolutely no doubt about it, that album helped me pull through at a time where I just couldn't have taken any more." In the autumn of 1976 he checked into a sanatorium, telling Gig magazine in May 1977: "I just needed to get away for a while and see things from a different perspective. There was nothing sinister. I needed to get into a regular pattern. A regular schedule. And it seems to be working."

Following the premature end to the band's eleventh US tour that July (after the death of Plant's son Karac), he largely disappeared from view, spending much of this time in his London home, Tower House, a large Gothic revival property in Kensington. The band didn't rehearse again until May 1978, when they met at Clearwell Castle to take stock. That winter they regrouped in Stockholm to make *In Through The Out Door*, but Page was still taking drugs and his contribution was far smaller than on previous LPs (though he mixed the tapes and took his customary production credit). Having sold his Tudor mansion in East Sussex, Plumpton Place, following the death of a friend there at a party in 1978, he bought the Old Mill House in Windsor in 1979 for a reported £900,000 and began to prepare for a renewed assault on the world's stages, though his unpredictable behaviour continued. As Mickie Most later recalled, "I went to Paradise Island in the Bahamas and Jimmy Page was there and he never came out of his hotel room in two weeks. I also went to his birthday party when he had a big house out in Windsor, which he bought from Michael Caine. They had roast pigs on spits and all sorts and he never turned up. He never even turned up for his own birthday party. So it was all a funny time."

On September 24th 1980, after the first rehearsal for their forthcoming twelfth US tour, the band congregated at the Old Mill House for the evening. That night, after a day-long vodka binge, John Bonham suffocated in his sleep, in a guest suite. Page, Plant and Jones quickly decided not to continue without him, and indeed Page later stated that in the aftermath of the tragedy he'd contemplated never playing guitar again. In fact, he has emerged as the principle custodian of the band's legacy, overseeing all archive releases and speaking of them with considerable pride. "Many people think of me as just a riff guitarist, but I think of myself in broader terms," he told Guitar World magazine in 1993. "As a musician I think my greatest achievement has been to create unexpected melodies and harmonies within a rock and roll framework. And as a producer I would like to be remembered as someone who was able to sustain a band of unquestionable individual talent, and push it to the forefront during its working career." A decade later he put it even more simply, telling Q magazine in 2003: "My life was Led Zeppelin. I lived and breathed Led Zeppelin. When I wasn't touring, I was at home writing

music for the group... It was a total obsession for me."

Page, Scarlet
b. March 1971
Jimmy Page's daughter, allegedly conceived at Bron-Yr-Aur half an hour after her father and Robert Plant had composed 'That's The Way'. Her full name is Scarlet Lilith Eleida Page, and she is now a successful rock photographer.

Pangbourne Boathouse
Jimmy Page's riverside home on the Thames in Berkshire, bought for £35,000 in 1967 and his base at the time of Led Zeppelin's formation. The house also served as a venue for the band's early rehearsals in September 1968.

Having travelled to Birmingham to hear Robert Plant sing in July 1968, he invited him to stay for a few days. Plant told International Times in March 1969: "I went down to Pangbourne where Jimmy lives. It was the real desperation scene, man, like I had nowhere else to go. There I was with my suitcase, getting off the train, and suddenly this old woman starts slapping my face and shouting about my hair!" When Plant arrived at the house, he told a 2005 press conference, he "knocked on the door and the door opened and this girl who was part of Dr. John's Night-Trippers backing group was dressed in a net curtain... my suitcase fell out of my hand." They spent their time chatting about music and listening to records (including the demo for Plant's Band Of Joy, which the singer had helpfully brought). Plant went on to tell Uncut magazine in May 2008: "I was welcomed into Jimmy's home and immediately realised that his interests and the whole landscape of his music and his life was very broad and pretty esoteric." When Page was out one day, Plant pulled out a few records to play, by artists including Howlin' Wolf Muddy Waters, Joan Baez, Fairport Convention and the Incredible String Band. Upon the guitarist's return they found that he had intended to play exactly the same ones, something they both took as a favourable omen. "We had a musical affinity, you could say… we got on well musically," Plant told the late radio interviewer Chris Tetley in 1982. "Though I was nineteen and a bit overawed by everything, I just about managed to hang in and not go well over the top as we started to think about looking for a drummer."

Page kept a motor-boat moored at the property (fitted with a stereo tape deck), and indulged his taste for art nouveau inside. The February 14th 1970 issue of Melody Maker explained that 'wandering around the interior revealed a surprising number of oddly-shaped rooms and passages, and down below the ground floor was a huge room housing the central heating, a dismantled antique bed, considerable quantities of junk and a motor launch bobbing about in an inlet, waiting for summer', as well as 'sloping floors and muddled piles of valuable paintings, records, model trains and books… in one room was a Mutoscope, a hand-cranked seaside peep-show… parts of the house were freezing cold… but all held the warmth of personality – and a welcome return

to traditional English eccentricity'. Page sold it in 1973, and in late 2007 it went on the market again, described as offering 'a very generous-sized mooring, an indoor heated swimming pool and a wide variety of rooms on three levels'.

Parker, Bobby
b. Aug. 31st 1937
US blues guitarist whose 1961 single 'Watch Your Step' bears similarities to the riff for 'Moby Dick'. According to the May 1993 issue of Guitar World magazine, Page flew to Washington DC in 1972 to hear Parker perform, with a view to signing him to the yet-to-be-formed Swan Song label. The two guitarists apparently jammed and Page reportedly gave Parker $2,000 to buy a tape deck and make a demo, but nothing more ever came of the idea. Legend also has it that Plant was inspired to start singing after hearing Parker's 'Blues Get Off My Shoulder'.

Pat's Delight
Original title for John Bonham's live drum solo (later recorded as 'Moby Dick'), named after his wife Pat, whom he married in February 1966, when he was 17.

Paul, Les
b. June 9th 1915
Born Lester Polsfuss, this Wisconsin native was a pioneer in developing the electric guitar, and a considerable influence on Jimmy Page, whose first electric guitar was a 1949 Gibson Les Paul (bought on hire purchase for £200). As Page told Melody Maker on December 27th 1969: "Les Paul – he's

the man who started everything, multi-track recording, the electric guitar – he's just a genius." He returned to the subject in Guitar Player magazine in July 1977, adding: "That's where I heard feedback first – Les Paul. Also vibratos and things. Even before BB King, you know, I've traced a hell of a lot of rock and roll, little riffs and things, back to Les Paul... I mean, he's the father of it all, multi-tracking and everything else. If it hadn't been for him there wouldn't have been anything, really."

see *Black Beauty*

Peel, John
b. Aug. 30th 1939 / d. Oct. 25th 2004
Legendary UK broadcaster and a noted early supporter of Led Zeppelin, who made their first radio broadcast on his BBC radio *Top Gear* show on March 23rd 1969 (it had been recorded on March 3rd). They returned on June 29th and August 10th (recorded on June 24th and 27th respectively), and also performed a legendary set for his *In Concert* radio show, aired on the evening of Sunday April 4th 1971. Several performances from all these broadcasts were included in the *BBC Sessions* boxed set, released in November 1997. Peel frequently compered at concerts and rock festivals, including the 1969 and 1970 Bath Festivals, at which Led Zeppelin played legendary sets, and Robert Plant attended his funeral.

Percy
Robert Plant's longstanding nickname in the band. Whether it derives from UK slang for the male generative organ or a popular TV gardener has never been definitively established.

see *Thrower, Percy*

Phillips, Sam
b. Jan. 5th 1923 / d. June 30th 2003
Proprietor of Sun Records and producer of early sides by Elvis Presley, Johnny Cash, Carl Perkins and others who had a major influence on the members of Led Zeppelin. The band were keen to record at his legendary Sun Studios in Memphis, but – as Page told LA's Rock Magazine in October 1970 – "Old Sam Phillips wouldn't do it. It was on the first tour and I suppose he thought 'who the Christ are they?', and really wasn't interested. It had always been a dream of mine to record at Sun."

see *Sun Records*

Physical Graffiti
The band's sixth LP, recorded at various times and in various places between 1970 and 1974, and finally released in February 1975 as their first album on their own Swan Song label. Though Bonham had assured the NME in July 1970 "We are not going to do the expected double album thing, simply because most of these are just padded with studio leftovers," by 1975 they had decided that they had enough decent material, both new and old, to merit a double.

The bulk of the recordings were made from November 1973. After Christmas (and having got over a brief threat to quit from Jones), they reconvened at Headley Grange and laid down a number of tracks Plant later described as 'real belters'. A decision was taken to combine these with off-cuts from earlier album sessions and make a double LP. As Page explained to Trouser Press in October 1977, "'Black Country Woman' and 'The Rover' were both done at the same time we did 'D'yer Mak'er'. 'Bron-Yr-Aur' was done for the third record. 'Down By The Seaside', 'Night Flight' and 'Boogie With Stu' were all from the sessions for the fourth album. We had an album and a half of new material, and this time we figured it was better to stretch out than to leave off. I really fancied putting out a song called 'Houses of the Holy' on the album."

Its complex, die-cut artwork (inspired by Jose Feliciano's 1973 LP *Compartments*) caused delays, as had that of their three preceding albums, so the original release date in July 1974 came and went. The finished sleeve showed 97 St. Mark's Place, in New York City, with inner sleeves that could be moved around to show different images in each window. These include such disparate figures as Charles Atlas, Elizabeth Taylor, Jerry Lee Lewis, The Queen, King Kong, Lee Harvey Oswald, Marlene Dietrich, Neil Armstrong and The Virgin Mary, with their old friend Roy Harper receiving a photography credit. Page was confident about the album from the outset. "It'll hit people in the groin more than some of the other things that we've done," he told Hit Parader magazine in November 1974. "There's a lot of instantaneous, or spontaneous, stuff that we did at Headley Grange – and that's where we

did the fourth LP. We had about three sides of that, and we also had some left over from the first, second, third, fourth and fifth LPs, and so we're going to put some of those things in just for the fun of it - and that makes up the double LP."

The album finally appeared halfway through their tenth US tour, and immediately became the fastest-selling record in the country. Despite being a double, sales were unprecedented and it generated $12,000,000 in America in its first year alone. It stimulated sales of the band's back catalogue to the extent that all five previous albums re-entered the Billboard Top 200 in March 1975 (*Led Zeppelin I* – #83, *Led Zeppelin II* – #104, *Led Zeppelin III* – #124, the untitled fourth LP – #116, *Houses of the Holy* – #92). "I love the album," Plant told the NME on February 1st 1975. "There are some real humdinger, roaring tracks on it – an then there are some others that are going to take a while… and then people will see."

Pickett, Kenny
b. Sept. 3rd 1942 / d. Jan 10th 1997
Lead singer of 1960s UK freakbeat heroes the Creation (for whom Richard Cole had tour-managed in Germany in 1967), and a Led Zeppelin roadie from 1968 to 1970. He flew to LA with the band on their first ever visit to the US at Christmas 1968. John Bonham's drum tech at the time, Glen Colson, later recalled: "He'd been a plumber, and he was also a tough guy… Basically Kenny and I had to do everything. We had a Transit van and between us we had to

carry a Hammond organ, a PA, a drum kit and two Marshall stacks... Kenny later did two tours of America with them, by himself, in a U-Haul truck. He drove all across America – just one roadie for the whole band. He didn't even have me to help him, as I never went to America with Zeppelin. He had to cope with the PA, the backline and the Hammond. He did that all on his own, night after night. He'd have to break down the gear after a show and drive straight to the next gig. And he did that for three years." Staggeringly, after leaving Led Zeppelin's employ Pickett went on to co-write Clive Dunn's January 1971 UK #1 'Grandad'.

Plagiarism

From the outset of their career Led Zeppelin faced accusations of borrowing from other musicians, principally American bluesmen, without crediting them. This was partially because Plant was an inexperienced lyricist when the band was formed, and partly because Page knew so many blues and folk records inside out that he would unknowingly incorporate elements from them into his playing. "I always tried to bring something fresh to anything that I used," he told Guitar World magazine in December 1993. "I always made sure to come up with some variation. In fact, I think in most cases you would never know what the original source could be. Maybe not in every case, but in most cases. And Robert was supposed to change the lyrics, and he didn't always do that – which is what brought on most of our grief. They couldn't get us on the guitar parts or the music, but they

nailed us on the lyrics. We did, however, take some liberties, I must say."

On their debut the band took the credit for 'Babe I'm Gonna Leave You', actually written by Anne Bredon and learnt from a Joan Baez LP. 'You Shook Me', meanwhile, was by Willie Dixon, with some lyrics interposed from Robert Johnson's 'Stones In My Passway'. 'I Can't Quit You Baby' is also by Dixon. 'Dazed and Confused', meanwhile, was adapted from US singer-songwriter Jake Holmes's debut LP. 'Black Mountain Side' was a folk club staple, which Page learnt from Scottish folk singer Anne Briggs, though Bert Jansch also played it. 'Communication Breakdown', meanwhile, bears similarities to Eddie Cochran's 'Nervous Breakdown', and 'How Many More Times' is based on Howlin' Wolf's 'How Many More Years', also incorporating a notable chunk from Albert King's 'The Hunter'.

Led Zeppelin II continued the practice. Though 'Whole Lotta Love' is based on an original riff by Page, the song clearly incorporates elements of Willie Dixon's 'You Need Love' (possibly via a cover included on the first Small Faces album from 1966). Dixon sued and was granted a settlement in 1985. Plant has since admitted "I just thought, 'well, what am I going to sing?' That was it, a nick. Now happily paid for." 'The Lemon Song' also contains elements of numerous blues songs, principally Howlin' Wolf's 'Killing Floor'. Indeed, early UK copies of the LP had the song listed under that title on the label, and another out-of-court settlement was eventually reached.

Plant's notorious invitation to 'squeeze my lemon till the juice runs down my leg', meanwhile, comes from Robert Johnson's 'Traveling Riverside Blues', though Johnson probably borrowed it himself. The 'Moby Dick' riff is influenced by bluesman Bobby Parker's 'Watch Your Step', while 'Bring It On Home' is directly adapted from Sonny Boy Williamson's original. On *Led Zeppelin III*, the guitar part of 'Bron-Y-Aur Stomp' is similar to Bert Jansch's arrangement of a traditional piece entitled 'The Waggoner's Lad', found on his 1966 *Jack Orion* LP, while 'Hats Off To (Roy) Harper' incorporates lyrics from Bukka White's 'Shake 'Em On Down'.

Thereafter the band's reliance on classic blues diminished, though 1975's *Physical Graffiti* saw a partial return to form, with 'Custard Pie' bearing comparison to Sonny Boy Fuller's 'Custard Pie Blues', Blind Boy Fuller's 'I Want Some Of Your Custard Pie' and Big Joe William's 'Drop Down Daddy', and the mighty 'In My Time Of Dying' seemingly borrowing from the version on Bob Dylan's debut, as well as and Josh White's 1933 'Jesus Make Up My Dying Bed' (and the track of the same name by Blind Willie Johnson). Finally, 1976's *Presence* contains their rendition of 'Nobody's Fault But Mine', with lyrics adapted from Blind Willie Johnson's version and an arrangement similar to one by John Renbourn. Evidently fed up with such accusations, Plant has since remarked: "First of all, it's public domain because he's been dead so long, and secondly it wasn't his song in the first place – nobody knows where it comes from."

Plant, Carmen
b. Nov. 21st 1968

Robert Plant's first child. "Carmen used to think she had two fathers," he told People magazine on December 20th 1976. "The one whose singing she heard through the speakers and the one on whose knee she was sitting." She can be seen paddling in a brook in *The Song Remains The Same* film, and went on to marry Plant's latter-day bassist, Charlie Jones.

Plant, Karac Pendra
b. April 12th 1972 / d. July 26th 1977

Robert Plant's first son. "We call him Baby Austin after that Bionic Man," the singer told People magazine on December 20th 1976. "He knows no fear, has no anticipation of danger. I envy him." Tragically, Karac died from a viral stomach infection as the band neared the end of its US comeback tour. Having played two shows at the Oakland Coliseum on July 23rd and 24th, they flew to Louisiana to prepare for a show at the New Orleans Superdome. Maureen Plant called their hotel there to announce that the five year-old was seriously ill and had been rushed to hospital. Two hours later she called again, to tell her husband that he'd died. Plant immediately returned to the UK, accompanied by John Bonham and Richard Cole. The tour was over. He later commented that "after losing my son, I found that the excesses that surrounded Led Zeppelin were such that nobody knew where the actual axis of all this stuff was… The whole beauty and lightness of 1970 had turned into a sort of neurosis."

Plant, Logan Romero

b. Jan. 27th 1979

Robert and Maureen Plant's second son. His arrival is thought to have hardened Plant's resolve not to undertake a major US tour in support of *In Through The Out Door*.

Plant, Maureen

b. 1948

Born Maureen Wilson, this Anglo-Indian beauty was Robert Plant's wife throughout Led Zeppelin's career. "My wife's the most beautiful woman I've ever seen," the singer told People magazine on December 20th 1976. "She has radiations, powers to take away all I'm thinking and make me say 'ahhhhhh'."

They met in 1966 at a Georgie Fame gig (though Fame failed to show up), and before long her family was giving the struggling musician a roof over his head. "My old lady comes from India, and her uncle was chief of the Calcutta mounted police during the 40s," Plant told Circus magazine in January 1976. "He can speak about 10 different dialects and he's a really great guy. In fact, one of the times that I worked before the Zeppelin days, I had a job as a production control manager in a factory that he ran. I got the sack because I ordered enough steel to keep three factories going for about a year, but I managed to remain his friend and one day I'd like to take him with me and go right up through Kashmir and then stop."

The couple married on November 8th 1968, and she joined the band in America early in 1969. Peter Grant later described her as 'waif-like' at this time. In general she adhered to the Led Zeppelin policy of keeping family away from tours. As her husband explained to the NME on June 23rd 1972: "I think I've got one of the finest ladies in the world, and it wouldn't do her any good [to come on tour] because she's not up on that stage. So she'd get tired and would want to know why we weren't doing this and that, and the very fact that I've just woken up and it's three o'clock in the afternoon and the shops shut at six, and there's no shopping to be done today and all that sort of thing... it isn't practical." Instead, she largely stayed in the UK, looking after their children Carmen, Karac and Logan. 'Thank You' (from *Led Zeppelin II*) was written for her, and during Plant's tax exile in 1975 (when they typically only saw each other at weekends) he wrote 'Tea For One' about his feelings for her. The couple separated in 1983, but remain on friendly terms.

Plant, Robert

b. Aug 20th 1948

Born Robert Anthony Plant in Bromwich, Worcestershire to a civil engineer and a housewife, Led Zeppelin's singer was educated at King Edward VI's Grammar School in Stourbridge. He'd become a devotee of American folk and blues well before his teens, and spent much of his time scouring second hand shops for obscure records. In an attempt to discourage him, his father once cut the plug off his record player, but it achieved little. As Plant told the Independent newspaper on April 15th 2005, "My father was a fine man in many respects. He never cursed; he was just this charming, charismatic guy who never touched upon anything that was iffy… He told everyone that he was frightened to death of me going into groups, but then when I became successful he couldn't stop telling everyone how well I was doing." To his parents' consternation, by the age of fifteen he was sitting in at whatever local musical venues would have him, such as the Seven Stars blues pub in Stourbridge, and later characterised himself as "the guy who couldn't grow a beard who used to play harmonica and sing all the old Muddy Waters stuff". After further study to obtain O and A-levels, and spending two weeks in an accountant's office, he decided to focus exclusively on music, though he was later to boast: "I laid the asphalt on half of West Bromwich High Street". It was not a decision he would regret: in September 1973 he told Creem magazine that "I could never be bored because I know that I could easily have been a chartered accountant… Some nights I just look out there and want to fuck the whole first row."

Before that became a possibility, however, he passed through the ranks of various short-lived bands, most with blues-derived names (Black Snake Moan, the Banned, The Tennessee Teens, the Delta Blues Band, the New Memphis Bluesbreakers), before meeting John Bonham in the Crawling King Snakes. "We were both proud owners of unbelievable egos," the singer later commented. When that band split he flitted in and out of numerous short-lived acts, including Listen, who made one single in November 1966 ('You'd Better Run' / 'Everybody's Gonna Say', CBS 202456). In 1967 he released a couple of flop solo 45s, 'Our Song' / 'Laughin' Cryin' Laughin'' (CBS 202656, March 31st) and 'Long Time Comin''/ 'I've Got A Secret' (CBS 2858, July 14th), both of which contained hints of his future power but failed to sell. That summer he formed the Band Of Joy, later telling Melody Maker that "the Band Of Joy was the launching pad for my ideas and theories on music."

He was already a charismatic frontman, as the group's bassist Paul Lockey confirmed in 1992: "Even in those days, 18-19 years old, people were taken aback. He'd walk into a party and all the women there would be just standing going 'ahhh!'. They were always really taken with Robert, even my wife! All the girls were just fascinated, and the guys were too in a different sort of way." US West Coast psychedelia was increasingly informing his musical taste, as evidenced on the Band Of Joy's demo, taped at London's Regent Sound studio in early 1968 and featuring covers of Buffalo Springfield's 'For What It's Worth' and Jimi Hendrix's 'Hey Joe', as well as a couple of originals, 'Adriatic Sea View' and 'Memory Lane'. Despite gigging in London's underground clubs, no record deal resulted and the band's personnel thus continually changed. The final line-up reunited him with John Bonham, but didn't last long. The band folded that

March, upon which Plant got back in touch with producers Tony Secunda and Denny Cordell, who'd shown an interest in the demo. A deal with EMI's Regal Zonophone label was briefly mooted, but came to naught. Plant did, however, meet singer Terry Reid through Secunda. As the spring of 1968 drew on, he gigged with bluesman Alexis Korner, whom he'd met at London's Speakeasy Club. They recorded one track together, a slow blues named 'Operator', but the partnership wasn't full-time, and before long the singer returned to the Midlands to fulfil a few dates with yet another band, Obbstweedle.

Plant was at a low ebb, but – unbeknownst to him – Terry Reid had recommended him to Jimmy Page as a possible frontman for the New Yardbirds. "I had nowhere to live, and the keyboards player's dad had a pub in Wolverhampton with a spare room," the singer told Q magazine in March 1988. "The pub was right over the road from Noddy Holder's father's window cleaning business, and Noddy used to be our roadie. We used to go to gigs with Noddy Holder's dad's buckets crashing around on top of the van! And that's when I met Pagey." At Reid's suggestion, Page, Grant and Chris Dreja had travelled to a teacher training college outside Birmingham to hear him in action with Obbstweedle, and liked what they heard. "When I auditioned him and heard him sing, I immediately thought there must be something wrong with him personality-wise, or that he had to be impossible to work with," Page told Trouser Press in October 1977, "because I just could

not understand why, after he told me he'd been singing for a few years already, he hadn't become a big name yet." Plant went on to tell Uncut magazine in May 2008 that "Even though I was hot and pretty self-confident, Jimmy, with all his sort of quietude, had a great advantage. I felt immediately this was a different kind of guy to anybody I'd met before... I was brash and bullish, and he was very retiring. And as much as I was tactile, he was quite the opposite."

The guitarist duly invited Plant to stay at his riverside pad in Pangbourne the following week, where their friendship was cemented when Plant pulled out some of Page's own favourites from his extensive record collection (including LPs by Joan Baez and the Incredible String Band). Plant was only too glad to accept the role of singer in the New Yardbirds, and recommended Bonham for the drum stool. Page already knew of the drummer by reputation, and as John Paul Jones was already on board. Led Zeppelin was airborne. The quartet began rehearsing that September, shortly after the singer's 20th birthday, and had soon recorded an album and headed for the US. "I don't really think anyone saw it all coming," Plant told Record Mirror in December 1969. "One week I was playing to half a dozen people at Birmingham Mothers, and the next there was standing room only." His early contributions to the band were limited by the fact that he was still under contract to CBS, so no songwriting credits for him appeared on their debut. By 1969, however, he was emerging as a striking lyricist and songwriter, with 'Thank

You' on *Led Zeppelin II* being his first major composition. It was dedicated to his long-term partner, Maureen, whom he'd married in October, shortly after the band had formed.

The band's success took him as unawares as anyone. "We were still very naïve," he told Mojo magazine of himself and Bonham in October 2005. "Up in the Black Country we were big fishes in a small pond. Suddenly we were in a kind of world situation, sitting on planes together, not knowing which cutlery to pick up." He thoroughly enjoyed visiting America, where the band first touched down on December 24th 1968. "There were a lot of fun-loving people to crash into and we started out on a path of positive enjoyment," he later told Rolling Stone. "Frank Zappa's girl group, The GTOs, were upstairs. We threw eggs, had silly water battles and had all the good fun that a 19 year-old boy should have." His first child, Carmen, had been born in November 1968 (only a

month before he left for their first US tour), and in 1969 he bought Jennings Farm, a fifteen-room farmhouse set in three acres near Kidderminster. Family was always important to him, as was the countryside, and in 1973 he also bought an 800-year-old farm in Wales, complete with 290 acres, 300 sheep and a pig named Madam. "Plunk on the side of a conical Welsh mountain, tucked away like in the fold of a good skirt – where we should all be," he joked to People magazine on December 20th 1975. The life of a country squire suited him well – as he told Disc on January 17th 1970: "I wake up in the morning and there are no buses, no traffic. Just tractors and the odd pheasant hooting in the next field."

This fed into his passion for Celtic history and lore, which strongly informed the band's musical development. One of his first compositions for them was 'Ramble On', of which he said in 1969: "That song was my baby, and I hoped everybody would suss it out and realise that this is where I want to go." His rustic inclinations found their fullest flower on 1970's *Led Zeppelin III*, but – much though he enjoyed country life – the singer was well aware that he couldn't afford to stagnate in a bucolic idyll. "It's so easy to get stale, you know," he told Melody Maker in April 1973. "There's a lot of bands do it. They reach a peak and think that that's it – the old country house bit, a year off and all that. Well, it doesn't work that way. There's only one way a band can function, and that's on the bloody stage." The band toured relentlessly for the first few years of its existence, though Plant wasn't a central figure in their legendary excesses. "I was a voyeur, watching it all happen," he claimed to People magazine on December 20th 1976. "To rock isn't necessarily to cavort. I still like to get carried away – but passively."

Though he and Page were not bosom buddies ("his path and mine seem to criss-cross – they meet at certain points along the way, and that's where we meet and play together," he told Melody Maker on March 28th 1970), they found each other rewarding songwriting partners. In April 1973 he told Disc: "Jimmy and I have developed a sort of sympathy between his acoustic playing and my lyrics and melodies, and I just couldn't imagine doing anything without him being there." He clarified further in Melody Maker of June 25th 1977, adding: "Right from the time Jimmy Page came up to see me in the Midlands and said he was gonna form this band, way back in 68, he and I have known that we're such different characters that we're good for each other." The singer elaborated upon their differences in Spin magazine in 2002. "There's definitely a warmth between us, and a patience," he said. "We're like Walter Matthau and Jack Lemmon. The reality is that Page is a very clever, talented guy who has a particular slant on music, and I was always his sidekick who had a different slant on music." Nonetheless, many of his memories of working with Page were fond – as he told Uncut magazine in May 2008 of their time at Bron-Yr-Aur in May 1970: "We were spectacularly close, and knew we'd got something going which was genuine, not some fabricated bullshit, and being together was something really special."

By nature a good-humoured extrovert, Plant thoroughly enjoyed being a rock star for the band's first few years. "I have such a good time strutting about that I don't think any place is any different to any other," he told the NME in August 1973. "It's quite an ego trip – but where else could you have so much fun earning a living? Life in this band is like a 24-hour a day riot." With the band at its peak of popularity and creativity, he spent the summer of 1975 travelling around North Africa, first with his wife and then with Page, before making his way to the Greek island of Rhodes for a family break. On August 4th he was involved in a serious road accident on, when a hired car driven by his wife careered off the road and into a tree. She was badly concussed, and he damaged his right leg so badly that there was doubt as to whether he would be able to walk properly again. The ensuing frustrations and delays affected the whole band, and ensured that no concerts could be performed in 1976. As Plant told Circus magazine that January, "I didn't know whether I was going to be able to work with the band again; I didn't know if my leg would heal. We had planned to do a world tour, but obviously that was nipped in the ankle, so to speak."

He recovered in time for a US tour the following July, stating at the time that "When I walked up the steps to the stage, all the premonitions and anxieties washed away and the exhilaration took over. I thought, 'Ah, it's been so *long!'* I just loved being back up there." Nonetheless, the tour was fraught with problems and far less joyful overall than previously. As Richard Cole wrote in *Stairway To Heaven*: 'At one point during the tour, Robert told me that the audiences were sometimes the only thing between him and just throwing in the towel. Their cheering motivated him to grit his teeth and push through the pain as though it didn't exist… He spent a lot of time by himself, whiling away many of his off-hours in his suite, resting his leg, watching TV and sampling whatever alcohol and drugs happened to be within reach.' The tour was almost finished when, on July 24th 1977, he received the terrible news of his five year-old son Karac's sudden death from a stomach infection. He immediately flew back to the UK, and the remaining dates were cancelled.

From the band's inner circle, only Bonham and Cole attended the funeral, something that is said to have upset the singer. Thereafter he became a virtual recluse, focusing on his family until the following May, when rehearsals for *In Through The Out Door* began. During his time off he remained at home, occasionally visiting the local pub. "We did nothing for a year and a half," he told People magazine on August 27th 1979. "I tinkered on the village piano and grew so obese drinking beer that nobody knew who I was." Indeed, he was barely seen in public until July 1978, when he played a gig with local band Melvin Giganticus and the Turd Burglars. While holidaying in Ibiza that August he performed with Dr. Feelgood (one of his favourite bands), and in September he appeared onstage with Swan Song signing Dave Edmunds in Birmingham. By the winter the band was ready to record again, and flew to Stockholm with his bandmates, though by then his relationship with Page had deteriorated. During their hiatus, Page and Bonham had developed serious drug habits, which made the sessions frustrating and undisciplined. As Richard Cole put it, 'While Bonham, Pagey and I were struggling with heroin, Robert never really became caught up in it. Maybe after months of painkillers he had taken enough drugs to last a lifetime.'

Instead he and Jones channelled their energies into the new record, which had was far less reliant on Page and Bonham than its predecessors had been. Plant's most notable contribution was perhaps 'All My Love', an emotional and highly personal ballad that was a surprising departure for the band. He was unsure how much he'd enjoy performing at the band's two Knebworth shows in August 1979, but agreed to a short European tour the following year. It would be the band's last, though he had agreed to a tour of the US that was cancelled when Bonham died in September 1980. According to a largely spurious article published in the NME days after Bonham's death, 'It is known that [Plant] has been stockpiling songs of his own' - and indeed he did embrace a solo career with greater speed than his bandmates.

Plumpton Place

Tudor mansion close to Plumpton Racecourse in East Sussex, bought by Jimmy Page for £100,000 from racehorse-owner Lord Manton in 1971. In his 1974 book *Led Zeppelin*, Howard Mylett describes visiting the house on December 29th 1972. According to him, it 'has over 50 acres, two tied cottages, beautiful lakes and a moat. Page's taste in art and decoration was not of the Ideal Home, glossy-magazine type; he had retained the original character of the house. The only conversion was a small recording studio upstairs... the stables housed goats, chickens, artwork, a Range Rover, one of the legendary 'Cord' American cars and a motorbike. He expressed a wish to obtain some swans for the lake.' Page told Hit Parader magazine in November 1974 that his home studio was "quite archaic, really. It's the remnants of what other studios would have thrown out, and is pieced together in my attic. It gives me enough of a guide, a sketch pad, sort of, to lay down ideas... to put the harmonies down and stuff. And I'd say that about 80% of the things we do are done that way. I do them at home and then later I play them for the group and get a set of opinions."

In an interview with the NME in February 1975, Page stated: "The situation with the house now is that when people come to the door, if they've got anything worthwhile to say, they're allowed in. If they're idiots, or cranks, or fanatics, they're welcome to walk around the grounds." He was frequently away on tour in the early 1970s, but spent much of the band's 1976-77 hiatus at the house. On September 17th 1977 he and Ron Wood (and a

band from Portsmouth named Arms & Legs) played an impromptu gig in the village pub, the Half Moon, on behalf of a charity named Goaldiggers. This prompted landlord Tony Hills to tell Melody Maker "down here, Jimmy Page is God" – a sly dig at Eric Clapton. That November Page told Melody Maker: "I've got a studio at home finally. It's taken me fifteen years to turn it into a reality... The console was installed last January, and it's taken all this time to sort out the acoustics. I've been listening to lots of live tapes of the band, going back to the Royal Albert Hall in 1969." The mixing for *In Through The Out Door* was later carried out at the studio, but in 1980 he sold up after a photographer friend named Philip Hale (aged only nineteen, according to one report) died of vomit inhalation during a party on October 24th 1979.

Polar Music

Abba's recording facility in Stockholm, where Led Zeppelin recorded *In Through The Out Door* in November and December 1978.

Pontiac Silverdome

Venue in Pontiac, Michigan where the band's gig on April 30th 1977 set a world record for the largest paid attendance at a single-artist performance. Having attracted 76,229 people, they also set another record by grossing $792,361.50. The band didn't much enjoy the show, however. "It was awful," John Paul Jones recalled in 1991. "It felt like a soundcheck in the dark. The audience was so far away – there was nothing coming back. You could hardly see them or even hardly hear them. And it was cold. It was everything you'd expect to be the worst of a huge gig."

see *Kezar Stadium / Tampa Stadium*

Poor Tom

Folk-blues shuffle recorded on June 5th 1970 at London's Olympic Studios, during the sessions for *Led Zeppelin III*, but unreleased until *Coda* appeared in 1982. The song was composed at Bron-Yr-Aur, and is in the ancient British 'murder ballad' tradition. It opens with one of John Bonham's most complicated drum patterns, though he didn't live to see it released. They never performed it live.

Pop Proms

Series of gigs held at London's Royal Albert Hall in June and July 1969. Led Zeppelin headlined on the first night, June 29th, with support from Blodwyn Pig and the Liverpool Scene. The gig consolidated the band's position in the UK, with Disc noting that the 3000-strong audience 'stormed the stage, danced in the aisles and the boxes, and were screaming so hard that the band did three encores'. For one of these ('Long Tall Sally') they were joined onstage by Blodwyn Pig's Jack Lancaster and the Liverpool Scene's Mike Evans, both on saxophone.

Premier Talent

New York-based entertainment agency, run by Frank Barsalona, that oversaw the band's first US tour, from December 1968 to February 1969, and other early US visits.

Presence

The band's seventh album, largely written and rehearsed in Malibu in the autumn of 1975, recorded at an unprecedented pace in Munich's Musicland Studios that November, and released in April 1976. Following Robert Plant's car accident in Rhodes on August 4th, the band had never been under such strain, with both Page and Bonham reportedly taking heroin, the singer confined to a wheelchair and John Paul Jones suffering from a hand injury. As Plant told Circus magazine in January 1976: "There won't be another album like it, put it like that. It was an album of circumstances; it was a cry from the depths, the only thing that we could do. I honestly didn't know what was going to happen and neither did anybody else." Page, meanwhile, told the NME in February 1977 that "before we went into Musicland we didn't actually know if we'd ever play together again... That's why, alone of all the albums we've recorded, *Presence* relates specifically to a point in time."

Unlike its predecessors, the album lacks any studio trickery, synthesizers or acoustic numbers: each song is a more or less straight rock performance, with a live, edgy feel (all of Jimmy Page's guitar overdubs were taped in one night). This was partially because it was recorded so quickly – taped and mixed in a mere 18 days. As Peter Grant told Tight But Loose in June 1993, "it was difficult in the writing and rehearsing stage, and then we were pressured to record it quickly." Part of the reason for this was that the Rolling Stones were booked in to record *Black and Blue* three weeks later. Plant told

Circus magazine in January 1976: "We worked pretty much straight through. We didn't – or, at least, *I* didn't – go out at all at night. Normally after hard work we always take our rewards, but that time there were no rewards for Robert." Page took charge of production, as usual, working long hours assisted by engineer Keith Harwood. It has been described as Page's album first and foremost, and indeed the guitar parts are especially dense and carefully layered, especially on 'Achilles Last Stand', destined to become a cornerstone of future gigs. Plant told the NME in February 1976: "Jimmy worked like a Trojan. It's his energy that got the album together so quickly. I mean, I was not really in any physical condition to hop around with gusto, inspiring the situation greatly". In fact, at one stage he did attempt to do just that, with near-disastrous results – he told Melody Maker the same month that "I was hobbling around in the middle of this great track when suddenly my enthusiasm got the better of me. I was running to the vocal booth with this orthopedic crutch when down I went, right on the bad foot. There was an almighty crack and a great flash of light and pain, and I folded up in agony. I'd never known Jimmy to move so quickly. He was out of the mixing booth and holding me up, fragile as he might be, within a second."

The album appeared in a typically enigmatic Hipgnosis sleeve ("the artwork is such that you could look at it and put your own interpretation to it," Page helpfully told Sounds in March 1976) and quickly sold a million, but initial orders were not sustained and sales tailed off sooner than expected. This may be partly attributed to the fact that the band couldn't tour in support of it, but it stands as their least commercial work by some distance. In addition, its long songs and complex arrangements sat uneasily with the prevailing punk climate, and when the band toured again in 1977, they tellingly included only two songs from it, 'Achilles Last Stand' and 'Nobody's Fault But Mine'.

Presley, Elvis
b. Jan. 8th 1935 / d. Aug. 16th 1977
The so-called 'King of Rock and Roll' and a massive formative influence on the members of Led Zeppelin. Indeed, Page has repeatedly stated that 'Baby Let's Play House' is the track that made him want to play guitar. On May 11th 1974, after performing a show attended by the band in Las Vegas, Presley expressed a desire to meet them, though John Paul Jones was absent. Their mutual promoter at the time, Jerry Weintraub, took Page, Plant, Bonham and Peter Grant up to the King's hotel suite. For the first few minutes, he ignored them, focusing on the television instead. Eventually he turned to them, asking whether tales of their antics on the road were true. Plant denied all, claiming that he loved nothing more than wandering around hotel corridors belting out Elvis classics. This broke the ice and led to two hours of chat, during which Presley revealed that 'Stairway To Heaven' was the only Led Zeppelin track he'd heard. Bonham and Presley spent much of the time discussing hot rods and Peter Sellers films.

Grant, meanwhile, was getting tired of standing. As he told Vox magazine in December 1994: "Usually people got 15 minutes with him – we had two and a half hours. The boys were busy talking to him and I went to sit on this settee. All of a sudden I heard this voice behind me saying "Jesus Christ". It was Elvis's dad, Vernon. I'd sat on him." Plant told Blender magazine in 2002 "Elvis was very funny, very self-effacing. It was a riveting and thoroughly entertaining two hours, which culminated in Elvis and me singing together in the corridor. We sang a song called 'Love Me', which goes 'Treat me like a fool, treat me mean and cruel, but love me'. Then he signed an autograph, which read: 'To Robert, a true friend. Treat me like a fool, Elvis Presley'." Page, meanwhile, later told Melody Maker that he had been "overawed when I met Elvis Presley".

The following year Jones finally met him, along with Richard Cole. Cole's foul language got things off to a bad start, but they were soon exchanging Monty Python quotes and even watches. The band's contact with the King continued sporadically thereafter: after his car accident on Rhodes in August 1975, Robert Plant received an unexpected fillip in the form of a get-well telegram from Presley, and two years later Presley's controversial manager, 'Colonel' Tom Parker, sought Peter Grant's advice as to how best present his client onstage in the UK (where he had never performed), but unfortunately he died before anything could be arranged.

The Press

"I do not have the time to become too engrossed in what the music press says," Jimmy Page told Record Mirror in February 1970. "Making music is my concern. The only press I have ever really objected to is the pseudo-intellectual underground papers who write in clichés and give rock and roll a pretension it does not need." In general, however, the music press was broadly favourable towards Led Zeppelin from the outset, albeit with notable exceptions such as Rolling Stone. Dismissive reviews at the start of their career soon changed to a respectful acknowledgement of their power and originality. Despite cultivating a certain mystique (by not appearing on television, leaving their name off their fourth and fifth albums and so on), all four members of the band were open and friendly towards US interviewers.

British critics were less warmly received, however, with Plant telling Australia's Go-Set magazine in February 1972: "They're a bunch of old queens." He returned to the theme in an interview with Melody Maker that July, commenting to interviewer Roy Hollingworth that "For some reason, English critics have never told the truth about us. For some reason, they've been out to get us a bit... There's been so much bullshit printed, it's just untrue." John Paul Jones weighed in too, telling Hollingworth: "Here we are [in the US] slaving away and getting consistently incredible reactions, and nobody back home can care anything about us... They say Jethro Tull are brilliant onstage – well, they do the same bloody thing every night...

each of our gigs is treated differently." Page was more philosophical, telling the NME on November 25th: "It's those few individuals trying to make a name for themselves with trite and caustic comments who get through on a personal level. I've realised now, though, that one or two exceptionally offensive remarks won't harm a group or a career. It would only be serious if the general consensus of opinion was against us."

Nonetheless, the Melody Maker's Chris Welch – one of the group's most vocal supporters from day one – was obliged to buy tickets to one of their Earl's Court shows from a tout in 1975, after publishing a less-than-glowing review of *Houses Of The Holy*. The band was also frustrated by the tabloid press on both sides of the Atlantic claiming that Page's interest in the occult had led to a curse on them. "When we talk about that time, we have to understand that the press itself was a completely different animal," Robert Plant told Mojo in June 1994. "Beer-swilling, monosyllabic guys who reviewed gigs from the beer tent." In December 2007, however, Page acknowledged that their woes with the media might have been at least to some extent self-inflicted. "Our musical journey was part of the problem where the press were concerned, because we were doing it without them," he told Mojo magazine. "And then there's the whole philosophy of the band: we don't release singles, and when we did interviews it involved one day with a load of journalists coming in on rotation. There was resentment about that, and I'm convinced that it affected the way the press viewed us."

Pretty Things

Durable British R&B act, of whom Jimmy Page had long been fond, and with whom he'd co-written 'You Don't Believe Me' on their 1965 *Get The Picture* LP (Fontana TL 5280). Plant was also a fan, telling French magazine Rock & Folk in February 1975 that "the Pretty Things have always been one of my favourite groups". When Swan Song was formed in 1974, they were eager to sign them, and the label's first UK release was their *Silk Torpedo* album, released in October 1974 and launched in Kent's Chislehurst Caves on Halloween night. A rumour that Led Zeppelin would be joining them onstage at the Marquee on May 27th 1976 caused pandemonium. In the event only Jones turned up to play on an encore of 'Route 66' as a gesture. see *Swan Song / Chislehurst Caves*

Proby, PJ

b. Nov 6th 1938

Trouser-splitting US entertainer whose October 1969 country rock / blues LP *Three Week Hero* (Liberty 83219) features Led Zeppelin's recording debut. All four members appear on 'Jim's Blues', with Plant contributing harmonica rather than vocals. Jones had agreed to arrange the album before he left session work behind, though it appeared well after the quartet's first effort, also recorded in October 1968. As Jones told Bonham's brother Mick in 2005: "I had to go back and finish off a PJ Proby record which I had already done the arrangements for. So, to keep the coffers full (because no one was earning any money), I booked all of us onto the session... I even got Percy in on tambourine, just so he wouldn't feel left out. So our first professional engagement was that PJ Proby record." They also appeared on the B-side to Proby's 'The Day That Lorraine Came Down' 45, the humorously-entitled 'Merry Hopkins Never Had Days Like These'. Jones was booked for the sessions by US producer Steve Rowland, who also used him, Bonham and Page on the Family Dogg's *A Way Of Life* LP (Bell SBLL 122) around the same time.

Punk

Though Paul Simonon of the Clash famously commented "just looking at their record covers makes me want to be sick" and Creem magazine stated n November 1979 that 'of all the old superfart bands it is certainly Led Zeppelin who have been and still are the most reviled by the New Wave', Jimmy Page and Robert Plant were all in favour of the punk movement that swept the music scene from 1975 onwards. Plant was already an admirer of pub rock bands such as Dr. Feelgood (whose basic approach presaged punk), and in 1976 the band shared a rehearsal space (and amiable banter) at London's Manticore Studios with Generation X, led by Billy Idol. Plant told Melody Maker in June 1977 that Johnny Rotten 'frightened me to death', but he and Page were greatly enamoured of the Damned. They watched them live at punk club the Roxy in January 1977 (supported by Eater), and Page was later rumoured to be in line for producing their debut. A drunk John Bonham clambered onstage at a Damned gig a week later, though he was heckled off almost at once. Though their own music was hardly compatible with punk, the NME acknowledged their ongoing relevance at the time of their Knebworth shows in August 1979, writing that 'They are one of the few groups of that era and that school of thought who can make some sense in the contemporary scheme of things."

Quaglino's

Upmarket Italian restaurant in London's Bury Place that served as the venue for a legendary private jam on the night of September 14th 1974, when Jimmy Page and John Bonham joined Stephen Stills, Graham Nash and Neil Young for renditions of Young's 'Vampire Blues' and 'On The Beach' (both included on his recently-released *On The Beach* LP). The Americans had played a concert at Wembley Stadium that day, along with Joni Mitchell and the Band, which all four members of Led Zeppelin had attended.

R

Rainbow Bar & Grill

Eaterie and nightspot on LA's Sunset Strip, where Led Zeppelin held court when in town. Richard Cole wrote in *Stairway To Heaven* that 'whenever we'd be flying into Los Angeles, I'd call from the air to let the Rainbow know we were on our way. I'd usually get Tony or Michael, who ran the Rainbow, on the phone and tell them 'We'll be landing at nine thirty… please have our tables cleared and some Dom Perignon ready… [The waitresses] would cordon off an area for Led Zeppelin… Usually, adolescent girls with layers of make-up, tight-fitting tops, short skirts and spike heels had the best chance of winning admission to our asylum.' According to the NME of December 20th 1975, Bonham was banned from the hostelry after a fight that had resulted in him requiring thirteen stitches.

Rainbow Theatre

Venue in Finsbury Park, London, where the band rehearsed in April 1980 for their forthcoming European tour, before switching to the New Victoria Theatre.

The Rain Song

This epic ballad is the second song on *Houses Of The Holy*, and was largely devised by Jimmy Page at his home, Plumpton Place. Its working title was 'Slush', perhaps a humorous reference to its soft-rock sound and mellow string arrangement. The band frequently played it live between late 1972 and 1975, including it immediately after 'The Song Remains The Same' in their set (allowing Page to use his famous double-necked Gibson guitar on both songs, and aping their running order on the LP). At that time Jones reproduced the string arrangement on his mellotron, though this was later replaced by his Yamaha GX1 synthesizer. "I used to approach the song with the greatest trepidation and fear," Jones later commented of performing it with a mellotron. "I wondered what was going to come out… Would it be anywhere near pitch? Would it be at half-speed? Would it be a string sound or a flute sound?" The song wasn't performed on their 1977 US tour, but reappeared at their 1979 dates in Denmark and at Knebworth, and was the only song from *Houses Of The Holy* performed on their 1980 European tour.

Ramble On

Tolkien-inspired folk-rock track included on *Led Zeppelin II*. "That song was my baby," Plant proudly stated shortly after the album's release in 1969, "and I hoped everybody would suss it out and realise that this is where I want to go." He has subsequently confessed to a degree of embarrassment about its lyrics, though he told Circus magazine in January 1976: "A lot of people say it's a sort of *Lord Of The Rings* type of thing. By then I had developed a wanderlust and that song was just a reflection of myself." John Bonham can be heard tapping a plastic rubbish bin before he comes in on drums. The song indicates the direction the band would take more fully on *Led Zeppelin III*, and during acoustic interludes at gigs, though it was never performed live.

Red snapper
Small, widely-eaten reef fish found off the Atlantic and Pacific coasts of the Americas and the Gulf of Mexico.

see *Shark Incident, the*

Reid, Terry
b. Nov. 13th 1949
Precocious singer who had released a string of records, both solo and with Peter Jay and the Jaywalkers (whom both the Yardbirds and Robert Plant's Band Of Joy had played alongside), when he became Jimmy Page's first choice of vocalist for the New Yardbirds in July 1968. Reid was managed by Peter Grant and produced by Grant's then-partner, Mickie Most, but decided he was too busy with his solo career to accept. When he bumped into Page and Peter Grant in Oxford Street soon afterwards,

he recommended Robert Plant instead, comparing him to 'a Greek fairy god'. Reid was also to tell Sounds on March 2nd 1974 that John Paul Jones had been about to join his band before opting for Led Zeppelin. Grant managed Reid until December 1969, when they agreed to part because too much of Grant's time was being devoted to Led Zeppelin.

Relf, Keith
b. March 22nd 1943 / d. May 14th 1976
One-lunged Yardbirds singer, and the chief instigator of the band's break-up in 1968. Having released a 45 as a duo named Together (with their former bassist Jim McCarty), he formed Renaissance. By 1975 he had moved towards Led Zeppelin's style with Armageddon, whose sole album contains some creditable hard rock. He died at home in Whitton, just outside London, from an electric shock while playing the guitar.

Remasters

The band's first compilation, overseen and re-sequenced by Jimmy Page and released in September 1990 as a 4-CD boxed set, and in October as a shorter double CD / triple vinyl package. "In the seventies we were basically mixing for vinyl," he explained to the Sunday Times on November 4th of that year. "The available sound spectrum wasn't as wide as it is with the advent of CD. You can hear more of everything now." The boxed set featured the CD debuts of the 1970 B-side 'Hey Hey What Can I Do?' and the BBC live 'Traveling Riverside Blues', as well as a newly-created fusion of 'Moby Dick' and 'Bonzo's Montreux'.

Rhodes

Greek island on which Robert Plant and his family had a serious car accident in the early afternoon of Monday, August 4th 1975. Having spent a couple of months in Morocco, first with his wife and then with Jimmy Page, the singer was keen to travel somewhere else sunny and slow-moving. He and Page thus went to the island with their families, intending to hook up with Phil May, lead singer of the Pretty Things (who were signed to Swan Song). Page left for Sicily on August 3rd, to inspect a property once occupied by Aleister Crowley, leaving the Plant family with his girlfriend Charlotte Martin and their four year-old daughter Scarlet. The following day Maureen Plant was driving Scarlet, her husband and their children Carmen (seven) and Karac (three) in a hired Mini when it veered off a narrow road and into a tree. Plant was in the passenger seat, and badly fractured his ankle and elbow, while his wife broke her leg, fractured her pelvis and suffered concussion for 36 hours. The children had only minor injuries.

The Plants were eventually taken to a local hospital by a fruit truck driver, while Peter Grant, holidaying in the South of France, arranged for a jet to be chartered (from construction magnate Sir Robert McAlpine), and flew over two Harley Street doctors (John Baretta and Mike Lawrence), as well as blood plasma. "I had to share a room with a drunken soldier who had fallen over and banged his head, and as he was coming around he kept focusing on me, uttering my name," the singer told Melody Maker in February 1976. "I was lying there in some pain, trying to get cockroaches off the bed, and he started singing 'The Ocean' from *Houses Of The Holy*." The Plants were flown back to England via Rome, at a reported cost of £7000. According to Richard Cole's memoirs, the plane circled over Heathrow for half an hour, not landing until after midnight: 'Even amid the chaos surrounding the accident, Zeppelin's accountants had the presence of mind to advise me that Robert would need to limit the number of days he spent in Britain, because of his tax exile status.' Covered in plaster, the singer was obliged to leave Britain for Jersey the following week, in order to avoid becoming liable for a full year's tax. From Jersey the band moved on to Malibu, where Plant indulged in some serious existential thoughts, prompted by the accident. "I sat looking at the ocean until the beach got washed up," he told Hit Parader in June, adding "my pain was not all physical... it was a contemplative thing as well. It was like I was going through something that I don't know if anybody else around me had gone through."

Rivers, Royd

UK folk singer who played in a duo with Cliff Aungier in the mid-1960s. Their sole LP, 1965's *Wanderin'* (Decca LK4696), was produced by Jimmy Page, who is also credited with the perfunctory sleevenotes ('Royd and Cliff's personal appearances have proved by the fantastic following they have acquired just what monster talents they are' etc). The record is a stark affair based on their club act, and the deal seems to have had something to do with Page's involvement with Immediate Records.

Robinson, Jimmy

Pseudonym under which Jimmy Page is believed to have produced the self-titled debut album by Led Zeppelin-influenced US hard rock act Detective in 1976. It was issued on Swan Song (SS 8417) in April 1977.

see *Des Barres, Michael*

Rock and Roll

Described by Page as 'a spontaneous combustion', this unapologetically heavy number was improvised early in 1971 during the first sessions for the band's untitled fourth LP at Headley Grange, while they were trying to nail 'Four Sticks'. Its genesis lay in Bonham impulsively bashing out the cymbal motif that begins Little Richard's 'Keep A Knockin" (and also underpins Eddie Cochran's 'Somethin' Else'). The other musicians, including Ian 'Stu' Stewart on piano, immediately joined in, with Plant making up lyrics on the spot. The tape was running, and – as Page later put it – "within fifteen minutes it was virtually complete". They began playing it live the same year (initially announced by Plant as 'It's Been A Long Time'), and it remained a staple set opener for much of their 1972 and 1975 tours.

Rockestra

Name under which Paul McCartney and Wings recorded two tracks at Abbey Road on October 3rd 1978, assisted by musicians including John Paul Jones, John Bonham, Hank Marvin, Pete Townshend and David Gilmour. The songs, Rockestra Theme and So Glad To See You Here, appeared on Wings' underwhelming *Back To The Egg* LP in June 1979. Jones and Bonham also appeared onstage with the Rockestra at the Concert For Kampuchea (organised by McCartney) in London's Hammersmith Apollo on Sunday December 29th 1979. The performance is thought to have been Bonham's last on a UK stage.

Rolling Stone

US music publication which started in 1967 and is still going today, albeit as a corporate shadow of its former self. It decided early that it didn't much care for Led Zeppelin, and therefore wrote numerous snide or dismissive reviews of their early albums and gigs. The band's debut apparently said nothing that Jeff Beck's debut 'didn't say as well or better three months ago', while *Led*

Zeppelin II was 'just one especially heavy song extended over the space of two whole sides' and *Led Zeppelin III* 'deviates little from the track laid by the first two'. Stung, the band declined to speak to the magazine until it changed its policy and began to court them. As Page explained to the NME in December 1972: "The situation we found ourselves in with Rolling Stone was purely political and stemmed from their side all along. The reasons are basically so trivial that it's really not worth going into." The band's policy was only relaxed in 1975, when the young Cameron Crowe was granted access to them, with the resulting cover story appearing on March 13th.

see *Crowe, Cameron*

Rose, Tim

b. Sept. 23rd 1940 / d. Sept. 24th 2002

US singer-songwriter who employed John Bonham to back him (alongside bassist Steve Dolan) on a UK tour as of June 1968. Bonham earned £40 a week, the best money he had ever had at the time. The set combined Rose originals with covers including 'Hey Joe' and 'Morning Dew' (the song that had made Rose's name), and included a solo spot for Bonham. Phil Collins, then playing with Flaming Youth, saw them play at the Marquee and has since remarked: "Within the first few minutes I was dumbstruck by the drummer. He was doing things with his bass drum that I'd never seen or heard before... he then played a solo and, again, I'd never heard or seen a drummer play like that. He played with his hands on the drums... He was, even then, a major influence on my playing."

Ian Paice, the drummer with Deep Purple, recalled: "Everything was going quite sweetly for the first couple of songs, which were basically acoustic. Then all hell broke loose. John played beautifully, but he played the same way he did in Zeppelin. So from this mellow little folky music it became 'drums with inaudible musical accompaniment'. Gloriously hilarious!" Having seen Bonham playing with Rose at London's Hampstead Country Club on July 31st 1968, Peter Grant and Jimmy Page managed to poach him for the Yardbirds early that August. According to Rose's affectionate account, Bonham didn't even tell him he was leaving, but simply upped sticks. The two never recorded together.

Roundhouse

Circular North London venue in which the recently-formed band played their first ever gig under the name 'Led Zeppelin', on November 9th 1968 – the day Robert Plant got married to Maureen Wilson. It also served as the venue for the couple's makeshift wedding reception that evening. Also on the bill were John Lee Hooker, the Deviants, John James, Tyres and DJ Jeff Dexter.

The Rover

Melodic rock track recorded during the *Houses Of The Holy* sessions at Stargroves in 1972, but ultimately included on 1975's *Physical Graffiti* (following some guitar overdubs in 1974). The song was conceived at Bron-Yr-Aur in 1970, and its initial arrangement was acoustic. Its lyrics celebrate the wanderlust which Page and Plant famously possessed – as the guitarist told Uncut magazine in May 2008, "It's got a real swagger about it. An intentional swagger." The inner sleeve to the original LP comments 'Guitar lost courtesy of [Ron] Nevison. Salvaged by the grace of [Keith] Harwood,' evidently a reference to problems encountered during the recording. Though they rehearsed it, the band never played 'The Rover' live, though an instrumental rendition was included once onstage in Australia in February 1972, and snatches of its opening were incorporated into 'Sick Again' during their 1977 US tour.

Royal Albert Hall

Victorian auditorium in London's Kensington Gore and the site of a famous gig by the band on January 9th 1970, which was filmed but went unreleased until the appearance of their live retrospective DVD in 2003. They had previously played two shows there on June 29th 1969, but Page was not entirely enamoured of the venue, telling LA's Rock Magazine in October 1970:

"It's a great atmosphere apart from some of the officialdom... Once you go past 11 o'clock at night they usually pull the plugs". A month later, it was reported in the NME that the band had been banned from the venue for fear of their fans damaging it, a ban that was evidently still in place in November 1972, when Page told the NME: "I'm personally a bit disappointed we can't play somewhere like the Royal Albert Hall, because I think it's an ideal place for a rock group – the atmosphere is so great. It's just a pity the place is falling to bits so badly." The following August 4th Melody Maker quoted Robert Plant commenting "the only time I ever get any nerves at all is when I play the Albert Hall in London," but the band never played there again.

see *Pop Proms*

Royal Orleans

The last track on side one of 1976's *Presence*. Its title refers to the hotel the band occasionally stayed in when in New Orleans, where – according to legend – John Paul Jones invited a transvestite back to his room in May 1973, believing him to be a woman. Having smoked a joint, the duo allegedly fell asleep with the end still smouldering, which caused a fire that wrecked the room but didn't hurt anyone. Jones, however, told Mojo magazine in December 2007: "That I mistook a transvestite for a girl is rubbish; that happened in another country to somebody else... Anyway 'Stephanie' ended up in my room and we rolled a joint or two and I fell asleep and set fire to the hotel room, as you do, and when I woke up it was full of firemen!" The track was also issued as the B-side to the 'Candy Store Rock' 45, but was never performed live by the band.

Rushock

Remote Worcestershire village in whose St Michael's Church John Bonham's funeral was held on October 10th 1980. It was attended by fellow Midlands musicians including Roy Wood, Denny Laine, Bev Bevan and Jeff Lynne, with wreaths from drummers Carl Palmer, Phil Collins, Carmine Appice and Cozy Powell, as well as Paul McCartney. Bonham was cremated at Worcester Crematorium, and his ashes were buried in Rushock churchyard. His headstone reads: 'Cherished memories of a loving husband and father / John Henry Bonham / Who died September 25th 1980 aged 32 years / He will always be remembered in our hearts / Goodnight, my love, God bless'. Tourists place drumsticks on his grave to this day.

Safer, Janine
Swan Song's publicity agent in New York from 1976-77. Her tenure at the label coincided with the band's fraught eleventh US tour.

Samwell-Smith, Paul
b. May 8th 1943
Yardbirds bassist whom Jimmy Page replaced in June 1966, following a shambolic performance at an Oxford University May Ball. According to Page, "Keith Relf was incredibly pissed. Everyone was dressed up in dinner jackets and Keith was rolling around the stage… He was shouting 'fuck you!' at the audience and eventually he just collapsed back into the drum kit… Paul just blew up and said 'I can't stand this anymore…'" Samwell-Smith went on to become a successful producer, working with Cat Stevens, Jethro Tull, Carly Simon and others.

Sander, Ellen
Reporter who joined the band on tour in the US in 1969 in order to pen an article for Life magazine. According to Richard Cole's memoirs, 'we took turns casually chatting with Sander, but none of us could find anything too endearing about her. She wasn't that much fun to be around. She didn't seem particularly fond of our music, and she clearly had contempt for our lifestyle.' The distaste in her resultant article may have been inspired by her final night with them, when (she later wrote), 'They were in a frenzy. I was absolutely terrified that I was going to be raped.' This is thought to be a reference to a drunken attempt to remove her clothes, led by John Bonham. Her article concluded: 'If you walk inside the cages of the zoo, you get to see the animals close up, stroke the captive pelts and mingle with the energy behind the mystique. You also get to smell the shit first hand.'

San Francisco
US hippie Mecca, home to the legendary Fillmore West auditorium, and scene of some of Led Zeppelin's most memorable early shows. "Peter told us if we didn't crack San Francisco, we'd have to go home," Plant has since recalled. "That was the place that was considered to be essential, the hotbed of the whole movement." Their first gigs there came on January 9th – 11th 1969, supporting Taj Mahal and Country Joe & the Fish. They went down a storm – as Page put it: "It felt like a vacuum and we'd arrived to fill it. First this row, then that row… it was like a tornado and it went rolling across the country."

Savalas, Telly
b. Jan 21st 1922 / d. Jan. 22nd 1994
Kojak actor who had a notable clash with the band and Richard Cole in May 1976, when they found themselves in the same first-class cabin on a flight to New York. The band was returning to the UK after

a year spent in tax exile, and their spirits were running high. Having traded a few insults with the bald thespian, cutlery started to be thrown and staff had to intervene. The incident was written up in the Sun newspaper.

Scandinavia

Barely a month after they'd got together in the summer of 1968, the quartet flew to Denmark and Sweden to fulfil outstanding Yardbirds dates. The first gig was in Copenhagen's Gladsaxe Teen Club on September 7th, and the last was at Malmö's Klub Bongo on the 17th. According to Plant, "In Scandinavia we were pretty green: it was very early days and we were tiptoeing with each other. We didn't have half the recklessness that became for me the whole joy of Led Zeppelin. It was a tentative start." Having grown in confidence considerably, they returned to Scandinavia (playing dates in Sweden, Denmark and Finland) in March 1969 and February 1970, and also gigged in Iceland in June 1970. The following June they visited Sweden, Denmark and Norway again, and once more in March 1973. Perhaps out of sentimentality, they chose to perform the warm-up dates for their massive Knebworth shows at Copenhagen's Falkonertheatre on July 23rd and 24th 1979, but received mixed reviews.

The Senators

Birmingham beat band in which John Bonham made his recording debut in 1964, when 'She's A Mod' appeared on the *Brumbeat* compilation (Dial DLP1). Recorded in the city's Hollick & Taylor Studios, the song was written by vocalist Terry Beale, who'd previously played in the Blue Star Trio and Terry Webb & The Spiders with Bonham. A re-recorded version also emerged on a 45, coupled with 'Lot About You' (Dial DSP 7001, 1964). The band's line-up also included Trevor McGowan (lead guitar), Graham Dennis (rhythm guitar) and Bill Ford (bass guitar).

Sessions

Both Jimmy Page and John Paul Jones were hardened veterans of London's recording session scene when the band was formed in 1968, and had arranged or played on innumerable hits and misses. Page had got out when he joined the Yardbirds in July 1966, but Jones was still at it and fast losing patience. "It was really frustrating because you never said anything musically the whole way through it," Page told Sounds on December 9th 1972. "There was no communication between us and the artist at any point. We were just a bunch of cogs, and that's why I got out of it... I suppose it was useful in that it helped a lot on discipline, coming to terms with being able to read music and so on... But I didn't know a single musician who was happy doing it." He went on to tell Q magazine in 2003 that "I knew I had to get out of it when I was doing a muzak session... It was the hardest job I'd ever taken on because it was constant reading, and yet the end result was something that made me want to vomit."

John Paul Jones was separately reaching the same conclusion. "You could be doing Cliff Richard in the morning,

Marc Bolan in the afternoon and Champion Jack Dupree in the evening," he told the Daily Telegraph in September 1999. "That's what it was like in the 60s, hundreds of musicians going from studio to studio, all day long, all week long." Jones had met Page in various studios throughout the decade, as he told Guitar Player magazine in July 1997 – "I used to see a lot of him just sitting there with an acoustic guitar, sort of raking out chords." When they agreed to form Led Zeppelin in mid-1968, their experiences as session men had taught them some important lessons. "There was hardly an ounce of attitude in the whole band," Jones later said. "Page and I had seen it all before. We just didn't want to make the obvious mistakes."

Shark Incident

Notorious jape that occurred at Seattle's Edgewater Inn motel on July 28th 1969, the day after the band had played the Seattle Pop Festival during their second US tour. The hostelry was built on stilts over water, and offered its guests the chance to hire rods and tackle so they could fish from the comfort of their own balconies. John Bonham was quick to see the possibilities of the concept, and – aided by Richard Cole, numerous members of Vanilla Fudge

and a copious quantity of alcohol – a red snapper was quickly caught (not a mud shark, as has been widely reported). Amidst much ribaldry, the unfortunate fish was duly employed to pleasure Jackie, a groupie from Portland, as Vanilla Fudge organist Mark Stein filmed the scene on a Super 8 movie camera. Cole has subsequently claimed responsibility for the incident, though other accounts have Bonham taking the initiative. Either way, according to the Fudge's drummer Carmine Appice, "It was pretty disgusting... pretty nutso."

Shaw, Sandie
b. Feb 26th 1947
Born Sandra Ann Goodrich, England's barefooted 1967 Eurovision winner was the first artist ever to cover a Led Zeppelin track. Her rendition of 'Your Time Is Gonna Come' appeared on her self-produced 1969 LP *Reviewing The Situation* (Pye NPL18323, UK-only). The album was not supported by her label or management and sold poorly, making original copies rare and expensive today.

Sheehan, Dennis
Welsh-born former roadie for Madeline Bell, who served as Robert Plant's personal assistant on Led Zeppelin's 1977 US tour, and accompanied him back to the UK that July following his son's death (along with John Bonham and Richard Cole).

She Just Satisfies
Backed with 'Keep Working', this rare R&B-styled 45 was released by Jimmy Page on February 4th 1965 (as Fontana

TF 533), following encouragement from his lover, Jackie DeShannon. On February 20th *Record Mirror* wrote: 'Though he's only 19, Jimmy Page has earned the musical respect of the most hardened of session men. He truly is an ace guitarist who has worked with all the top names. He also plays harmonica, percussion and writes songs, including eight on a recent trip to the States with Jackie de Shannon. He also likes Indian music, and painting 'gives me peace of mind'. Now Jimmy sings on record: 'She Just Satisfies', out now. Jimmy's a six-footer, black-haired, gentle-mannered. A decidedly brilliant young man – just hope his disc gets the credit it deserves. He likes: Bob Dylan, James Brown and the Famous Flames.'

Page has since described the single as 'a joke' and 'best forgotten', adding to the NME in September 1973: "There's nothing to be said for that record except it was very tongue-in-cheek at the time. I played all the instruments on it except for the drums and sang on it too, which is quite, uh... unique." In fact it's a perfectly creditable R&B effort, with surprisingly tough vocals on the A-side. The B-side is an instrumental, unusually long for its time, and both tunes were co-written with Barry Mason. The drummer was Bobby Graham. No follow-up was recorded, Page explained in Trouser Press in 1977, "Because I wanted to do 'Every Little Thing' with an orchestra, and they wouldn't let me do it... and my contract ran out before I could do anything else. Simple as that."

Shepperton Studios

Located in Surrey, in the summer of 1975 these film studios served as the location for secretive reshoots of the incomplete or sub-standard live sequences for the band's Song Remains The Same movie. These were undertaken in strict secrecy. As Page told Mojo magazine in December 1997, the band was "miming to our own soundtrack and doing a variation of the one thing we'd tried to avoid doing – miming on Top Of The Pops."

Sherman, Bobby

b. July 22nd 1943
US pop singer who co-owned 'the Starship' with entertainment mogul Ward Sylvester. Led Zeppelin hired the private Boeing B720 aeroplane for their 1973 and 1975 US tours.

see *Starship*

Showco

Dallas, Texas-based lighting and sound company founded by Jack Maxson and Rusty Brutsché in March 1970, which contributed effects to the band's live shows as of 1973. Before then, the band had made do with whatever individual venues could offer. As Page told the NME in April 1973: "It's nothing phenomenal, it's just that we had no lights before, so we thought it might be fun and add a little extra atmosphere. Everybody else has been doing it for years, but before we always let the music speak for itself." Brutsché – who travelled to Japan with the band in September 1971 – explained to the Business Wire in March 2000: "We were one of the first to realise the amount and scale of equipment that the major arena concerts required. Jack was a recording engineer and I was a musician. We learned that most public address systems were built for the amplification of a single announcer over crowd noise. The dynamics of live music and the power required to generate the sounds we hear at concerts today were almost unthinkable at that time."

Other vital members of their team were Kirby Wyatt and Ian 'Iggy' Knight (heads of the lighting team) and Allen Branton (chief spotlight operator). According to Led Zeppelin's official 1975 US tour programme, 'The sound system, designed by Showco, is a 24,000 watt, 4-way system, the largest indoor sound system ever. The lighting system is a 310,000 watt system, more than double any previously created system… More than 4000 pounds of cable is necessary for each Led Zeppelin show.' The firm oversaw the band's spectacular Knebworth shows in August 1979, and also worked on their final tour, 'Led Zeppelin Over Europe', the following summer.

Sick Again

The driving rock track that closes 1975's *Physical Graffiti*. Its lyrics concern the sordid groupie scene in LA – as Page told the NME in December 1974: "The competition thing out there is incredible, and you've got to keep out of the middle of it or else it gets to you too. There's a song on the new album called 'Sick Again' that about sums it up." The song was often played live by the band, coming second in their set on

their 1975 and 1977 US tours (presaged by the introduction to 'The Rover' in 1977). They also played it at Knebworth in August 1979, though it didn't feature on their European tour the following year.

Since I've Been Loving You

This powerful, semi-improvised slow blues appears on *Led Zeppelin III*, and was recorded almost live. Its intro is similar to the Yardbirds' 'New York City Blues', while its verse sections have been likened to 'Never' by Moby Grape (one of Plant's favourite US West Coast bands). It features what many – including its engineer, Terry Manning – regard as Jimmy Page's most lyrical electric guitar solo, though the guitarist told Disc in October 1970 that "it could have been better – but, you know, you are never satisfied with a performance". He also expressed dissatisfaction with John Bonham's audibly squeaky bass drum pedal on the recording. The track had first been attempted in the studio in late 1969, and featured prominently throughout Led Zeppelin's live career.

Singapore

Conservative Far Eastern territory that refused Jimmy Page and Robert Plant entry for a scheduled concert on February 14th 1972, on account of their long hair. The duo were en route for Australia, so briefly visited Bombay instead, playing an impromptu club gig for which they were paid a bottle of Scotch.

Singer Bowl

New York venue where Led Zeppelin

played an eventful gig on July 13th 1969, alongside the Jeff Beck Group and Ten Years After. Alvin Lee, lead guitarist with the latter, had recently made some disparaging remarks about Page in the UK music press, and Led Zeppelin were bent on revenge. First up for punishment was their keyboard player Chick Churchill, who – according to the memoirs of security man Don Murfet – 'was unlucky enough to be caught without back-up in a locker room by a vengeful rabble of roadies, who scared the crap out of him before ruthlessly stripping him of his clothes. Then they stripped him of his dignity by dumping him naked and trussed like a lamb to the slaughter in the starkly lit corridor outside.' When Ten Years After went onstage, Alvin Lee became the focus of their efforts: 'Hidden in the anonymity of the shadows in a corner in front of the stage, the Zeppelin crew pelted Alvin Lee mercilessly from the moment he took the stage with anything that came to hand – including hot dogs, burgers, orange juice and probably much messier and more painful missiles.' According to Richard Cole in *Stairway To Heaven*, 'On that hot, 100-degree afternoon, the situation only got worse for Lee. The orange juice quickly dried and his hands and the guitar became sticky. His fingers just couldn't manoeuvre properly from fret to fret. He was forced to slow his pace. He struggled through the group's remaining songs'. Then, during Jeff Beck's set, a drunk Bonham staggered onstage, replaced Micky Waller on the drumstool, played a striptease beat and proceeded to remove all his clothes. Only the diplomacy of Peter Grant

averted an arrest and a possible end to their third US tour.

Singles

Perhaps mindful of the Yardbirds' string of latter-day flops, Led Zeppelin pursued a strict policy of not issuing singles in the UK. A handful of promo copies of 'Communication Breakdown' / 'Good Times Bad Times' were pressed and sent to DJs in November 1969, and sell for hundreds of pounds today. Though 'Whole Lotta Love' became a hit in the US the following month, its UK release was cancelled after only 500 copies had been pressed. "The single had been reduced in playing time, and was only ever meant for issue on radio stations for promotional purposes," explained Bonham. Instead, Page told Record Mirror on September 20th 1969, "I'm going off on holiday, and when I come back the group is really going to work hard and spend time on producing a single… I'd like to do a single and have success with it, but only if we were happy with the recording." This never happened, and surviving copies of both 45s sell for astronomical sums today.

Several further singles appeared in the US and elsewhere, principally to stimulate album sales through radio play, but the UK was not granted any except a promo issue of 'D'Yer Mak'er' / 'Over The Hills And Far Away' in 1973 and a giveaway of 'Trampled Underfoot' / 'Black Country Woman' in 1975. As Grant explained to Melody Maker on June 22nd 1974: "We just decided not to put singles out because of that trip you have to go through, or had to at that time… You had to go and wine and dine these people and all that crap, and they weren't keen on anything that didn't sound poppy. I think Led Zeppelin failed their audition." An additional benefit was that an absence of singles forced fans to cough up for albums. As Plant explained to UK TV show *The Old Grey Whistle Test* in late 1974: "I think albums are a true statement of a group's work. You have time in an album to indicate exactly what you've been up to over a period of time creatively. If you take a single off an album and stick it out, it's just part of an album. It might as well stay on the album."

SIR

Acronym for Studio Instrument Rentals, a rehearsal facility in LA that the band used while working up material that would end up on *Presence* in late 1975. As Robert Plant told Circus magazine in January 1976, "It was hard in the beginning; I had to sit in an armchair with my leg up in the air while the band was on the stage. And I'd go into another room where Detective were playing and Michael Des Barres was singing, aping all of my movements and looking in the mirror at the same time… But anyway, slowly and painfully we began working on the album, and it gradually came together."

Sitar

India's national stringed instrument. Jimmy Page was arguably the first English pop musician to own one, which he had imported from Bombay in 1964. It was his that was used on the Yardbird's 'Heart Full Of Soul', but

– somewhat surprisingly – he never used it on record, and no Led Zeppelin recordings feature it. As he explained to ZigZag magazine in November 1972, "To use an instrument which has been developed over thousands of years as a quick gimmick, well…"

Sleepy

Obscure British psychedelic band who supported Led Zeppelin at one of their very first gigs, at London's Marquee Club on Friday October 18th 1968. The band managed two singles on CBS (to which Robert Plant was still under contract), both issued in 1968.

Sloppy Drunk

Never-released outtake from the band's untitled fourth LP, on which Plant plays guitar and Page mandolin. Plant told Disc in February 1971 that "you can imagine it being played as people dive round the maypole". Its title was presumably inspired by Big Joe Williams' 'Rather Be Sloppy Drunk', and it has been speculated that it ended up on *Physical Graffiti* as 'Boogie With Stu'.

Slush

Possibly unreleased track dating from the *Houses Of The Holy* sessions in April 1972, though many suspect that it was merely a working title for 'The Song Remains The Same' or 'The Rain Song'.

Smith, Henry

Nicknamed 'the Horse', this amiable US-born individual served as an assistant road manager during the band's early tours. He discovered the theft of Jimmy Page's favourite guitar at Winnipeg

Airport in April 1970, and assisted Richard Cole in unplugging the Flock's equipment at the Bath Festival in 1970.

Sol
Recording studio located in Cookham, Berkshire, acquired by Jimmy Page from engineer Gus Dudgeon in 1981, and used to master the 1970 recordings 'We're Gonna Groove' and 'Poor Tom' for 1982's *Coda* compilation. It was subsequently used by artists including Elton John and Jeff Beck.

Solo Performances
Shoddy late 70s bootleg consisting of 23 minutes of Jimmy Page's unfinished soundtrack for Kenneth Anger's *Lucifer Rising* film (taped by an audience member at a screening of the incomplete film in LA in September 1976), as well as both sides of the single Robert Plant made with Listen in 1966, and both of his solo singles from 1967. The record came in a black and white picture cover showing Page, Plant and John Bonham.

The Song Remains The Same (song)
The opening track to *Houses Of The Holy* was originally conceived as an instrumental to be called 'The Overture', which would have segued into 'The Rain Song'. Jimmy Page told Guitar Player magazine in 1993 that "I had all the beginning material together, and Robert suggested that we break down into half-time in the middle. After we figured out that we were going to break it down, the song came together in a day... I always had a cassette recorder around." Plant's lyrics celebrate the universality of music. "Every time I sing that, I just picture the fact that I've been round and round the world, and at the root of it all there's a common denominator for everybody," he told the NME in June 1973. His vocals were slightly sped up on the record, and in January 1976 he admitted to Circus magazine: "'The Song Remains The Same is possibly one of the few songs that I don't think I really did justice to'." Nevertheless, it was a regular feature of their live performances up to 1980, when it was dropped for their European tour.

The Song Remains The Same (film)
Billed as 'a *real* film in which we've tried to say something by extending Zeppelin's musical feelings and re-enacting their fantasises' and half-jokingly described by Peter Grant as 'the most expensive home-movie ever made', this was the sole film made by the group during its existence, and a notable mis-step. As Jones put it to Tight But Loose in 1997, "it was a massive compromise. We never knew what was happening. When we first had the idea, it was a relatively simple one – to film some shows and then release it as a film. Little did we know how difficult it would all become."

Plans to make a concert film had been mooted as early as January 1970, when the band's performance at the Royal Albert Hall was filmed. That June Peter Grant told Disc that "a camera team will be travelling with them to Iceland on June 22nd, and the whole thing should be tied up within a couple of months". John Bonham, meanwhile, told Melody Maker in July that the film "will probably be an hour-long semi-documentary and will feature some footage from the Royal Albert Hall concert. One of the highlights of the film will be a sequence featuring my four year-old son Jason playing his drums." The Albert Hall footage, however, was eventually deemed too dark to be usable, and plans to cut it with film shot at their Bath Festival appearance on June 28th were abandoned. Over the next couple of years demand for live performances became impossible to meet, so – as Page told Mojo magazine in December 2007 – "The idea was that people who couldn't get to see Zeppelin play live could go to the cinema and watch us there."

The final decision to make a concert movie was taken at short notice in July 1973, when the band's three-night stand at New York's Madison Square Garden (from the 27th to the 29th) was filmed by Joe Massot. Unfortunately, the footage had serious gaps in it, so it was later interspersed with segments supposedly reflecting each member's fantasies (as well as Peter Grant's). Grant was seen as a Chicago-style gangster (alongside Richard Cole), while Plant was filmed in full Arthurian mode, as well as riding and enjoying the outdoors with his family. Jones's offering sees him reading a bedtime story to his daughters before heading off into the night as a highwayman, crudely symbolising the duality of his existence. According to him subsequently, "the individual sequences weren't originally planned. They only happened because there were giant holes in the concert footage… a couple of days in advance I'm suddenly told that a film crew was coming down

to my house to film a sequence, and what was I going to do? That's the amount of planning that went into it." Page, meanwhile, is shown climbing a Scottish hillock one night in December 1973. "I was exhausted at the end of it because I had to stand up all the time," he panted to the NME in February 1975. "I really had to bring out all my yoga training for that." According to Massot, "He insisted that his segment be shot on the night of a full moon. It was quite difficult lighting the mountain at night… it was a weekend and overtime for the crew, but Jimmy wanted it to be right." Massot's replacement, Peter Clifton, would later claim that he'd had to reshoot Page's nocturnal segment because the guitarist was worried that his backside looked too large in the first version. Bonham arguably emerges with the most credit, as he is simply seen doing some DIY, visiting a pub, roaring around in a hot rod and showing off some of his cattle.

A rare example of Peter Grant operating outside his field of experience, the production was fraught with difficulties and delays. The live sequences were incomplete and didn't show the band at its best, prompting clandestine reshoots for certain songs and links at the UK's Shepperton Studios. The film was then edited during the band's 1975-76 tax exile from the UK, leading to considerable upsets with Clifton. Page told Melody Maker in November 1977 that "we had considered shelving the film, to film the forthcoming American tour… but then, after Robert's accident we had to fill the gap and go ahead". The process was far from harmonious. Plant told Circus magazine in January 1976: "The attitude and antics of the people involved with film, the way they follow their own odd trips, are really beyond my comprehension altogether. I could never imagine being involved in movies by myself. If I had to repeat the work on that film again, I would refuse to do it." Page, meanwhile, told Trouser Press in October 1977 that "We'd gotten to the point where we were so far into it we couldn't pull out. We'd put so much money into it."

After innumerable delays and disagreements with the film-makers, the finished product finally had its world premiere in New York on October 20th 1976, in front of guests including Mick Jagger, Carly Simon, Bad Company's Simon Kirke and David Bowie's guitarist Mick Ronson. On November 4th it was simultaneously premiered in London's Warner West End and ABC Shaftesbury Avenue cinemas. The band attended the beginning of both these screenings, and a press party was held after the show, at the Floral Hall in Covent Garden. According to security man Alf Weaver's 2001 memoirs, *The First Rock N Roll Bodyguard*, 'Four different traditional beers would be available at the party, including Robert and Bonzo's favourite, Banks's. Special arrangements were made with the Midlands-based Wolverhampton & Dudley Breweries to deliver the booze... There was also a cockle-and-whelk stall, a mobile fish-and-chip shop and a bloke on a tea urn serving egg-and-bacon sarnies. A nice little disco, too.' Reviews were lukewarm, however, with many cinemas unable to

get the sound across satisfactorily (rather than being quadraphonic, Page explained in interviews, it was in 'quint'). Circus magazine commented that the film felt like it had been made 'by junior college students who had just discovered LSD', while Melody Maker wrote that 'Zeppelin as mere mortals, giving specific insight into their private lives and fantasies, were largely depressing – embarrassing even... by the second hour the repetition is wearing. It's just like being at a live gig, but you can't walk around.' Rolling Stone, meanwhile, branded the film 'a tribute to their rapaciousness and inconsideration', concluding that 'their sense of themselves merits only contempt'.

By November, Page himself was expressing doubts, telling Melody Maker on the 20th: "When you've been on something for that amount of time, there is always that slight reservation: have we gone over the top?" Though Plant had claimed "we're as pleased with it as we possibly could be" in the paper that February, he was less effusive in subsequent years, dismissing it to Mojo magazine in 1994 as "a load of old bollocks". Ultimately, perhaps Ahmet Ertegun, the head of Atlantic and allegedly the only man Peter Grant looked up to, proved the film's most eloquent critic: during a specially-arranged advance screening in New York in the summer of 1976 he fell fast asleep.

The Song Remains The Same (album)
The soundtrack to the band's concert film was recorded by Eddie Kramer at

New York's Madison Square Garden over the nights of July 27th, 28th and 29th 1973, and released over three years later, in late September 1976. Page had begun to mix the music in the summer of 1975, returning to the project with Eddie Kramer at New York's Electric Ladyland studios in the winter of 1975-76. The duo spent a huge amount of time attempting to perfect it, with final mixes being carried out by Page at London's Trident studios in August 1976, while Kramer prepared the audio for the cinema release at Todd A.O. studios in California. By the time the resultant double LP finally appeared, it was badly out of date. Page acknowledged its imperfection almost as soon as it became available, telling Nick Kent of the NME on November 20th: "My idea prior to Robert's accident, which has dictated virtually everything we've done since, was to do a chronological affair with tracks dating back to 1970." He concluded with the equivocal words "It's just a reasonably honest statement of where we were at the particular time." He also stated: "There are loads of howling guitar mistakes on there. Normally one would have been inclined to cut them out, but you can't do that when it's a soundtrack."

The front cover and accompanying publicity materials was designed by Hipgnosis and depicted a run-down cinema based on Old Street Studios, a London rehearsal space used by the band before their ninth US tour in 1973. Inside the gatefold were adulatory notes by Cameron Crowe and an eight-page colour booklet showing stills from the film. It was undoubtedly a lavish package, but failed to top the US charts, stalling at #2 behind Peter Frampton's *Frampton Comes Alive*.

Son Of Dracula
Unfunny 1974 musical comedy film, released through Apple Films and starring Harry Nilsson and Ringo Starr. It features a cameo from their drinking buddy John Bonham as the drummer in Dracula's band, the Count Downes, in Tramp nightclub (alongside Nilsson, Peter Frampton and members of Badfinger). The song they are playing is a 1950s classic by the El Dorados, 'At My Front Door'. Screenings have been rare over the years, and it has yet to appear on DVD.

South Bound Saurez
Jaunty, piano-led outing featured on 1979's *In Through The Out Door*. It is not clear what 'Saurez' means, though it is a wine-producing region in Uruguay. Written by Robert Plant and John Paul Jones, it's one of only two songs by the band that does not feature a credit for Jimmy Page (the other being 'All My Love'). It has been pointed out that there are mistakes in his contribution to the song, but that he chose to leave them in. The band never performed it live.

Spence, Lewis
b. Nov 25th 1874 / d. March 3rd 1955
Scottish folklorist and antiquarian, whose 1949 volume *The Magic Arts in Celtic Britain* has been cited by Robert Plant as an inspiration for the lyrics to 'Stairway To Heaven'.

Spinal Tap

Fictional rock band whose 1984 film *This Is Spinal Tap* may well have been influenced by aspects of Led Zeppelin's career. For example, one of their drummers died by 'choking on vomit' (albeit someone else's), they perform a memorable gig with a supposedly awe-inspiring Stonehenge set (as did Led Zeppelin at Oakland, California in 1977) and their lead guitarist Nigel Tufnel performs solos using a violin against his guitar strings, a clear parody of Jimmy Page's bowing technique. Led Zeppelin's 1976 *The Song Remains The Same* movie has long been compared to *This Is Spinal Tap*, meanwhile. As Page told Mojo magazine of its 'fantasy' sequences in December 2007: "You can look at those sequences as either an attempt to break new barriers, or just Spinal Tap. I don't think there's really any in-between."

Spirit

US West Coast band with whom Led Zeppelin shared stages in 1969, and of whom they are known to have been fans, performing a cover of their 'Fresh Garbage' onstage. It has been pointed out that the acoustic introduction to 'Stairway To Heaven' bears slight similarities to Spirit's brief instrumental 'Taurus' (included on their self-titled January 1968 debut LP). Bonham's drum solo in 'Moby Dick' also echoes Spirit drummer Ed Cassidy's solo on 'It's All The Same', included on their December 1968 *The Family That Plays Together* LP.

Springfield, Dusty

b. April 16th 1939 / d. March 2nd 1999
English pop and soul singer who knew Jimmy Page and John Paul Jones through their prolific session work, and was backed by Jones on bass during a residency at London's Talk Of The Town club in early 1968. Her high opinion of the duo's abilities has been cited as part of the reason that they were signed to Atlantic on November 1st 1968. The following year the label issued a promotional LP (Atlantic TL ST-135) to US record shops for in-store play, combining cuts from her *Dusty In Memphis* LP with excerpts from the band's forthcoming debut. This is now a significant rarity.

SS

Abbreviation for 'Schutzstaffel', the brutal secret police under Hitler's Nazi's regime. With questionable taste, Jimmy Page chose to sport their peaked caps, trousers and jackboots onstage during Led Zeppelin's ill-fated 1977 US tour.

Stairway To Heaven

Arguably the band's signature tune, this eight-minute epic closed side one of their untitled fourth LP and has gone on to become the most-played song in the history of US FM radio (with over 4 million airings), as well as being the biggest-selling piece of sheet music in rock history. Its beginnings were hesitant, with Page devising the guitar parts over several months, beginning at Bron-Yr-Aur in May 1970. These were laid down in London's Island Studios in December, while Plant's lyrics were largely improvised by the fire at Headley Grange in the New Year, as Page strummed his guitar. "I was holding a pen and paper, and for some reason I was in a terrible mood," he later explained. "Then all of a sudden my hand was writing out the words… I just sat there and I looked at the words and I almost leapt out of my seat." Jones later overdubbed multi-tracked bass recorders and electric piano, while (after a few false starts) Page improvised his guitar solo. Plant went on to tell Australia's Go-Set magazine in February 1972: "A thing like 'Stairway To Heaven' can take on so many different meanings, because really it has no direct meaning."

The song was first performed live at Belfast's Ulster Hall on March 5th 1971, with Page using a double-necked Gibson. Jones later joked that the audience was "bored to tears waiting to hear something they knew", but bootlegs indicate otherwise. Melody Maker's Chris Welch was there, and wrote in his review of the gig a week later that the song was 'an excellent ballad, it displayed Robert's developing lyricism'. The song quickly became a live staple, typically serving as their closing number and being omitted from set-lists very rarely. Plant would often ask 'Does anyone remember laughter?' just after singing the words 'And the forests will echo with laughter'. Bonham once confessed to falling asleep onstage while awaiting his drum cue, and Plant found it harder to perform in the light of his son's death. Nonetheless, Page told Cameron Crowe in the March 13th 1975 issue of Rolling Stone: "I thought 'Stairway' crystallized the essence of the band. It had everything there and showed the band at its best… Every musician wants to do something of

lasting quality, something which will hold up for a long time, and I guess we did it with 'Stairway'."

Stargroves
Located in East End, Newbury, Berkshire, this was Mick Jagger's country home in the 1970s, and venue for numerous Led Zeppelin recording sessions in 1972, using the Rolling Stones' mobile studio. Some of the tracks taped there were included on *Houses Of The Holy*, including 'Dancing Days' and 'The Crunge'. Others appeared on *Physical Graffiti* in 1975, such as 'The Rover' and 'Black Country Woman'. Earlier sessions had been held by the band there in 1970, though (as engineer Andy Johns subsequently told Guitar World magazine) "Jimmy didn't want to stay there because Mick wanted too much money". According to Richard Cole in *Stairway To Heaven*, 'As with any Led Zeppelin gathering, there was some ongoing horseplay at Stargroves. It cut the tension that had built up, and seemed to regenerate the band's spirits for the following day's work. In a curious way, it was also how the band members showed affection for each other.'

Starship
Private Boeing aircraft commandeered by the band for their 1973 and 1975 tours of North America, at a cost of around $2500 a day. They'd encountered turbulence in a smaller Falcon Jet they'd chartered in 1972, and as Page and Bonham both suffered from a fear of flying, they were determined to travel in greater comfort and safety for their next US tour. The Starship had been

modified by its owners, entertainment mogul Ward Sylvester and former teen idol Bobby Sherman, to allow greater comfort to its passengers. Of an original 138 seats, only forty were left intact. Where the others had been in the main cabin there was a bar, chairs, tables, an artificial fireplace, revolving armchairs, a sofa running the length of the craft (opposite the bar), as well as a large television and a range of videotapes. The bar had an electric organ built into it, to facilitate singalongs (typically led by Jones), and to the rear were a kitchen and two private rooms, one with scatter cushions on the floor and the other with a waterbed (complete with white fur throw) and en suite shower. There were even two pretty young air hostesses, Suzee and Bianca, whose job had an unexpected perk – the rolled-up, cocaine-encrusted $100 bills left scattered around the plane after each flight. The plane's function was not just to fuel the band's egos and taste for excess; it also made logistical sense. Check-ins, security and hassles from fans were now a thing of the past, as the Starship allowed them to centre themselves in one city at a time – Chicago, for example – and fly to and from nearby cities where they were performing. This saved them from much of the tedium of endless hotels, which they had long since tired of, as well as having to stop over in towns that couldn't offer much in the way of entertainment.

Rumours of bacchanalian parties have long circulated, though Howard Mylett perhaps came closer to the truth when he wrote in his 1976 book 'Led Zeppelin' that 'on-flight activities [on the 1975 US tour] were subdued, with John Bonham sitting quietly drinking and adjusting the bowler hat that seemed to have become a permanent fixture. John Paul Jones played games of chess and backgammon with reporters, and Jimmy, Robert and Peter rested in the bedrooms'. Plant, however, told Blender magazine in 2002 that his fondest memory of the craft was "oral sex in turbulence". According to Richard Cole in *Stairway To Heaven*, 'On the flights to concerts, the mood on the Starship was relatively quiet. But pandemonium reigned on the post-concert flights.'

Led Zeppelin were the first act to hire the refitted plane, in July 1973. They band had their logo sprayed onto the Starship's fuselage, and the Swan Song

192

logo added to its tail. For the 1975 tour they had a different design, in red and blue, with their name smaller and accompanied by several stars. As time went on John Bonham conquered his early fear of flying to the extent that he occasionally co-piloted the plane. The band sought to use it again for their 1977 US tour, but it was grounded at Long Beach Airport, forcing them to find an alternative, 'Caesar's Chariot'. Other acts to have hired the Starship include the Rolling Stones, Deep Purple and Elton John. The last musician to charter it was Peter Frampton, in 1976. Thereafter it repeatedly changed hands before going into storage at Luton Airport, outside London. It was broken down and sold for parts in July 1982.

see *Caesar's Chariot*

Staysea

34-foot sea-going cruising boat acquired by John Bonham in April 1972. According to his brother Mick's memoirs, 'After a couple of days of cleaning and getting the boat spotless, John decided that a cruise down the river was in order. Large quantities of food and Newcastle Brown Ale were stowed away… Unfortunately for us the lock-keeper disputed ownership of the boat and wouldn't let us through. In the end we had to make do with a cruise up and down a three-mile stretch of the river until all the provisions had been disposed of '.

Steiner, Rudolph

b. Feb. 25th 1861 / d. March 30th 1925
Austrian philosopher and pioneer of liberal teaching. In the aftermath of his son Karac's death in 1977, Robert Plant considered training to become a teacher. "For a while I wanted to do something else," he has commented. "I considered teacher training. My daughter went to the Rudolph Steiner school, and I liked their philosophy, which was both gentle and productive. I wanted to be surrounded by that sweetness. I would have got a lot out of it. But in the end, I decided I really love doing what I do."

Stewart, Ian

b. July 18th 1938 / d. Dec. 12th 1985
Universally known as 'Stu', this short-lived member of the Rolling Stones (and long-lived 'sixth member') was on hand for the sessions for Led Zeppelin's untitled fourth LP at Headley Grange, playing piano on 'Rock and Roll'. He also lent his name and superb piano-playing to 'Boogie With Stu'. His association with Page went back to the early 60s, when they were both regulars at London's R&B clubs, and he even played on the Yardbirds track 'Drinking Muddy Water', included on the 1967 *Little Games* LP.

St. Mark's Place

Location of the New York tenement that can be seen on the front cover of 1975's *Physical Graffiti*. In subsequent years numbers 96-98 housed – amongst other things – a vintage clothes boutique named after the album.

Stryder

Robert and Maureen Plant's blue-eyed Merle dog, immortalised on *Led Zeppelin III*'s 'Bron-Y-Aur Stomp' in 1970.

Studley Conservative Club
Warwickshire boozer in which John Bonham's 'pub' scenes for *The Song Remains The Same* were filmed in the spring of 1973.

Sullivan, 'Big' Jim
b. Feb. 14th 1941
Along with Page, the doyen of 1960s London session guitarists. On his website he writes of Page: "We got on well on sessions. Sometimes I would play lead and sometimes Jimmy. I used to do most of the country solos and he the rock ones. We would change over sometimes and I would be the rocker. We also did a lot of folk sessions together. Jimmy was into blues and I was into jazz and country blues. The rhythm section that played on a lot of the 60s group records consisted of Jimmy, myself, John Baldwin (or John Paul Jones, as he liked to be called) and Bobby Graham on drums. The amount of recordings we did together was amazing, and when he said he and John were going to leave he said I should join them too. I said I was married and would stay in sessions a while longer." Like Page, Sullivan was a keen exponent of the sitar, even recording his own album in 1967, *Sitar Beat* (Mercury SML30001). Page and Sullivan are also thought to have collaborated with obscure Bedford singer-songwriter John Williams on the 1968 *Maureeny Wishfull Album*, though Sullivan has no recollection of it. In December 1972 Page told Sounds: "I didn't know any musician who was happy doing sessions, and yet most of them are still there. And a lot of them were better musicians than I was – Jim

Sullivan, for instance. There's somebody who should have said 'right, that's it, I'm going to have a go', but he never did."

The Summit
Compilation LP issued on budget label K-Tel (NE 1067) in 1980, in aid of 'The Year Of The Child'. It included Led Zeppelin's 'Candy Store Rock', alongside tracks by ELO, Dire Straits, Supertramp and others.

see *By Invitation Only / Supertracks*

Sunday Lyceum Concerts
Series of gigs organised by Tony Stratton-Smith at London's Lyceum Theatre in 1969. On October 12th Led Zeppelin were paid the highest-ever fee for a one-off concert by a UK band for their effort, untypically described by Rolling Stone as 'an unprecedented success... the screaming audience proved that it's the music that does it for them, not the hype'. Stratton-Smith went on to found Charisma Records.

Sun Records
Based in Memphis, Tennessee and founded by Sam Philips, this label was the home of early rock and roll classics by Elvis Presley, Johnny Cash, Carl Perkins and others. As such, Robert Plant and Jimmy Page were keen to visit its legendary studios after being given the keys to the city at a ceremony in April 1970. According to local Atlantic promo man Philip Rauls, 'Appearing like a couple of bashful children asking for their mother's permission, Jimmy Page sought approval from road manager Richard Cole... While exiting my car,

Page and Plant began surveying the property and stuffing their shirts into their trousers and straightening out their appearance as if approaching sacred grounds.' Unfortunately, however, the studios were shut, so they had to content themselves with visiting Hot Line Record Distributors instead, where they helped themselves to handfuls of records on Sun, Chess, King and Stax.

see *Phillips, Sam*

Sunset Sound Recorders

Recording facility located at 6650 Sunset Boulevard in Hollywood, California, where Jimmy Page flew with Peter Grant and Andy Johns in February 1971, in order to mix the band's untitled fourth LP. As Page later explained, "Andy Johns said he knew a place where we could mix the album, Sunset Sound in LA. He convinced us it was the best place to do it, the best missing room… we wasted a week wanking around. From that point on Andy crapped himself and he disappeared." Plant was no more charitable, adding: "We were just disgusted at the amount of time it had taken to get the album finished. The sound of the mixing room that Andy Johns had taken Jimmy to was really duff." When they returned to London for a playback at Olympic, only 'When The Levee Breaks' was deemed usable. It was clear that another mix would be required, which was carried out at Olympic over the course of that Spring.

Sunshine Woman

This boogie number was recorded by the band for Alexis Korner's 'Rhythm & Blues' programme for the BBC World Service on April 14th 1969. It has never been officially released, but an off-air recording has surfaced.

Superhype

Publishing and recording company formed by Jimmy Page and Peter Grant in September 1968, named in ironic reference to press accusations that Led Zeppelin was built on hype, not talent. It has been suggested that its original name was to have been 'Superhip', but that Grant was unable to resist the subsequent pun. It was Superhype and not Led Zeppelin that Atlantic signed that November. The labels on early UK pressings of *Led Zeppelin I* give publishing credits for numerous songs to 'Superhype Music', though this was swiftly amended to 'Warner Bros. / 7 Arts'.

Supershow

1969 concert film featuring Led Zeppelin alongside jazz-rock and blues artists such as Colosseum, Roland Kirk, Buddy Guy, Jack Bruce and Eric Clapton. The band filmed their segment, a memorable seven-and-a-half-minute rendition of 'Dazed and Confused', in front of a live studio audience in a disused linoleum factory in Staines, Middlesex on March 25th. They had got involved through a friend of Page's, though Peter Grant wasn't sure it was a good idea and didn't attend the filming. Directed by John Crome, the film had a limited cinema run in London at the end of the year (premiering at the Lyceum on November 14th), and has gone largely unseen ever since.

Supertracks

Compilation LP issued on Vertigo Records (as SPORT 1) in 1976, in support of the Sports Aid Foundation. It included 'Trampled Underfoot' by Led Zeppelin, as well as tracks by the Rolling Stones, Jethro Tull, Pink Floyd and others

see *The Summit / By Invitation Only*

Sutch, Screaming Lord

b. Nov 10th 1950 / d. June 16th 1999

Eccentric rock singer and self-styled peer of the realm (born plain David Sutch), through the ranks of whose band, the Savages, passed musicians including Deep Purple's Ritchie Blackmore. The young Bonham once cycled a reported 48 miles just to get his autograph, but – despite releasing a string of 45s – by the autumn of 1969 Sutch still hadn't put out an LP. As Bonham told the NME the following June, he and Page had encountered Sutch in a LA's Thee Image club that September, and Sutch had suggested they repair to Hollywood's Mystic Studios for a jam session on some rock and roll standards, for possible release as his debut album. They agreed, as did Jeff Beck and Noel Redding, but "on the complete understanding that under no circumstances would he mention our names… it now seems he took us all in."

Unbeknownst to them, Sutch subsequently overdubbed new lyrics and guitar solos (without crediting the other guitarist) and had the recordings issued by Atlantic as *Lord Sutch And Heavy Friends* (Cotillion SD 9015) on May 25th 1970, with Page also credited as producer. Sutch gleefully described the LP to Melody Maker as 'modern rock and roll with the real Zeppelin sound, that driving beat with loads of excitement', but the musicians were unimpressed. Bonham told the NME in June 1970: "Sutch is a great bloke, but he used our friendship to sell his album." Page, meanwhile, commented that "everybody thought 'oh, Jimmy Page played that heap of crap', and it became more than an embarrassment." Peter Grant may have had some explaining to do as well: he had in fact arranged the deal with Atlantic. The disc climbed to #84 in the US charts, and has since been named in more than one poll as the worst album ever recorded.

Swan Song

The band's own record label, started in 1974 after their five-year contract with Atlantic came up for negotiation at the end of 1973. By then they were tired of having to fight for total creative control of their work, and as similar ventures had already been undertaken by the Beatles (Apple), the Rolling Stones (Rolling Stones Records), Elton John (Rocket), Emerson Lake & Palmer (Manticore) and the Moody Blues (Threshold), it was a natural step for them to take. Other names mooted included Slut, Slag, Eclipse, Deluxe, Stairway and Zeppelin, but the final name was taken from the title of a lengthy unreleased acoustic instrumental by Page. The logo was inspired by an 1869 painting named 'Evening: Fall Of Day' by William Rimmer, which hangs in the Boston Museum of Fine Art.

The label's formation was announced in the NME on April 4th 1974, with Grant explaining that it would be "a good investment in terms of money and artistic satisfaction." Surprisingly shabby offices were found above the British Legion at 484 King's Road in London's Chelsea (according to Richard Cole, the place "had no furniture and there was never anyone there"), and initial signings included Maggie Bell, Bad Company (outside Europe) and the Pretty Things. Jimmy Page told Hit Parader magazine in January 1975 that "I see this label as something that could be really good because of the kind of people we have… in all of these cases the record companies totally ignored them, and they're great talents – every one of them. They just haven't come across the right way… With Swan Song we have a situation where it won't happen, where people who have talent will be able to be heard." He clarified further in Trouser Press in October 1977, stating: "We didn't really want to get bogged down in having to develop artists, we wanted people who were together enough to handle that type of thing themselves."

Perhaps most importantly, the label gave Led Zeppelin something to take a pride in at a stage when their own career was at such a peak that ennui was in danger of setting in. They played no gigs and released no new music in 1974, so it gave them a focus beyond themselves. Swan Song's US launch was divided between a lunch reception at New York's Four Seasons hotel, where swans were hired to paddle about in the swimming pool (though an unfortunate mix-up led to geese being delivered instead, two of which were released into the traffic by Cole and Bonham), and a party in Bel Air attended by Ahmet Ertegun, Groucho Marx, Bryan Ferry, Bill Wyman, David Geffen and others. Plant emphatically rejected the suggestion by French magazine Rock & Folk in February 1975 that the band stood to make millions from the venture, stating: "That's not the reason for the label. If that were the case, we would have signed groups that sell a lot more albums." Nonetheless, the label did extremely well initially, with Bad Company's debut topping the US charts, though other signings did slower business.

By December 1977 Page was telling Melody Maker: "We've had a bit of a shake-up in the record department. After having gone through two label managers, we've found out we can do it better ourselves." Atlantic executive and long-term group confidant Phil Carson later revealed that "at one point I arranged to get a leave-of-absence from Atlantic so that I could actually work with Peter on a daily basis, to try and re-establish Swan Song in the late 70s. Unfortunately, Peter never made it to any of the meetings." Grant later conceded that he simply hadn't had the time to make the label the success it could have been. "What I regret is not getting someone in to run it properly," he told Tight But Loose in 1993. "I tried to run it like a 9 to 5 job, driving up to London for three hours every day. It just wore me out. Then I'd get home and Danny Goldberg or Steve Weiss would be on the line from America…

and just to do Zep justice was a 24-hour job." Inevitably, Swan Song's affairs became chaotic, and when its offices in London's King's Road were cleared in 1982, unplayed demos were found by acts who'd subsequently achieved stardom.

Sylvester, Ward

US entertainment mogul who co-owned 'the Starship' with pop singer Bobby Sherman. Led Zeppelin hired the private Boeing B720 aeroplane for their 1973 and 1975 US tours.

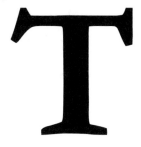

Tampa Stadium

Florida venue at which the band broke the Beatles' then-world record for concert attendance and gross, with an audience of 56,800 and a take of $309,000 on May 5th 1973 (the Beatles had played to 55,600 fans, earning $301,000, at New York's Shea Stadium on August 15th 1965). During the gig the band reportedly released 700 doves. Their next date there, on Friday June 3rd 1977, was less triumphant: heavy rain forced them to abandon their set after fifteen minutes, causing fans to riot. According to Richard Cole, 'Despite the continuing rain, much of the crowd remained at the stadium... Fights broke out in the audience, fans fighting with fans. Forty policemen in riot gear, most of whom had been stationed outside the stadium, dove into the crowd, flailing their billy-clubs... Sixty fans ended up in hospital.' A furious Peter Grant demanded that promoters Concerts West, who hadn't made adequate provision for the downpour, print a full-page apology to the band in the local paper the following day, which read in part: 'You are the best and deserve the best – not the worst treatment'.

see *Kezar Stadium / Pontiac Silverdome*

Tangerine

Melodic country-pop song included on *Led Zeppelin III*. Penned by Page alone, its roots lay in the Yardbirds, who had recorded an earlier, unreleased version entitled 'Knowing That I'm Losing You'. As Page told ZigZag magazine in November 1972, "I wrote it years earlier, after an old emotional upheaval, and I just changed a few of the lyrics." The subject of the song is thought to be US songwriter Jackie De Shannon, with whom Page had a passionate affair in the mid-60s. Led Zeppelin's recording features a memorably elegant pedal steel guitar solo, and the song was performed live by them in 1971-72, as well as at their Earl's Court shows in May 1975. Bonham proved an unexpectedly adept harmony singer on the latter occasions, after the first of which Plant announced "That is the first time the four of us have sung together on stage, or on record."

Tasty Pop Sundae

Ludicrously-named BBC radio show hosted by Chris Grant and aired on Sunday mornings in 1969. Led Zeppelin were featured alongside teeny-bop acts Marmalade and Vanity Fare on June 22nd, having taped their performance on Monday June 16th at Bond Street's Aeolian Hall. The programme was renamed after Grant took over from David Symonds's *Symonds On Sunday*, which the band was originally scheduled to appear on. Despite Grant's corny introductions ("There they are, Led Zeppelin! Great new pop combo!"), the band turned in a fine performance, including a unique recording of Sleepy John Estes' 'The Girl I Love

She Got Long Black Wavy Hair', a roaring rendition of 'Communication Breakdown' and an early taste of 'What Is And What Should Never Be'. Grant's unintentionally comic interviews with the band fully suggested that his own tastes lay more in the direction of the Marmalade and Vanity Fare, and were not broadcast.

Tax exile

Though Led Zeppelin drew considerable inspiration from England, both artistically and spiritually, its draconian tax demands forced them into exile in 1975, first in Montreux, Switzerland, and then in Jersey. They settled on the latter as it was close to the UK, meaning they could shuttle over for Christmas, landing shortly after midnight on December 25th. As Plant told the NME the following February: "It's a very sad situation, you know, to have to leave one's own country for the sake of money. The government in England is almost saying, 'Well, never mind, they'll come back you know, they're English and they'll come home.' And they're damn right! The number of times we have come so close to getting on a plane and going home! The spirit of Albion is really embedded in everyone's soul." Nonetheless, they stayed away for the required period, which involved Plant being separated from his wife and children following their car accident on holiday in Rhodes on August 4th 1975. The singer vented his spleen in a letter to Melody Maker, also published in February 1976: "We all want to go home, but there's an outrageous state of affairs taking place in England...

It's a very pitiful situation where a lot of the more established musicians have to flee... If it weren't for this tax, we'd be doing an English tour at least once a year for sure." Ironically, six years earlier they had been feted by politicians for their contributions towards the British economy.

see *Jersey* / *Grant, Anthony* / *Dunwoody, Gwyneth*

Tea For One

The lengthy slow blues that closes *Presence*. Its lyrics were inspired by the homesickness felt by Plant, who'd been separated from his wife Maureen (for tax reasons) so soon after their car accident on Rhodes in August 1976. As he told the NME in February 1976: "There's one song I wrote when I was very sad and missing Maureen in Malibu, and it's very personal." Page told Trouser Press in October of that year: "Tea For One was the only time I think we've ever gotten close to repeating the mood of another of our numbers, 'Since I've Been Loving You'. The chordal structure is similar, a minor blues." They never performed the track live, though parts of its guitar solo were incorporated into 'Since I've Been Loving You' in concerts from 1977.

Television

Other than a couple of very early appearances, Led Zeppelin pursued a policy of not appearing on television. This was partially to sustain their mystique and encourage fans to see them live, but also because, as Page explained to the *Sunday Mirror* on January 4th 1970: "I don't think TV people anywhere know how to present a group, especially from the point of view of getting the right sound. So, if viewers can't see or hear us at our best, then we'd rather stay off the small screen." Grant was contemptuous of the medium as well, explaining to *Tight But Loose* in June 1993 that "we did the Marquee [in 1968] and offered BBC2 the chance to film it, and they didn't even turn up." He was emphatic on the point, declining an offer of $1m for the band to perform a gig transmitted by satellite from West Germany on New Year's Eve 1969 and refusing to sell any TV rights for *The Song Remains The Same* movie in 1976.

Ten Years Gone

This epic was included on 1975's *Physical* Graffiti, and was – according to Robert Plant – "painstakingly pieced together from sections [Jimmy Page] had written." The singer went on to explain to Rolling Stone in March 1975 that "I was working my ass off before joining Zeppelin. A lady I really dearly loved said, 'Right. It's me or your fans.' Not that I had fans, but I said, 'I can't stop, I've got to keep going.' She's quite content these days, I imagine. She's got a washing machine that works by itself and a little sports car. We wouldn't have anything to say anymore… Ten years gone, I'm afraid." The band performed it on their 1977 US tour, and at their first Knebworth concert on August 4th 1979, though it was absent from their second show there a week later.

Thailand

Far Eastern kingdowm in which Led Zeppelin stopped on their way back to the UK from Australia in March 1972. Plant expressed a never-fulfilled desire to play there to Melody Maker that November, as did Page to Disc soon afterwards ("the sort of groups that do those sort of places are Marmalade, Tremeloes and Bee Gees, but they haven't had anybody to go over and sort of rock it up"). Plant's thoughts strayed back to Bangkok a month later, when he told the NME about his tour of the city's red light district with Page and Richard Cole. "We were taken by this guy who spoke strictly Queen's English, and it seemed to be the policy to show all visiting rock bands the brothels. I mean, it was interesting and that, but they couldn't understand why we didn't do anything." This is at variance with Cole's recollection, recounted in *Stairway To Heaven*: 'We were like kids in a candy store… the three of us indulged in everything from massages to good, old-fashioned sex.' A proposed tour of the Far East was cancelled following Plant's car accident on Rhodes in August 1975.

Thank You

The tender love song that closes side one of *Led Zeppelin II* was written by Plant for his wife, Maureen. "Robert wrote 'Thank You' on his own," Page told Trouser Press in October 1977. "That was the first one, and it's important, because it's when he began to come through as a lyricist. I'd always hoped that he would." The song was often played live by the band until 1973, and typically featured an extended organ solo from Jones. It occasionally cropped up as an encore thereafter, and can be heard on the band's *BBC Sessions* boxed set.

That's The Way
Light folk-pop track written by Page and Plant during their stay at Bron-Yr-Aur in 1970, originally entitled 'The Boy Next Door'. Plant told Uncut magazine in May 2008 that "We wrote 'That's The Way' one morning, and the lyrics were good... And the magisterial movement of the chords in the stanzas between the verses, it was all one could ever wish for." Page later described the song's genesis: "Coming down a ravine, we stopped and sat down. I played the tune and Robert sang a verse straight off." According to Plant onstage in 1994, the guitarist's daughter Scarlet was conceived half an hour after it was written. It featured prominently in their live sets between 1970 and 1972, and was revived for their Earl's Court dates in May 1975.

Thomas, Ray
Jimmy Page's guitar technician for many of the band's tours. Page told the NME in October 1974 that "We use so many tunings that Raymond, the road manager, spends most of his time re-tuning the guitars." Thomas was also responsible for replacing broken strings (and straps), often mid-concert. He later died from drug-related causes.

Three Men In A Boat
Walsall boozer and a pillar of the Birmingham music scene. Peter Grant bombarded it with telegrams in July 1968 (sending an estimated 40 in all), in his campaign to persuade John Bonham to join the nascent Led Zeppelin.

Thrower, Percy
b. Jan. 30th 1913 / d. March 18th 1988

UK gardening expert and TV personality who supposedly served as inspiration for John Paul Jones's 1968 wisecrack about 'watching plants grow', which gave rise to Robert Plant's durable nickname, 'Percy'.

Tight But Loose
Phrase used by both Plant and Page in interviews during their 1977 US tour, to describe the band's onstage chemistry. They even suggested that it might be a title for their next album, but events intervened and the idea had long since been abandoned by the time they finally taped *In Through The Out Door* in late 1978. Instead, it became the name of the band's long-running fanzine, edited by leading expert Dave Lewis.

Tolkien, JRR
b. Jan. 3rd 1892 / d. Sept. 2nd 1973
Scholar and author, whose fantasy novels *The Hobbit* and *The Lord Of The Rings* exerted considerable influence over Robert Plant. This is most discernable in *Led Zeppelin II*'s 'Ramble On', whose lyrics seem to echo the travails of Tolkien's hero, Frodo Baggins, with direct references to 'Mordor' and 'Gollum'. It has also been speculated that Tolkien's work informed the lyrics to 'The Battle Of Evermore' and 'Misty Mountain Hop' (from the band's untitled 1971 album), and 'Over The Hills and Far Away' (from 1973's *Houses Of The Holy*).

Tonsillitis
The band's eagerly-anticipated 1977 US tour, due to start in Texas on February 27th, had to be postponed until April

1st when Plant contracted tonsillitis. Unfortunately for Page, the band's equipment had been shipped to the States before the decision was taken, meaning that he had nothing but a dulcimer to play until he travelled across the Atlantic a month later. He told Circus magazine in June that the situation had him "pacing around like a caged lion… Climbing the walls, sleepless nights, you bet your life."

Top Gear

Much-loved BBC radio show presented by the late John Peel, which broadcast Led Zeppelin's first radio performance on March 23rd 1969 (it had been recorded on March 3rd). The band returned on June 29th and August 10th (recorded on June 24th and 27th respectively), performing a selection of album material, including extemporisations as well as a largely-improvised 'Traveling Riverside Blues' and the as-yet unreleased 'What Is And What Should Never Be'. The former performance was taped the day after their famous appearance at the Bath Festival, while the latter offered the band a chance to stretch out for longer than a typical radio session permitted. Though it was aired as part of *Top Gear*, it paved the way for the long-running *In Concert* series (which began in January 1970) and included a rendition of Page's famous 'White Summer' solo acoustic showcase.

Touring

Described by Jimmy Page in 1977 as 'a stag party that never ends', Led Zeppelin had a vigorous touring schedule throughout their existence, pausing only in 1974 and 1976. In total they played well over 600 concerts, including eleven US tours and visits to the UK, Sweden, Canada, Japan, Iceland, France, Italy, Finland, Holland, Belgium, Germany, Switzerland, Ireland, Australia, New Zealand and Austria. They were always dynamic onstage – as John Paul Jones later commented, "Page always looked as though he was looking at the floor, but we'd watch each other's hand movements all the time. There would often be seemingly amazing unrehearsed stops and starts. We'd all go BANG – straight into it. The audience would think, 'How did they do that?' It was because we were paying attention."

Their first gig was at Denmark's Gladsaxe Teen Club on September 7th 1968, and though early shows were poorly remunerated (with $200 being the smallest fee they ever received in the US), by the end of their first tour their asking price had risen to around $1500. That had soon rocketed to astonishing levels, causing Boston promoter Robert Chernov to state in September 1970: "I have never seen anyone as vicious or money-minded. These guys are worse than General Motors ever thought of being." By this time they had stopped employing opening acts, and charged a minimum fee of $25,000 per performance. From the start of their career they were criticised in the UK for not playing enough gigs on home turf, causing Page to tell the NME in April 1969 that "There just aren't the big venues in which to play. What is needed is a club in every major city which is something between the size of the Marquee and the Roundhouse." The band resented claims that they were only playing for the money – something that partially motivated 1971's 'Back To The Clubs' tour – but Peter Grant was well aware of the huge sums that were there for the taking, and for the first five years of their existence they toured relentlessly.

Though they broke attendance records everywhere they went, by 1972 life on the road had lost much of its initial appeal. A riot at Milan's Vigorelli stadium in July 1971 badly shook the band, and they became more security-conscious. As Richard Cole wrote in his autobiography, 'Even in the earliest days of Zeppelin there had been occasional threats, but – perhaps naively – we ignored them. By 1971, however, the threats had become almost weekly occurrences.' The relentless round of hotels and airports also began to take its toll. As Page told Disc in November 1972: "The last US tour just got silly. There were something like 28 dates in 30 days. We were playing an average of three hours every night, sometimes more than that, and it was really doing us in." Press agent Bill Harry commented later that "people don't realise how very tedious it can be sitting around waiting for hours and hours in recording studios, concerts, airport lounges and hotel rooms, waiting for some action to start. Sitting all day in a hotel, the band felt like prisoners."

Interviewed by the NME in LA in June 1973, during their ninth US tour, Plant conceded "There's a bit of boredom when you're stuck in Mobile, Alabama,

or places like that. A few lamp standards may fall out of windows, things like that…" In fact, the band developed a fearsome reputation for their destructive antics. As Richard Cole put it, their rampages 'weren't designed to create chaos, but rather to deal with excess energy and cope with the boredom of life thousands of miles from home.' Their escapades ranged from schoolboy high-jinks (buckets of water over doors, food fights, destroying hotel rooms, throwing TVs out of windows) to more sinister activities, such as tearing clothes off journalists (see *Sander, Ellen*), encouraging dogs to pleasure groupies, or pleasuring them with dead fish (see *the Shark Incident*). Typically Cole and Bonham were the ringleaders, with the other band members joining in as the mood took them. As Atlantic executive Phil Carson later explained, "Some people may find it difficult to understand, but high spirits build up in a group on the road… often they're difficult to relate later – you had to have been there."

Immediately before close of their 1973 US tour at Madison Square Garden (filmed for *The Song Remains The Same*), Page told the NME: "It's been an incredible tour, but we're all terribly worn out. I went past the point of no return physically quite a while back, but now I've gone past the mental point… It seems like so long since we had a break. I cannot remember when we were not working." Plant, meanwhile, told the paper in June: "My little boy's just started to walk, and I haven't seen him bloomin' walk yet. Those are the things that upset you about being on the road." Nonetheless, he'd told Melody Maker that April that "It's so easy to get stale, you know. There's a lot of bands do it. They reach a peak and think that that's it – the old country house bit, a year off and all that. Well, it doesn't work that way. There's only one way a band can function, and that's on the bloody stage. I think we're going to play more dates this year than we've ever played in our lives."

After the tour ended on July 29th, however, John Paul Jones told Peter Grant that he could no longer tolerate the pace and long absences from his family. Matters hadn't been helped by a death threat made against Page – as he told the NME in September 1973: "Actually it was a lot more serious than I thought – the guy was a real crazy and had all these photographs on the wall with circles around them. It was a real Manson situation". Looking back on the 1973 US tour, Page told Mojo magazine in December 2007 that "You couldn't just get off the plane and click back into real life. We'd had months and months of being bombarded, if you like, with intense images and sensations. I can remember coming back and suddenly the dimensions of the room you're in seem different from how they'd been before. It took time to settle down." The band therefore took 1974 off, and didn't play a single gig all year. They saw little of each other when they weren't working, as Plant told Mojo magazine in December 1997: "When we got off a plane, the band said goodbye or sometimes didn't even do that – you'd leave each other at the carousel, thumbs up and we'd be gone." John Paul Jones confirmed this in the same magazine in December 1994: "We never socialised. That's why it lasted so long, I think. We got on the road and everyone was really pleased to see each other. We got back to Heathrow and everyone goes, 'Bye!'" When it was time to regroup they would soon warm up again, as he told Blow By Blow magazine in 1992: "You could be off for a couple of months, and you go back and it's like the night after. You see the people, you see the programme, you see the roadie on the side and it just triggers it all off."

By February 1975, when the band was in the middle of its tenth US tour, Plant told the NME: "You know, you're talking to the new Robert Plant. My perspective has been changed on a lot of things. I've been through so many tours that now I see that there are ways and means of making it more enjoyable without having to rush into anything, or burning yourself out. If there's any raping or looting about… well, it's done with good taste, I suppose." The singer emphasised this to Rolling Stone's Cameron Crowe the following month, claiming: "Nowadays we're more into staying in our rooms and reading Nietzsche." Page seemed similarly calm, telling interviewer Lisa Robinson: "This time I'm going to get some Afghani hangings, and my rooms are going to look like, well, like mosques. You get loads of carpets and lay them on top of each other and have everything candlelit. My home's like that, you see, and I'd like to bring my home on tour." Homesickness affected

Jones and Bonham the worst, however. "Bonzo loved drumming, but he hated being on tour," Jones later remembered. "I used to sit up with him, just talking or listening to the radio." He went on to tell journalist Ritchie Yorke that "Touring makes you a different person, I think. You always realise it when you come home after a tour. It usually takes weeks to recover after living like an animal for so long."

The mental toll of touring was perhaps hardest on Page, who told Street Life magazine in May 1976: "Doing those concerts in front of so many people, there was so much energy being stored up. I felt like a kettle with a cork in the top. I'd stay up for five nights on the trot... I built up to such a pitch that I couldn't see myself coming down again." The band did not in fact play any gigs at all that year, but in early 1977 they were rehearsing in London for another US visit. A Swan Song press release of February 2nd quoted Plant promising 'blood, thunder and the hammer of the gods' – and indeed the tour was marked by bloodshed and a stormy atmosphere. Mid-tour in June, the singer told Creem magazine that "one thing that does upset me is that I see a lot of craziness around us. Somehow we generate it, and we revile it." The tense atmosphere was exacerbated by rioting fans and increased drug use by the band and their entourage. Page and Bonham were dabbling with heroin, as was Richard Cole, while Peter Grant was using ever more cocaine. "They were touring continuously and lost their sense of reality," commented Grant's old friend and former business partner, Mickie Most. "Add to that taking substances and it's a bad mix... You're living in a world where no one says 'no' to you... anything you want, it'll be there. You can almost commit murder. Rape. Pillage. Driving cars into swimming pools at parties. It's a terrible thing really." Remembering the tour in Uncut magazine in May 2008, Plant said: "There was no way of containing the energy in those [venues]. It was just insane. And we became more and more the victims of our own success. And the whole deal about the goldfish bowl and living in it, that kicked in... so everyone retired to their own corners within the environment, the hotels. Everybody had their own way of dealing with it."

According to Richard Cole in *Stairway To Heaven*, 'Something was different about this tour... From the beginning it just didn't feel right to me... The soul that had driven Zeppelin since 1968 seemed to have weakened, and drugs played too much of a role in everyone's life... the band members had drifted as far apart as they ever had on a tour. There was constant tension.' Most, meanwhile, had this to say in retrospect: "I know it came with the territory, to be outrageous and do things you knew you could get away with, but there was something unpleasant about it all. It might have seemed fun at the time, but in retrospect it wasn't very nice." The notorious 'Oakland incident' of July 24th 1977 was the lowest point. Page went on to tell Q magazine in 2003 that "a lot of the violence that went on was kept away from the group, so we rarely knew anything. It was only near the end that I saw it truly manifesting itself. It had got very heavy by then, and it was so far removed from what the true spirit of the band was all about. The bad elements in the organisation grew out of all control".

The tragic death of Plant's son Karac days later ended their last US tour on a desperate note. It would be more than two years before they played again, at Knebworth in August 1979. Those two enormous shows attracted a mixed response from critics and fans. Plant told Uncut that "there were moments at Knebworth that were spectacular. But the price you have to pay to get to those moments, I didn't think was worth it anymore." Nonetheless, the shows awakened enough enthusiasm in the band to tour Europe the following June and July. At the tour's end, Plant finally agreed to another US tour (which would have been their twelfth), but it was cancelled after Bonham's death on September 25th. Though Plant, Page and Jones have reunited publicly on three occasions (at Live Aid in 1985, at Atlantic Records' 40th anniversary party in 1990 and at the Ahmet Ertegun memorial concert in 2007), their reputation as the greatest live act of the 1970s rests on their performances with Bonham that decade. As Page remarked in 1973: "We've never ever gone out there and chewed gum and sort of messed about – we've always played our bollocks off."

Tous en Scene

French TV programme on which Led Zeppelin appeared on June 19th 1969, playing 'Communication Breakdown' and 'Dazed and Confused'. They travelled to Paris for the filming midway through a UK tour, and their performance was originally broadcast on September 5th. Some of it is included on the 2003 *Led Zeppelin* DVD.

Tower House

Imposing Victorian mansion in Melbury Road, Kensington that has served as Jimmy Page's London base since April 1974, when he paid a reported £350,000 for it (apparently outbidding David Bowie). He bought it from the actor Richard Harris, who had to go to the Bahamas for tax reasons. The house was designed by William Burges, and has strong Gothic influences. Page was strongly drawn to it for its historical connections. "I had an interest going back to my teens in the pre-Raphaelite movement and the architecture of Burges," he has said. "What a wonderful world to discover."

Train Kept A-Rollin'

Penned by Tiny Bradshaw, Howard Kay and Lois Mann in 1951, this rock and roll standard was featured on the Yardbirds' 1965 *Having A Rave-Up* LP, and went on to become one of the first two songs Led Zeppelin ever played together, along with Garnett Mimms's 'As Long As I Have You'. They subsequently played it as a set opener at gigs in 1968 and 1969, and surprised many by reviving it for their final 'Over Europe' tour in 1980.

Trampled Underfoot

This funk-rock track evolved out of a rehearsal jam and – having been honed to perfection – was included on 1975's *Physical Graffiti,*. It was largely inspired by Robert Johnson's 'Terraplane Blues' (as confirmed by Robert Plant at Earl's Court in May 1975), though it also bears similarity to Stevie Wonder's 1972 hit 'Superstition'. "When we first ran through it, John, Paul and Jimmy started off the riff, but then we thought it was a bit souly for us," John Bonham told Melody Maker in June 1975. "Then we changed it around a bit. It's great for me. Great rhythm for a drummer. It's just at the right pace, and you can do a lot of fills." The song is powered by a clavinet riff (as was 'Superstition'), and features a memorable guitar part on which Jimmy Page employs wah-wah and backwards effects. It was issued as a single in the US in April 1975 (backed with 'Black Country Woman', as Swan Song SS 70102), and reached a disappointing #38. Nonetheless, it quickly became a fixture of their live shows, and was played on every tour up to 1980, typically serving as a showcase for John Paul Jones's keyboard prowess.

Traveling Riverside Blues

Raw blues recorded by Robert Johnson in 1936, memorably performed by Led Zeppelin during their BBC session on June 24th 1969, and included on their *BBC Sessions* boxed set in 1997. Johnson's original also includes the notorious words 'Squeeze my lemon till the juice runs down my leg,' incorporated by Robert Plant into 'The Lemon Song' on *Led Zeppelin II*.

Turquoise

Greeny blue colour in which the words 'Led Zeppelin' appeared on the front of the early UK copies of their debut album in March 1969. This was soon switched to orange, (supposedly at the order of Peter Grant, because that was easier to read from a distance), making the former variants considerable collectables today. The labels on the discs that came inside the turquoise-lettered sleeves gave publishing credits for numerous songs to 'Superhype Music', which was swiftly amended to 'Warner Bros. / 7 Arts'.

TV International

Company responsible for the giant video screens on the band's 1977 US tour, and at Knebworth in August 1979, under the direction of Chris Bodger.

Untitled

Led Zeppelin's fourth album, released in November 1971, carried no title but is commonly referred to as 'Led Zeppelin IV'. Though the band was hurt by the mixed critical reaction to *Led Zeppelin III*, they were determined to continue ploughing their own furrow for its follow-up. As Plant told Disc in October 1970: "Now we've done *Zeppelin III*, the sky's the limit. It shows we can change, shows we can do these things. It means there are endless possibilities and directions for us to go in. We are not stale and this proves it." Initial sessions were held at Island's studio in London's Basing Street in December 1970 (simultaneously with Jethro Tull, who were making *Aqualung*), but they decamped to Headley Grange in January 1971, where they had already rehearsed and where they could enjoy the flexibility of using the Rolling Stones' mobile recording truck. As Robert Plant told Rick McGrath in August: "We put up all the equipment in one room and stuck all the mike leads through a window, straight into the recording van. So anything that we did just went straight down on tape."

Assisted by engineer Andy Johns and copious amounts of cider from the village shop (according to Richard Cole), the band found the atmosphere highly conducive to creativity and had the album finished by February. A double LP was originally mooted, and Page even suggested releasing it as four separate EPs, but such ideas had been abandoned by the time he flew to the US to mix it with Andy Johns. That wasn't a success, so remixes were prepared back at Olympic Studios in London, delaying the completion of the master until the summer. The album finally appeared on November 8th 1971, in a controversial sleeve that didn't feature their name or a title anywhere (much to Atlantic's consternation). As Page told Guitar World magazine in 1993, "It was a meaningless protest really, but we wanted to prove that people were not buying us for the name." Instead each band member was represented by a symbol (which has given rise to the LP's nickname, 'Four Symbols').

The image of the old man on the front was found by Robert Plant in a Reading junk shop, and has given rise to much speculation. Jimmy Page told the BBC that "some people say it has allusions to Holman Hunt, but it hasn't. It actually comes from the idea from the tarot card, the hermit and so the ascension to the beacon and the light of truth." The tower block on the back was shot by famed rock photographer Keith Morris. One of the buildings pictured has a barely legible Oxfam poster on it, reading 'Someone dies from hunger everyday'. Page had hoped it would be easier to read, explaining at the time that "the negatives were a little bluff". The original disc came in a grey inner sleeve with credits relating to the music and artwork, as well as the lyrics to 'Stairway To Heaven'. As Page told Guitar World magazine in 1993: "The typeface for the lyrics to 'Stairway' was also my contribution. I found it in a really old arts and crafts magazine called Studio, which started in the late 1800s. I thought the lettering was so interesting, I got someone to work up a whole alphabet."

Despite lacking the band's name or a title, upon its release on November 8th 1971 the album was a huge seller on both sides of the Atlantic. It was kept off the top spot in the US by Carole King's *Tapestry*, but has gone on to become their best-selling album of all. As Jimmy Page later commented: "I've really got fond memories of those times, and the album was done with such great spirit. Everyone had a smile on their face. It was great."

see *Four Symbols / Zoso*

Valens, Mrs.

Rocker Ritchie Valens' bereaved mother, who received an unexpected co-songwriting credit on 'Boogie With Stu', as the lyrics owed something to her late son's 'Ooh My Head'. As Page later explained: "What we tried to do was give Ritchie's mother credit, because we heard she never received any royalties from any of her son's hits, and Robert did lean on that lyric a bit. So what happens? They tried to sue us for all of the song! We had to say bugger off."

Vanilla Fudge

Formed in 1967, this US band specialised in heavy covers of contemporary hits. Jimmy Page had first met them when they played some dates in London in 1967, and – as a fellow Atlantic act – Led Zeppelin toured the US as support to them in late 1968 and early 1969, after Jeff Beck cancelled (Peter Grant saw the opportunity at once). The two groups got along well, despite the fact that the English upstarts upstaged them at every show. As drummer Carmine Appice put it in May 2000: "We always wondered who would blow us off - and it was Led Zeppelin. Our shows with them were always lots of fun. We all became real good friends. We would

sometimes switch rhythm sections in the middle of 'How Many More Times'." Jones confirmed this in 2005, stating to Bonham's brother Mick: "There was this bit in Dazed and Confused where we all stop to let Page and Plant do all the screaming and high bits, then we come back in with the fast riff… when Jimmy and Robert turned around they found Bogert and Appice and not Jones and Bonham. We'd swapped places while they were out front, and because we were always in the dark at this point, no one had noticed!" Appice and bassist Tim Bogert later formed Beck, Bogert and Appice with former Yardbird Jeff Beck. In 2007 the reformed Vanilla Fudge recorded a Led Zeppelin tribute album entitled *Out Through The In Door*.

see *Appice, Carmen / Shark Incident*

Vigorelli Stadium

Venue in Milan, Italy, where Led Zeppelin played a government-sponsored festival on July 5th 1971. When the 12,000 fans in attendance stood to cheer them after the opening songs, local police and soldiers over-reacted, spraying tear gas and weighing in with batons. Despite Plant's best efforts to quell the crowd, a riot ensued during which much of the band's equipment was destroyed or stolen (despite their roadies' best efforts to rescue it). Terrified, they took refuge in their dressing room, which fans vigorously attempted to break into. The quartet later acknowledged the event to be the single experience that had most united them. As Page put it to Ritchie Yorke in the NME in October 1971: "Italy is a word never mentioned in my hearing. It causes a big argument, or a nervous breakdown." The band never played there again.

Violin bow

Bowing the strings of an electric guitar was a practice that quickly came to be associated with Jimmy Page, and was credited to him as an innovation. Other guitarists were doing it too, however – in the April 30th 1966 edition of Melody Maker, for instance, it was reported that 'The Move are constantly experimenting with new sounds, and lead guitarist Roy Wood can even play his guitar with a violin bow,' while on June 4th it reported that 'The Creation, a new recording group, features an unusual sound on their first single. Lead guitarist Eddie Philips uses a violin bow on his electric guitar, which gives the group a highly distinctive sound'. Page learnt the idea from session violinist David McCallum in the mid-60s, and told Radio 1's *Insight* programme on July 27th 1975: "It obviously looks gimmicky... but the fact is that it's very musical, it sounds like an orchestra at times, the cello section, violins, it's quite amazing!"

Wales

British territory that served as a source of inspiration for Jimmy Page and Robert Plant. "If I wasn't into rock I would be living somewhere like Wales, in a commune," Page told Disc in April 1972. Several Led Zeppelin classics were penned by the duo at a cottage named Bron-Yr-Aur (outside Machynlleth, in Gwynedd) in May and October 1970. Plant had spent childhood holidays there, and was an avid fan of Celtic mythology, naming his son Karac after the Welsh warrior Caratacus in 1972. In 1973 he bought an 800-year-old farm in Wales, complete with 290 acres, 300 sheep and a pig named Madam. "Plunk on the side of a conical Welsh mountain, tucked away like in the fold of a good skirt – where we should all be," he joked to People magazine on December 20th 1975. When on tour he conceded that his thoughts occasionally strayed there, telling the NME on June 11th 1977 that rowdy fans are "the element that makes you wonder whether it's better to be halfway up a tree in Wales."

Walsh, Joe
b. Nov. 20th 1947

In April 1970, when Jimmy Page was asked by Ritchie Yorke of the NME which guitarists he admired, he replied: "There's a friend of mine called Joe Walsh who's got a group going round the Cleveland area called the James Gang. I heard them and they were very good." That October he explained to Melody Maker that his 1959 Gibson Les Paul guitar had been obtained from Walsh. "At the time, [Page] didn't have that kind of money," Walsh later claimed, "so I gave him mine." Walsh was to have opened for the band (along with the Pretty Things) at the Oakland Coliseum on August 23rd and 24th 1975, but the shows were cancelled following Plant's car accident in Rhodes. By the time the band did return to the US in 1977, he had gone on to mega-stardom in the Eagles.

Walter's Walk

Houses Of The Holy outtake, recorded at Stargroves on May 15th 1972 but not released until the *Coda* compilation appeared in 1982. It has been speculated that Plant's contribution was overdubbed at a later date, as his vocal timbre is more reminiscent of his work on *In Through The Out Door* than the band's early 70s recordings. It was never played live in its entirety, though parts of it cropped up during 'Dazed and Confused' at gigs in 1972.

Wanking Dogs

Pseudonym under which the band performed on a Danish TV show on February 28th 1970, following a threat of legal action from Eva Von Zeppelin. That night they played a gig in Copenhagen's K.B. Hallen as 'the Nobs' (also quoted as 'The Four Knobs').

see *The Nobs*

The Wanton Song

Sexually-charged hard rock number that evolved during a rehearsal jam and was included on 1975's *Physical Graffiti*. For his solo Page ran his guitar through a Leslie speaker cabinet, as well as putting backwards echo on it. The song was played at certain European and US concerts in 1975, but not thereafter.

Washbourne, Ray

Peter Grant's personal assistant, and the man charged with the difficult task of breaking John Bonham's death to him on September 25th 1980.

Waterloo Station

Iconic London railway station in which Peter Grant attempted to organise a gig in 1972. His scheme was for special trains to convey fans from all over the country, but ultimately it was decided that too much chaos would be caused to commuters, and the idea was abandoned. "I thought it was a great idea," he told Melody Maker that July. "You know, we could have had Led Zeppelin specials coming in on the platforms, it was going to work, but the station authorities said there was one late train that would get in the way. Shame, it would have been great – imagine Led Zep playing Waterloo Station. A completely covered hall, and very good acoustics."

A Way Of Life

Birmingham-based band active from 1966-67, featuring John Bonham on drums, along with Reg Jones (vocals), Mike Hopkins (lead guitar) Chris Jones (rhythm guitar), and Tony Clarkson (bass). They largely played cover versions with harmony vocals, and developed a considerable local following, though they rarely earned more than £20 a night and often had to steal petrol in order to turn up at all. The sheer volume of Bonham's drums also made them unpopular with venues – as Reg Jones commented in 2001: "He was so loud we never used to mike up his drum kit at gigs, and we still constantly got complaints about the volume." Nonetheless, they supported the Kinks at the Handsworth Plaza on Saturday June 17th 1967. Occasionally fellow local drummer Alan 'Bugsy' Eastwood would play alongside Bonham, giving a the band a distinctive sound. Later line-ups featured Danny King (bass and vocals) and Dave Pegg (bass), but the band split when bookings dried up, largely owing to Bonham's volume.

Clarkson later cropped up in the World of Oz, while Pegg went on to a lengthy and distinguished career with Fairport Convention. Eastwood played with the Exceptions, as well as releasing numerous solo 45s and an album, *Seeds* (President PTLS 1037), in 1971. The band had an impromptu reunion in October 1978, when Bonham attended a gig by the Jones brothers' new band, Grit, at Shenstone College in the Midlands, and joined them onstage for a couple of numbers. Coincidentally, *A Way Of Life* was also the title of an album by the Family Dogg that Bonham, Page and Jones played on as session musicians in the autumn of 1968.

Wearing and Tearing

Latter-day hard rock number, devised

at rehearsals for the band's August 1979 Knebworth gigs and recorded on November 21st 1978, during the *In Through The Out Door Sessions* at Abba's Polar Studios in Stockholm. There was talk of issuing it as a souvenir single of the gigs (backed with another LP out-take, 'Darlene'), but, as Page explained to Melody Maker in August 1979, "Time ran out because of rehearsals, and unfortunately we never got round to it." In the end it was released posthumously on *Coda*.

Webb, Keith
b. 1934 / d. 2007
Drummer in Terry Reid's band who greeted the nervous Robert Plant and John Bonham on their first ever arrival in America, at LA's Chateau Marmont hotel on Christmas Eve 1968. Standing outside in the baking heat, he waved champagne in their direction, saying: "Come on in, welcome to America, and Merry Christmas." Plant told Rolling Stone in 1975: "Bonzo and I were amazed."

Webb, Stan
b. Feb. 3rd 1946
Long-standing Chicken Shack guitar ace and a drinking buddy of John Bonham's. In 1972 the duo participated in a legendary binge, along with Mick Abrahams of Blodwyn Pig. It began in the afternoon at Soho's Coach and Horses pub, where they ordered cocktails containing every liqueur behind the bar, before Bonham ripped Led Zeppelin publicist Bill Harry's trousers and shirt. The furious Harry vowed never to work with them again, but the drummer was too rampant to care. Next the trio turned up at Harry's office in Oxford Street, hoping to find Jethro Tull bassist Glen Cornick. Having kicked the door down, they failed to nail their cowering quarry, so contented themselves with hurling loo rolls around and trashing Harry's office before covering Chrysalis executive Doug D'Arcy in masking tape and dumping him on a nearby roundabout. Bonham and Webb then called Richard Cole, who drove up from the countryside to join in the fun, along with Atlantic's Phil Carson. A theatrical costumier was their next port of call, and – having hired Arab robes – they checked into the Mayfair Hotel dressed as Sheikhs. After exposing themselves to some women in the lift, they entered their suite and ordered fifty steaks from room service. These were duly hurled around, and a massive terracotta sculpture of a Maharajah and a horse was smashed, before they departed in a hired Rolls Royce, snatched Led Zeppelin's secretary from the street and went to the Speakeasy club, where they continued to expose themselves. The incident allegedly led to Bonham being banned from the vast majority of decent hotels in the city for the rest of his life.

Weiss, Steve
The band's long-serving US lawyer, who worked for them from the start, having already acted for the Yardbirds.

Welch, Chris
Melody Maker journalist and longtime advocate of the band, who conducted numerous important interviews with

them throughout their lifespan. He travelled with them to places including Ireland and Germany, and even joined them onstage at Frankfurt's Festhalle on July 18th 1970 to accompany 'Whole Lotta Love' on timbales. Though he'd been one of their most vocal supporters from day one, after penning a less-than-glowing review of *Houses Of The Holy* in 1973 he briefly fell from favour. As a result he was obliged to buy his own tickets to one of their May 1975 Earl's Court shows from a tout – only for Robert Plant to dedicate 'Moby Dick' to him from the stage. In subsequent years Welch has continued to write warmly and insightfully about the band.

We're Gonna Groove

Propulsive R&B classic by Ben E King and James Bethea, with which the band opened their early live sets, and which kicks off 1982's *Coda* compilation. That rendition was taped at London's Morgan Studios on June 25th 1969. Six months later, on January 9th 1970, they opened their gig at London's Royal Albert Hall with the song – a potent performance that can be seen on their 2003 DVD retrospective.

What Is And What Should Never Be

The lengthy track that follows 'Whole Lotta Love' on *Led Zeppelin II*. Lurching from mellow, jazzy sections into out-and-out hard rock, it notably employs stereo 'panning' between speakers and features an early instance of Jimmy Page playing his beloved Gibson Les Paul guitar, as well as a particularly complex bass part from John Paul Jones.

When The Levee Breaks

The dense, hard-hitting closing track on the band's untitled fourth LP is a rewrite of a 1929 blues number by Memphis Minnie, who shares the songwriting credit with Led Zeppelin. It was one of several songs they had attempted in London's Island Studios in December 1970, before decamping to Headley Grange a month later. Robert Plant had introduced the song to the sessions, and had reworked the original lyrics. Jimmy Page told Guitar World magazine in 1993: "We tried 'Levee' in just an ordinary studio, and it sounded really laboured. But once we got Bonzo's kit set up in the hall in Headley Grange and heard the result, I said, 'Hold on! Let's try this one again!'"

It opens with a monolithic and much-sampled drum pattern from Bonham, recorded by Andy Johns one evening in early 1971, when the other band members were out having a drink. "We got his drums and put him in the hallway," Johns later explained, "and then hung two MI60 mikes from the staircase and pointed them towards the kit… I remember sitting there thinking it sounded utterly amazing, so I ran out of the truck and said 'Bonzo, you gotta come in and hear this!' He shouted 'Whoa! That's it! That's what I've been hearing!'" The rest of the song was built around Page's gritty riff and some wailing, heavily echoed harmonica by Plant. The song's apocalyptic atmosphere proved hard to recreate live, and it was only performed twice, early on their 1975 US tour.

White Summer

Jimmy Page's solo acoustic showcase for much of the band's early live career. He'd been playing it since Yardbirds days, adding to it all the while. Its origins lay in Davy Graham's 'She Moved Thru the Bizarre', an arrangement of the traditional Irish folk song 'She Moved Through the Fair'. A version appeared on the Yardbirds' *Little Games* LP in 1967, but it was never released by Led Zeppelin. It did, however, show up briefly as background music for a section of the band's *Song Remains The Same* film in 1976. Page would typically play it alone onstage, though Bonham would occasionally contribute percussion. Between 1968 and 1970 it typically segued into 'Black Mountain Side', though later in their career it preceded 'Kashmir'. A famous performance of it was taped for UK TV's *Julie Felix Show* on April 26th 1970. Page told the NME in October 1974 that "I used to do a long instrumental called 'White Summer', in strange tunings. It went on for about 20 minutes – until everyone fell asleep. Then we'd play a bit of rock n' roll."

Whole Lotta Love

Starting with a suggestive chuckle from Plant and Jimmy Page's quintessential riff, the first track on *Led Zeppelin II* is arguably the song that defines Led Zeppelin above all others. Jones has suggested that the riff emerged during an onstage improvisation, though Page told Uncut magazine in May 2008 that this is "Absolutely incorrect. It was put together when we were rehearsing some music for the second album. I had a riff, everyone was at my house, and we kicked it in from there. Never was it written during a gig." Plant's lyrics, meanwhile, were inspired by US bluesman Willie Dixon's 'You Need Love' (perhaps via a cover version included on the Small Faces' 1966 debut LP), and Dixon successfully sued Led Zeppelin over them in 1985. The cacophonous middle section (in which Plant wails orgasmically over sounds including a steel mill, napalm being fired and a squalling theremin) was carefully devised by Page and engineer Eddie Kramer, but edited from the single release, which climbed to US #4 in late January 1970 (backed with 'Living Loving Maid'). Having issued it in numerous other territories, Atlantic sought to release it in the UK on December 5th 1969, but only 500 copies escaped to Manchester before Peter Grant blocked it. These now sell for large sums. In October 1970 Plant's former mentor Alexis Korner took an instrumental version of the song to #13 into the UK charts with CCS. This was also used as the theme to *Top Of The Pops* – a show that Led Zeppelin had made it clear they'd never appear on. Fittingly, the song closed the band's last ever concert, at Berlin's Eissporthalle on July 7th 1980.

Williams, John

Obscure Bedford singer-songwriter who is thought to have collaborated with Page and 'Big' Jim Sullivan on the 1968 *Maureeny Wishfull Album*, though Sullivan has no recollection of the project today. Williams also recorded a self-titled solo LP in 1967 (Columbia SX6169), produced by Vic Keary, which featured two tracks published by 'James

Page Music'. The rest were published by 'Mark Music', presumably owned by Page's friend and occasional collaborator Jon Mark. It is not known what became of Williams.

Wilson, BJ
b. March 18th 1947 / d. Oct. 8th 1990

Drummer with Procol Harum, who was considered as a possibility for the nascent Led Zeppelin before Jimmy Page encountered John Bonham.

Wilson, Robert
Coroner for East Berkshire who ruled in October 1980 (following evidence from Jimmy Page, Bonham's assistant Rex King and others) that John Bonham's death had been been accidental, through inhalation of vomit following heavy drinking. Pathologist Edmund Hemden, who conducted the post-mortem, explained to the inquest (held in Windsor) that the huge amount of alcohol the drummer had consumed had caused his lungs to fill with fluid, making breathing impossible.

Winchester Cathedral
Ancient Gothic place of worship whose choirmaster John Paul Jones allegedly considered becoming in late 1973, having grown disillusioned with Led Zeppelin's hectic touring schedule. Peter Grant allegedly persuaded him against the idea, perhaps sickened at the recollection of the New Vaudeville Band's 1966 novelty hit of the same name, on the back of which he'd organised tours of the US for a hastily-assembled version of the group.

Wolverhampton Wanderers
Midlands football team ardently supported by Robert Plant, who was unsuccessfully approached to be their Honorary Secretary in the early 70s. He regularly attended their games during his tenure with Led Zeppelin, however, and even played in some testimonial matches. After his car accident on Rhodes in August 1975, they rewarded his loyalty by inviting him to build up his fitness by training with them.

Wonder, Stevie
b. May 13th 1950

Blind US singer, songwriter and record producer. Similarities have been pointed out between his 1972 hit 'Superstition' and Led Zeppelin's 'Trampled Under Foot' (included on 1975's *Physical Graffiti* LP). Both songs start with funky riffs played on a Hohner Clavinet, but beyond that the likeness is slim. Wonder was also the inadvertent cause of great embarrassment to the whole band and Roy Harper in Los Angeles one evening in 1975. As Richard Cole describes it, 'One late afternoon, to relieve the monotony, I suggested that the band dress up in drag... Without much coaxing, the trio of groupies who were with us that day took off their clothes and Jimmy, Robert and Bonzo squeezed their way into them... We almost forgot we were supposed to meet George Harrison for a dinner date. When he arrived at the hotel, he had Stevie Wonder with him. George took one look at Bonzo, Robert and Pagey in drag and he fell on the floor laughing. The hysterics were contagious and soon everyone was shrieking – everyone, that is, except Stevie. "What's so funny?" Stevie kept saying… The laughter stopped, and we we just wanted to crawl into a hole, dresses and all.'

Wood, Ron
b. June 1st 1947
Guitarist with the Rolling Stones as of 1975, and a friend of Jimmy Page's since the mid-1960s, when he'd played guitar with the Birds and shared stages with the Yardbirds. On February 14th 1975 he joined Led Zeppelin onstage at Long Island's Nassau Coliseum for 'Communication Breakdown', while on September 17th 1977 he and Page played an impromptu gig in Page's local pub, the Half Moon in Plumpton.

Wood, Roy
b. Nov. 8th 1946
Leader of The Move and a major figure in the 1960s Birmingham music scene that also yielded Robert Plant and John Bonham. In May 1978 John Bonham played drums on 'Keep Your Hands on the Wheel', included on his *On the Road Again* LP. "John was a very good friend of mine," Wood told Goldmine magazine in 1994. "We used to live in the same area. In fact, I was working down at Rockfield Studios in Wales and John and Robert came in. They were rehearsing down at Clearwell Castle with Zeppelin, which was only just down the road from the studio. They were looking to record a new album and they came in to see what the studio was like, because they'd never recorded there before. I think I was working on that track at the time and I think I played drums myself on the album. I got my kit set up and John was messing around on the kit and I said, 'Do you fancy having a go on this one?' And he said 'all right', and we just went for it, it was great."

Woodstock
The most famous music festival of all time, held in upstate New York between August 15th and 18th 1969 and attended by an estimated 500,000 people. Typifying their unconventional approach, Led Zeppelin declined to appear, despite a report to the contrary appearing in Record Mirror on May 31st. Peter Grant later explained to Tight But Loose: "We were asked to do Woodstock and Atlantic were very keen, and so was our US promoter, Frank Barsalona. I said no because at Woodstock we'd have just been another band on the bill." Instead they played dates in Boston and Toronto. A more prosaic explanation for their non-appearance has also been suggested, however: existing contracts forbade them from accepting further engagements.

Yamaha GX1

Keyboard on which John Paul Jones composed much of *In Through The Out Door*. "I'd got a brand new instrument, the Yamaha GX1," he told Mojo magazine in June 2004, "and suddenly there was no one else to play with. I was at rehearsals and Robert turned up, and between us we pretty much wrote the album."

Yardbirds, the

The leading British R&B group of the 1960s after the Rolling Stones, and the launchpad for Eric Clapton, Jeff Beck and Jimmy Page. When Clapton left the band in January 1965, Page declined to join (disliking the way that Clapton's departure had been described to him as 'a holiday'), and proposed Beck instead. As the band built an increasing following in America, Page persisted with session work in the UK, as well as releasing a solo single (see *She Just Satisfies*). On the evening of May 16th 1966, Page, John Paul Jones, Keith Moon and pianist Nicky Hopkins joined Beck in London's IBC Studios to lay down a track entitled Beck's Bolero. Such was the chemistry (particularly between Beck and Page) that there was immediate, if idle, talk of forming a band to be called Lead

Zeppelin, albeit with the omission of Jones. That was premature, but a month later Page was again invited to join the Yardbirds, this time to replace bassist Paul Samwell-Smith (who was leaving after an especially chaotic gig at an Oxford University ball, attended by Page, who'd been driven down by Beck). Frustrated by the limitations of session work, Page accepted (despite the considerable drop in earnings), and played his first gig with them at London's Marquee Club on June 21st. The news was announced on the front of Melody Maker four days later, on the 25th.

It quickly became obvious that his talents were wasted on bass, so he and Beck became twin guitarists for a while (with rhythm guitarist Chris Dreja shifting to bass). Beck's insecurity and Page's insouciance – coupled with their inevitable competitive edge – didn't make for a harmonious atmosphere, though. After a short UK tour supporting the Rolling Stones in September and October, they filmed a brief live scene for Michel Antonioni's film *Blow-Up*, playing 'Stroll On' in a nightclub. The only single to feature both guitarists – the brilliant 'Happenings Ten Years Time Ago' / 'Psycho Daisies' – appeared in the UK that October (as Columbia DB8024), and peaked at a disappointing #43. That month they embarked on some fractious US dates as part of 'Dick Clark's Caravan Of Stars', which involved endless coach journeys and surviving on hamburgers. Beck missed numerous US shows, supposedly owing to tonsillitis, and after another six-week visit to the US ending in late November, he left the band in December ('Beck's Bolero' finally appeared in March 1967, as the B-side to his UK solo hit 'Hi Ho Silver Lining').

The group remained a quartet thereafter, though their commercial glory days were behind them. A single, 'Little Games' / 'Puzzles', was released in the UK in April 1967 and flopped. Peter Grant took over their management from Simon Napier-Bell the following month, shortly before they embarked on tours of France, Japan and America. Following the failure of their last 45 in the UK, the *Little Games* LP was released only in the US that July, where it failed to sell (peaking at #80). It is of interest to Led Zeppelin fans for the indications it gives of the direction the band would take, such as the folky 'White Summer' (never recorded by Led Zeppelin, but a regular feature of the acoustic portion of their gigs) and the guitar-bowing on 'Tinker Tailor Soldier Sailor' and 'Glimpses'.

Though the band were no longer having hits (a 45 coupling Manfred Mann cover 'Ha Ha Said The Clown' with 'Tinker Tailor Soldier Sailor' reached only US #45 in July, while 'Ten Little Indians' / 'Drinking Muddy Water' peaked at #96 in October, with neither being released in the UK), they were still making good money on the US live circuit, under Grant's astute management. Page's increasingly experimental, heavy guitar playing sat uneasily with Relf and McCarty's desire to go in a folkier direction, however, and EMI had all but lost interest in the band in the UK, where the release of their final 45, 'Goodnight Sweet Josephine' / 'Think About It' was cancelled. It crept out in the US in March 1968 (with a different take on the A-side), peaking at a miserable #127, and the exhausted musicians returned to the UK at a low ebb in the early summer. Shortly afterwards, Relf and McCarty announced that they'd had enough, to Page's disappointment. As he told the NME in November 1972: "I never wanted the Yardbirds to break up at all – it was me who was trying hardest of all to keep them together. Keith Relf had other ideas."

In an article published in Go magazine in the US on June 21st, under the headline 'Yardbirds Split But The Name Goes On', it was announced that the band was to be renamed 'The Yardbirds Featuring Jimmy Page'. The piece went on to state that the guitarist was already auditioning drummers and singers to join him and Dreja, and that he wanted a singer who could also play keyboards, and intended to feature mellotron prominently in the new set-up. Though none of this came to be, towards the end of the Yardbirds' lifespan they had started to play two songs that would crop up in Led Zeppelin's repertoire: the instrumental 'White Summer' and 'I'm Confused', a re-arrangement of Jake Holmes's 'Dazed and Confused'. Their final gig was played on Sunday, July 7th 1968 at Luton Technical College in Bedfordshire, following which Relf and McCarty formed Together, while Page and Dreja agreed to fulfil some outstanding dates in Scandinavia that autumn.

see *the New Yardbirds*

Your Time Is Gonna Come

Devised by John Paul Jones (who contributes the lengthy organ intro), this soulful number was included on the band's debut, with lyrics echoing the Ray Charles classic 'I Believe To My Soul'. The band never performed the song live, though Robert Plant extemporised a snatch of it onstage in Tokyo on September 24th 1971.

You Shook Me

Blues standard penned by Willie Dixon and J.B. Lenoir, a bludgeoning rendition of which appeared on Led Zeppelin's March 1969 debut. The song had also appeared in August 1968 on *Truth*, the solo debut of Page's former Yardbirds bandmate Jeff Beck. Beck was said to be furious at the time, though Page categorically denied stealing his arrangement. By 1971 Beck had long since forgotten any annoyance he might have felt at the time, telling Rolling Stone on June 24th that his first impression of Led Zeppelin's rendition was that "it wasn't the same, but the choice, the approach, was in the same bracket... I just thought, well – I'm quite honoured, really. I do wish them the best of luck." The song remained a regular feature of Led Zeppelin's live performances until 1973.

Zacron

see *Drew, Richard*

Zeppelin, Eva Von

Scion of the famous airship-making family, and an early thorn in Led Zeppelin's side. Her determination for them not to use her family name, or the image of the stricken Hindenburg on the front of *Led Zeppelin I*, called for some careful diplomacy. "They may be world-famous, but a couple of shrieking monkeys are not going to use a privileged family name without permission," she blasted on Danish TV shortly before the band made an appearance in February 1970. Page explained to *Melody Maker* that "The whole thing is absurd. The first time we played Copenhagen she turned up and tried to stop a TV show. She couldn't, of course, but we invited her to meet us to show we were nice young lads. We calmed her down, but on leaving the studio, she saw our LP cover of an airship in flames and exploded! So – it's shrieking monkeys now. But she is quite a nice person." The band went on to play their concert on February 28th as the Nobs, a decision that received widespread publicity and showed up not only their whimsical sense of humour, but also Frau Von Zeppelin's pomposity. She didn't trouble them again.

Zoso

Though it wasn't intended to be interpreted as a word, this is a popular approximation of Jimmy Page's symbol on the band's untitled fourth LP. Its inspiration came from Aleister Crowley's book *The Equinox of the Gods*, but – as Page told ZigZag magazine in November 1972: "It wasn't supposed to be a word at all, but something entirely different and with a different meaning altogether." Quite what that meaning was, he didn't explain. Apparently the only person he did ever tell was Robert Plant, who has since forgotten.

APPENDIX ONE

THE ALBUMS

LED ZEPPELIN
(Atlantic 588 171)

Released: Jan. 12th 1969 (US) / March 28th 1969 (UK)
Highest chart position: #10 (US) / #6 (UK)

Side One
1. Good Times Bad Times (*Page / Jones / Bonham*)
2. Babe I'm Gonna Leave You (*Bredon / Page*)
3. You Shook Me (*Dixon*)
4. Dazed And Confused (*Holmes / Page*)

Side Two
1. Your Time Is Gonna Come (*Page / Jones*)
2. Black Mountain Side (*trad. arr. Page*)
3. Communication Breakdown (*Page / Jones / Bonham*)
4. I Can't Quit You Baby (*Dixon*)
5. How Many More Times? (*Page / Jones / Bonham*)

Robert Plant – lead vocals, harmonica
Jimmy Page – electric, acoustic and pedal steel guitars, backing vocals
John Paul Jones – bass, organ, backing vocals
John Bonham – drums, timpani, backing vocals

with Viram Jasani (tabla drums on 'Black Mountain Side')

Produced by Jimmy Page
Director of engineering – Glyn Johns

Recorded and mixed in Olympic Studios, London in September /
October 1968

Back cover photo – Chris Dreja
Cover design – George Hardie

Executive producer – Peter Grant

'Very occasionally a long-playing record is released that defies immediate classification or description, simply because it's so obviously a turning point in rock music… This Led Zeppelin album is like that. This album makes you feel good. It makes you feel good to hear a band with so much to say and the conspicuous ability to say it as they feel it; to translate what's in their heads to music' – **Felix Dennis, Oz, March 1969**

'The popular formula in this, the aftermath era of such successful British bluesmen as Cream and John Mayall, seems to be: add to an excellent guitarist who, since leaving the Yardbirds and / or Mayall, has become a minor musical deity, a competent rhythm section and a pretty soul-belter who can do a good spade imitation. The latest of the British groups so conceived offers little that its twin, the Jeff Beck Group, didn't say as well or better three months ago' – **John Mendelsohn, Rolling Stone, March 15th 1969**

'Jimmy Page triumphs! While long-hailed as one of the British guitar-slinging heroes, he has been a rather mystical figure to British fans... He proves to be technical, tasteful, turbulent and torrid. His band is imaginative and exciting. Robert Plant is a new singer of stature, and John Paul Jones and John Bonham are more than adequate. Their material does not rely on obvious blues riffs, although when they do play them they avoid the emaciated feebleness of most so-called British blues bands... This Zeppelin is really in a gas new bag!' – **Melody Maker, March 29th 1969**

'Led Zeppelin never flag on this LP, which should be played at full volume. On no account allow your mother to turn it down – let alone off' – **Beat Instrumental, April 1969**

'Way-out blues sounds that go mad at times, that's the forte of this new group... Robert Plant is an inconsistent lead vocalist who sometimes sounds good and sometimes sounds bad... John Paul Jones, well-known helper-out on various records hitherto, is on bass and organ, and John Bonham on drums. All three back Plant vocally. They perform their over-dramatic songs well and thump up a storm on their instruments, but I felt they overdid it a bit at times' – **Allen Evans, NME, April 5th 1969**

LED ZEPPELIN II
(Atlantic 588 198)

Released: October 22nd 1969
Highest chart position: #1 (US) / #1 (UK)

Side One
1. Whole Lotta Love (*Page / Bonham / Plant / Jones*) 5:34
2. What Is and What Should Never Be (*Page / Plant*) 4:44
3. The Lemon Song (*Page / Bonham / Plant / Jones*) 6:19
4. Thank You (*Page / Plant*) 4:47

Side Two
1. Heartbreaker (*Page / Bonham / Plant / Jones*) 4:14
2. Living Loving Maid (She's Just a Woman) (*Page / Plant*) 2:39
3. Ramble On (*Page / Plant*) 4:23
4. Moby Dick (*Bonham / Jones / Page*) 4:21
5. Bring It On Home (*Page / Plant*) 4:20

Robert Plant – lead vocals, harmonica
Jimmy Page – electric, acoustic and pedal steel guitars, backing vocals
John Paul Jones – bass, organ, backing vocals
John Bonham – drums, timpani, backing vocals

Produced by Jimmy Page
Engineered by Eddie Kramer, George Chkiantz, Andy Johns and Chris Huston

Mixed at A&R Studios, New York
Director of engineering and mixing – Eddie Kramer

Recorded between January and August 1969 in Olympic Studios, London / Mirror Sound, Los Angeles / Mystic Studios, Los Angeles / Morgan Studios, London / A&R Studios, New York / Juggy Sound, New York / Atlantic Studios, New York / Mayfair Studios, New York / Hut Studios, Vancouver

Artwork by David Juniper
Executive producer – Peter Grant

'It's difficult to capture stage excitement on record, but Led Zeppelin come very near to it' – **Disc & Music Echo, November 1st 1969**

'On first hearing, the numbers on this album seem weak plagiarisms of those on the group's first record… but getting into the cuts is wholly worthwhile, and the key is in the production' – **International Times, November 6th 1969**

'Music for the paranoiac 20th Century city man – another brilliant album from the remarkable Led Zeppelin… This brings out more of the group, particularly Robert Plant, and also shows that the Zeppelin isn't confined to one groove… Perhaps the most remarkable thing about Led Zeppelin II is that the group manages to maintain the element of surprise, so obvious when you first hear them… Led Zeppelin have been one of the success stories of 1969, and this extremely good album will serve to quicken their stride towards a place among the world's top groups' – **Nick Logan, NME, November 8th 1969**

'Wow! Led Zeppelin don't disappoint with this LP, a really LOUD and raunchy item, plenty of crashing guitar work, sensual rhythms and everything you'd expect from the reputation group. Page works on some good guitar within the framework of the basic sounds, and there's a lot going on. Nice middle to the fold-out sleeve, 20th Century Fox art. This one should be a smash with anyone who likes well-played nouveau rock – and some tracks show delicacy too' – **Record Mirror, November 8th 1969**

'Much looser than the group's first… still almost worth buying anyway for Plant's tortured voice and Page's guitar, which at times sounds as disturbing as car tyres screaming to a crash' – **Time Out, November 22nd 1969**

'Seems as if it's just one especially heavy song extended over the space of two whole sides' – **John Mendelsohn, Rolling Stone, December 27th 1969**

LED ZEPPELIN III
(Atlantic 2401 002)

Released: Oct. 5th 1970 (US) / Oct. 23rd 1970 (UK)
Highest chart position: #1 (US) / #1 (UK)

Side One
1. Immigrant Song (*Page / Plant*) 2:23
2. Friends (*Page / Plant*) 3:54
3. Celebration Day (*Page / Plant / Jones*) 3:28
4. Since I've Been Loving You (*Page / Plant / Jones*) 7:24
5. Out On the Tiles (*Page / Plant / Bonham*) 4:05

Side Two
1. Gallows Pole (*trad. arr. Page / Plant*) 4:56
2. Tangerine (*Page*) 2:57
3. That's the Way (*Page / Plant*) 5:37
4. Bron-Y-Aur Stomp (*Page / Plant / Jones*) 4:16
5. Hats Off To (Roy) Harper (*trad. arr. Charles Obscure*) 3:42

Robert Plant - vocals, harmonica
Jimmy Page – acoustic, electric and pedal steel guitar, backing vocals
John Paul Jones - bass guitar, organ, mandolin, backing vocals
John Bonham - drums, percussion, backing vocals

Produced by Jimmy Page
Engineered by Andy Johns (London and New York) / Terry Manning (Memphis)

Recorded at Ardent Studios, Memphis / Headley Grange, Hampshire (with the Rolling Stones' Mobile Studio) / Island Studios, London / Olympic Studios, London

Mixed at Island Studios, London / Electric Lady Studios, New York / Ardent Studios, Memphis

Artwork by Zacron (Richard Drew)
Executive producer – Peter Grant

'Credit must be given to BRON-Y-AUR, a small derelict cottage in South Snowdonia, for painting a somewhat forgotten picture of true completeness which acted as an incentive to some of the musical statements' – August 1970

'It's out! Led Zeppelin's third album has finally exploded over our heads, and it's their best yet… a beautifully creative programme which spans as many moods as a widescreen epic. The best way to dig 'III' is to put on headphones, close eyes and light a cigarette… Production is up to their usual pace-setting standard, and there is no evidence here of a 'drying-up' of ideas. In many ways this is a much better album than 'II', with many varied approaches, and they maintain a steady standard of taste and execution. But the main quality is that indefinable Zeppelin magic' – **Chris Welch, Melody Maker, October 10th 1970**

'Perhaps it's because we all waited so long and expected so much, that this album leaves you feeling deflated… the overall effect lacks that funky, exciting live feeling they captured before… the album seems to lack sparkle. Don't Led Zeppelin care anymore?' – **Disc, October 10th 1970**

'Their third album deviates little from the track laid by the first two, even though they go acoustic on several numbers. Most of the acoustic stuff sounds like standard Zep graded down decibel-wise, and the heavy blitzes could've been outtakes from *Zeppelin II*. In fact, when I first heard the album my main impression was the consistent anonymity of most of the songs… I must mention a song called 'That's the Way', because it's the first song they've ever done that has truly moved me. Son of a gun, it's beautiful' – **Lester Bangs, Rolling Stone, November 26th 1970**

'So this is the group that toppled the Beatles from the top spot as the world's most popular group! That's a very heavy title to keep off the ground. *Zeppelin III* is the first wax offering since the band received the title, and thus is the album which will be compared to *Sgt. Pepper* etc. Whereas volumes I and II were original and heavy, this does not progress, but merely moves along in the same groove… The opening tracks on each side, 'Immigrant Song' and 'Gallows Pole' are, with 'Tangerine' and, to an extent, 'Hats Off To (Roy) Harper', the only ones which deserve to be on an album with such great advance sales' – **Beat Instrumental, November 1970**

[UNTITLED]
(Atlantic 240 1012)

Released: November 8th 1971
Highest Chart position: #1 (UK) / #2 (US)

Side one
1. Black Dog (*Page / Plant / Jones*)
2. Rock And Roll (*Page / Plant / Jones / Bonham*)
3. The Battle Of Evermore (*Page / Plant*)
4. Stairway To Heaven (*Page / Plant*)

Side two
1. Misty Mountain Hop (*Page / Plant / Jones*)
2. Four Sticks (*Page / Plant*)
3. Going To California (*Page / Plant*)
4. When The Levee Breaks (*Page / Plant / Jones / Bonham / Memphis Minnie*)

Robert Plant - vocals, harmonica
Jimmy Page – acoustic, electric and pedal steel guitar, backing vocals
John Paul Jones - bass guitar, organ, mandolin, backing vocals
John Bonham - drums, percussion, backing vocals

with Sandy Denny (vocals on 'The Battle Of Evermore')

Produced by Jimmy Page
Engineered by Andy Johns
Mixed by Andy Johns and George Chkiantz at Island Studios, London / Olympic Studios, London

Recorded between December 1970 and March 1971 at Headley Grange, Hampshire (with The Rolling Stones' Mobile Studio) / Island Studios, London / Sunset Sound, Los Angeles.

Design co-ordination – Graphreaks
Inside illustration – 'The Hermit' by Barrington Colby
Photography by Keith Morris
Executive producer – Peter Grant

'Side one contains perhaps the band's best recorded material to date. For me it smashes everything Zeppelin have done before into the ground… this one gives you the best of both worlds – the excitement of the rock and rolling Zeppelin and the beauty of the acoustical side, which they are more and more into' – **Sounds, November 20th 1971**

'By far their best album to date, and has a depth and maturity to it which can only result from recording and performing experience. It has many moods and many styles and seems more emotionally loaded than any of their other albums; they seem to convey a wisdom through experience into their music now' – **Disc, November 20th 1971**

'It might seem a bit incongruous to say that Led Zeppelin – a band never particularly known for its tendency to understate matters – has produced an album which is remarkable for its low-keyed and tasteful subtlety, but that's just the case here… What's been saved is the pumping adrenaline drive that held the key to such classics as 'Communication Breakdown' and 'Whole Lotta Love', the incredibly sharp and precise vocal dynamism of Robert Plant, and some of the tightest arranging and producing Jimmy Page has yet seen his way toward doing' – **Lenny Kaye, Rolling Stone, December 23rd 1971**

'This album presents a less-heavy Zeppelin and seems to turn on the amazing vocals of Robert Plant. On one extreme there's Rock And Roll which is a fast-moving number following the musical idiom indicated in its title and at the other extreme there's The Battle Of Evermore. Evermore is a much gentler number than I've heard Zeppelin perform before. It features Plant on vocals against a soft backing of acoustic guitar and mandolin. The high points of the number come when harmonies are introduced. Going To California is another opportunity for Plant to experience his abilities and it comes off well. It's relieving to discover that Zep. have not trapped themselves in the 'heavy bag' but are competent in other fields of music without ever forsaking their originality' – **Beat Instrumental, November 1971**

HOUSES OF THE HOLY
(Atlantic K50014)

Released: March 28th 1973
Highest chart position: #1 (UK) / #1 (US)

Side One
1. The Song Remains the Same (*Page / Plant*) 5:32
2. The Rain Song (*Page / Plant*) 7:39
3. Over the Hills and Far Away (*Page / Plant*) 4:50
4. The Crunge (*Bonham / Jones / Page / Plant*) 3:17

Side Two
5. Dancing Days (*Page / Plant*) 3:43
6. D'yer Mak'er (*Bonham / Jones / Page / Plant*) 4:23
7. No Quarter (*Jones / Page / Plant*) 7:00
8. The Ocean (*Bonham / Jones / Page / Plant*) 4:31

Robert Plant - vocals
Jimmy Page – guitars
John Paul Jones - bass, synthesised bass, organ, mellotron, synthesiser
John Bonham – drums

Produced by Jimmy Page
Engineered by Eddie Kramer, George Chkiantz and Keith Harwood

Recorded between January and August 1972 at Stargroves and Headley Grange (with the Rolling Stones' Mobile Studio) and Island Studios, London

Mixed at Olympic Studios, London / Electric Lady Studios, New York

Artwork by Hipgnosis

Executive producer – Peter Grant

'The 14-month wait was worth it. Led Zeppelin, without shouting their claims, have come up with an album that will stand as one of rock's best. Plant's voice is often electronically distorted, the rhythms are complex, the lyrics enigmatic, but after a few plays the songs assume larger proportions. Cool, clear, measured, mysterious and beautiful, Zeppelin have taken group-rock further than any. This is a landmark of an album' – **Record Mirror, March 31st 1973**

'After the initial brilliance of 'The Song Remains The Same' a malaise began to creep in, reaching a nadir in the sadly indulgent 'D'yer Mak'er'… there is not one song (with the exception of 'The Song Remains The Same') that has any buzz of excitement… Perhaps a cool appraisal of this album will spur them on to greater efforts' – **Melody Maker, March 31st 1973**

'Both Plant and Page are strangely sluggish and vacant, exploding only occasionally on tracks like 'The Rain Song', 'Over The Hills And Far Away' and 'Dancing Days'. And they seem to have run out of good melody lines, as witnessed by 'The Crunge' (a straight jam that barrels along on a couple of chords)… on two or three hearings it comes over as an incredibly inconsistent piece of work' – **Disc, March 31st 1973**

'It shows what a superb guitarist Jimmy Page is, as well as highlighting Robert Plant's vocal talents. They both shine throughout the album, almost obliterating the talents of John Bonham on drums and John Paul Jones on bass / keyboards and a variety of modern electronics… I'm a little disappointed that Zep haven't come on just a little heavy in places, but from an advancement point of view this is a fine album' – **Sounds, April 7th 1973**

'Several tracks are simply bad jokes (maybe worse), like the schlocky, string-drenched torpor of 'The Rain Song', not to mention 'The Crunge', an absolute dog of a song. Then there's 'D'yer Mak'er', which sounds like an inept 50s paean… As far as I can see, the whole problem throughout is that the music just doesn't go anywhere. Three of Jimmy Page's compositions are strictly lukewarm rock and roll, his fourth ('The Rain Song') is rather dire, and the four cuts not penned by Page are uniformly poor" - **Phonograph Record, May 1973**

'One of the dullest and most confusing albums I've heard this year… Led Zeppelin's forte has always been rockin' the blues; if they took themselves seriously they'd realize that they are foolish to step outside that genre… While they've been busy denying their blues-rock roots, Robert Plant's vocals have lost their power and the band's instrumental work has lost its traces of spontaneity… Page and friends should realise their limitations and get back to playing the blues-rock that moves mountains. Until they do, Led Zeppelin will remain Limp Blimp' – **Gordon Fletcher, Rolling Stone, June 7th 1973**

PHYSICAL GRAFFITI
(Swan Song SSK 89400)

Released: February 24th 1975
Highest chart position: #1 (UK) / #1 (US)

Side One
1. Custard Pie (*Page / Plant*) 4:13
2. The Rover (*Page / Plant*) 5:37
3. In My Time Of Dying (*Bonham / Jones / Page / Plant*) 11:05

Side Two
1. Houses Of The Holy (*Page / Plant*) 4:02
2. Trampled Under Foot (*Jones / Page / Plant*) 5:37
3. Kashmir (*Bonham / Page / Plant*) 8:32

Side Three
1. In The Light (*Jones / Page / Plant*) 8:46
2. Bron-Yr-Aur (*Page*) 2:06
3. Down By The Seaside (*Page / Plant*) 5:13
4. Ten Years Gone (*Page / Plant*) 6:32

Side Four
1. Night Flight (*Jones / Page / Plant*) 3:36
2. The Wanton Song (*Page / Plant*) 4:07
3. Boogie With Stu (*Bonham / Jones / Page / Plant / Stewart / Valens*) 3:53
4. Black Country Woman (*Page / Plant*) 4:24
5. Sick Again (*Page / Plant*) 4:42

Produced by Jimmy Page
Engineered by Ron Nevison and Andy Johns (Headley Grange) / Eddie Kramer (Stargroves) / George Chkiantz (Olympic) / Andy Johns (Island)
Mixed by Keith Harwood (Olympic) / Eddie Kramer (Electric Lady)

Recorded between July 1970 and October 1974 at Headley Grange (with Ronnie Lane's Mobile Studio) / Stargroves (with the Rolling Stones' Mobile Studio) / Olympic Studios, London / Island Studios, London
Mixed at Olympic Studios, London / Electric Lady Studios, New York

Package concept and design: AGI (Mike Doud – London / Peter Corriston
– New York)
Photography by Elliot Erwit, BP Fallon and Roy Harper
Tinting by Maurice Tate
Window illustration by Dave Heffernan
Executive producer – Peter Grant

'The first Led Zeppelin album since the first that I can imagine myself
wanting to explore beyond the call of duty... by turns brain-numbingly
intrusive, exhilarating, over-stretched, effectively concise, obvious and full
of little surprises. If the albums were sold separately, I'd buy sides three and
four. Throughout the album the bedrock and momentum is supplied by
John Bonham... without being outstanding, John Paul Jones supports him
adequately... the many guitars of Jimmy Page are deployed with accuracy
and style' - **Steve Peacock, Sounds, March 8th 1975**

'This two-record set, the product of almost two years' labour, is the band's
Tommy, Beggar's Banquet and *Sgt. Pepper* rolled into one: Led Zeppelin's bid
for artistic respectability... *Physical Graffiti* only confirms Led Zeppelin's pre-
eminence among hard rockers. Although it contains no startling breakthroughs,
it does afford an impressive overview of the band's skill... Throughout the
album, Page and the band tap a strange lot of sources, although the result is
always pure Zeppelin" – **Jim Miller, Rolling Stone, March 27, 1975**

'More direct and self-assured than anything that preceded it... after repeated
listenings, the 83-minute set emerges as one of the decade's most viscerally
engaging albums. Its excitement is just about uninterrupted... Sides 3 and
4 are not as uniformly terrific as the first two, but there's enough variety
to justify a double album... All in all, a massive chunk of super-sound' –
Phonograph Record, March 1975

'*Physical Graffiti* is, in fact, better than the other five offerings, the band being
more confident, more arrogant in fact, and more consistent. The choice
of material is varied, giving the audience a chance to see all sides of the
band. Equal time is given to the cosmic and the terrestrial, the subtle and
the passionate... This is not pop music, but a harder stuff, more heady and
potent, like a round of whiskeys and coke' – **Creem, May 1975**

PRESENCE
(Swan Song SSK 59402)

Released: March 31st 1976
Highest chart position: #1 (UK) / #1 (US)

Side One
1. Achilles Last Stand (*Page / Plant*) 10:25
2. For Your Life (*Page / Plant*) 6:20
3. Royal Orleans (*Bonham / Jones / Page / Plant*) 2:58

Side Two
1. Nobody's Fault But Mine (*Page / Plant*) 6:27
2. Candy Store Rock (*Page / Plant*) 4:07
3. Hots On For Nowhere (*Page / Plant*) 4:43
4. Tea For One (*Page / Plant*) 9:27

Robert Plant – vocals, harmonica
Jimmy Page – electric guitars
John Paul Jones – bass guitar (4 and 8-string)
John Bonham – drums, percussion

Produced by Jimmy Page

Engineered and mixed by Keith Harwood and Jimmy Page

Tape engineer – Jeremy Gee

Recorded and mixed in November and December 1975 at Musicland Studios, Munich, Germany

Sleeve design – Hipgnosis

Executive producer – Peter Grant

'From the opening bars of the remarkable 'Achilles Last Stand', the unity of Zeppelin, in the eighth year of their existence, is striking... Zeppelin have come among us again, this time with a whole album of dynamic compositions delivered with a fervour that shows how anxious the band were to get down their new ideas... an album that has pace, direction and tremendous style' – **Melody Maker, April 10th 1976**

'The rumours were right: this album is unadulterated rock and roll. It's fantabulous. The music is really basic and simple, almost every song an archetypal Zeppo riff, but while they've kept the basic framework, everything within has been stripped down, polished, and reassembled. The sound is monolithic, with a definite feel of the room they're in... the real star of the show is Bonzo, who is dynamite. He's everywhere, bulldozing songs along mercilessly... In terms of urgency and aggression and an all-out attack on rock and roll, this is Zeppelin's best album yet' – **Sounds, April 10th 1976**

'Led Zeppelin's seventh album confirms this quartet's status as heavy-metal champions of the known universe... Although Page and Plant are masters of the form, emotions often conflict and the results are mixed. A few bars from one piece convince the listener he's hearing the greatest of rock & roll, then the very next few place him in a nightmarish 1970 movie about deranged hippies... At their best, the riffs are clean and purifying. The two dreary examples of blooze ('Tea for One', 'For Your Life') may stretch even the diehards' loyalty, but make no mistake: *Presence* is another monster' – **Stephen Davis, Rolling Stone, May 20th 1976**

THE SONG REMAINS THE SAME
(SSK 89402)

Released: September 28th 1976
Highest chart position: #1 (UK) / #1 (US)

Side One
1. Rock and Roll (*Bonham / Jones / Page / Plant*) 4:03
2. Celebration Day (*Jones / Page / Plant*) 3:49
3. The Song Remains the Same (*Page / Plant*) 6:00
4. Rain Song (*Page / Plant*) 8:25

Side Two
1. Dazed and Confused (*Page*) 26:53

Side Three
1. No Quarter (*Jones / Page / Plant*) 12:30
2. Stairway To Heaven (*Page / Plant*) 10:58

Side Four
1. Moby Dick (*Bonham / Jones / Page*) 12:47
2. Whole Lotta Love (*Dixon / Bonham / Jones / Page / Plant*) 14:25

Robert Plant – vocals
Jimmy Page – acoustic guitar, electric guitar
John Paul Jones – bass guitar, keyboards
John Bonham – drums

Produced by Jimmy Page
Mixed at Electric Ladyland Studios, New York

Recorded live at Madison Square Garden, New York
Engineer – Eddie Kramer
Mastered at Sterling Sound, New York

Artwork by Hipgnosis / George Hardie
Liner notes by Cameron Crowe

Executive producer – Peter Grant

'In this ephemeral, up to the minute, 48 thrills in 48 hours rock 'n' roll world, does three year-old Led Zeppelin interest you? Especially when they were spotlighting what is arguably their worst album? You betcha. Zep is, after all, the supposed premier live band and not all of us have heard the live bootlegs. We've waited eight years for this. Well, tough titties, because in one word this effort is B-O-R-I-N-G... The exception is side one. 'Rock And Roll' kicks off at high speed, doing just what the title describes... They keep it up for 'Celebration Day', 'The Song Remains The Same' and 'The Rain Song'. The rest, without visual support, is a mish-mash of the good, the bad and the ugly" – **Sounds, October 16th 1976**

IN THROUGH THE OUT DOOR
(Swan Song SS59 410)

Released: September 28th 1976
Highest chart position: #1 (UK) / #1 (US)

Side One
1. In the Evening (*Jones / Page / Plant*) 6:49
2. South Bound Saurez (*Jones / Plant*) 4:12
3. Fool in the Rain (*Jones / Page / Plant*) 6:12
4. Hot Dog (*Page / Plant*) 3:17

Side Two
1. Carouselambra (*Jones / Page / Plant*) 10:31
2. All My Love (*Jones / Plant*) 5:53
3. I'm Gonna Crawl (*Jones / Page / Plant*) 5:30

Robert Plant – vocals
Jimmy Page – acoustic guitar, electric guitar
John Paul Jones – bass guitar, keyboards
John Bonham – drums

Produced by Jimmy Page

Engineered by Leif Masses

Assistant engineer – Lennard Östlund

Recorded in November and December 1978 at Polar Studios, Stockholm, Sweden

Artwork by Hipgnosis

Executive producer – Peter Grant

'Two of the songs performed at Knebworth were only tasters for things to come. In Through The Out Door is the grand reunion. The renaissance after the trials and tribulations of recent years, it ties up the inconclusive ends of the rather disjointed Presence album and their patchy live double effort… 'Carouselambra' is the sharpest spearhead on the album. Magnificent with its flowing mane of keyboards, steered and nurtured by Bonham… 'All My Love' is the peacock of side two. It's an heroic song, couched in the same tones as the opening to 'Stairway To Heaven'…' – **Record Mirror, September 1st 1979**

'Sadly, John Bonham's exuberance on *In Through the Out Door* is matched only by Robert Plant's appetite for inanity... Of the seven songs only one has orchestral guitar rumble, and Plant's singing has fallen to the occasion in the other six. With this paucity of good music to work with, Plant fails to create phrasing good enough to disguise the lyrics, which are horrible... 'In The Evening' has the only great guitar riff on the entire album. The rest of the songs are based on John Paul Jones' keyboard work. Though an excellent musician, Jones functions best behind Jimmy Page, not in front of him... Side two consists of three of the least effective songs the band has ever recorded' – **Charles M. Young, Rolling Stone, October 18th 1979**

CODA
(Swan Song 79 0051)

Released: November 19th 1972
Highest chart position: #6 (US) / #4 (UK)

Side One
1. We're Gonna Groove (*Bethea / King*) 2:40
2. Poor Tom (*Page / Plant*) 3:01
3. I Can't Quit You Baby (*Dixon*) 4:17
4. Walter's Walk (*Page / Plant*) 4:31

Side Two
1. Ozone Baby (*Page / Plant*) 3:35
2. Darlene (*Bonham / Jones / Page / Plant*) 5:06
3. Bonzo's Montreux (*Bonham*) 4:17
4. Wearing and Tearing (*Page / Plant*) 5:31

Robert Plant – vocals, harmonica
Jimmy Page – acoustic guitar, electric guitar, producer, electronic treatments
John Paul Jones – bass, piano, keyboards
John Bonham – drums, vocals

Produced by Jimmy Page
Engineered by Andy Johns / Vic Maile / Eddie Kramer / Leif Masses / John Timperly
Mixed at Sol Studio, Cookham, Berkshire
Mixing engineer – Stuart Epps

Recorded at Morgan Studios, London (June 25th 1969) / Olympic Studios, London (June 5th 1970) / Royal Albert Hall, London (January 9, 1970) / Stargroves (with the Rolling Stones' Mobile Studio, May 15th 1972) / Polar Studios, Stockholm (November 1978) / Mountain Studios, Montreux (September 12th 1976)

Sleeve design by Hipgnosis

Executive producer – Peter Grant

'They really were pretty great, and these eight outtakes – three from their elephantine blues phase, three from their unintentional swan song – aren't where to start discovering why. But, despite the calculated clumsiness of the beginnings and the incomplete orchestrations of the end, everything here but the John Bonham Drum Orchestra would convince a disinterested party – a Martian, say' – **Robert Christgau, Village Voice, December 1982**

'A resounding farewell from the greatest heavy metal band that ever strutted the boards… the album chronicles a ten-year adventure in high guitar drama and maximum blast. If the record seems a bit of a cheat timewise – it clocks in at 32:40 – the song selection is a marvel of compression, deftly tracing the Zeppelin decade with eight powerful, previously unreleased tracks, and no unnecessary elaboration' – **Kurt Loder, Rolling Stone, January 20th 1983**

APPENDIX TWO

THE SINGLES

US releases

03/69   *Communication Breakdown / Good Times Bad Times*
(Atlantic 2613) #80

11/69   *Whole Lotta Love / Livin' Lovin' Maid (She's Just A Woman)*
(Atlantic 2690) #4

11/70   *Immigrant Song / Hey Hey What Can I Do*
(Atlantic 2777) #16

12/71   *Stairway To Heaven*
(Atlantic PR-175, promo only)

12/71   *Black Dog / Misty Mountain Hop*
(Atlantic 2849) #15

02/72   *Rock And Roll / Four Sticks*
(Atlantic 2865) #47

05/73   *Over The Hills And Far Away / Dancing Days*
(Atlantic 2970) #51

09/73   *D'yer Mak'er / The Crunge*
(Atlantic 2986) #20

04/75   *Trampled Under Foot / Black Country Woman*
(Swan Song SS 70102) #38

06/76   *Candy Store Rock / Royal Orleans*
(Swan Song SS 70110) *did not chart*

12/79   *Fool In The Rain / Hot Dog*
(Swan Song SS 71003) #21

UK releases

11/69	*Good Times Bad Times*	(1-sided acetate, Atlantic 584 268)

11/69 *Good Times Bad Times*
(1-sided acetate, Atlantic 584 268)

11/69 *Communication Breakdown / Good Times Bad Times*
(promo only, Atlantic 584 269)

12/69 *Whole Lotta Love / Livin' Lovin' Maid (She's Just A Woman)*
(withdrawn, Atlantic 584 309)

05/73 *D'Yer Mak'er / Over The Hills And Far Away*
(promo only, Atlantic K 10296)

04/75 *Trampled Under Foot / Black Country Woman*
(giveaway, die-cut sleeve, Swan Song DC1)

04/75 *Trampled Under Foot / Black Country Woman*
(wrong cat. #, Swan Song SSK 19403)

08/79 *Wearing & Tearing / Darlene*
(unreleased Knebworth souvenir, existence
unconfirmed)

APPENDIX THREE

THE CONCERTS

First Scandinavian tour[1]

07/09/68 Copenhagen – Gladsaxe Teen Club
07/09/68 Copenhagen – Brondby Pop Club
08/09/68 Nykobing – Raventlow Park
08/09/68 Roskilde – Fjordvilla
12/09/68 Stockholm – Gronalund Tivoli
13/09/68 Stockholm – Inside Club
14/09/68 Knivsta – Angby Park
15/09/68 Gothenburg – Liseberg Amusement Park
17/09/68 Malmö – Klub Bongo

First UK tour

04/10/68 Newcastle – Mayfair Ballroom
18/10/68 London – Marquee Club
19/10/68 Liverpool University
25/10/68 Surrey University
09/11/68 London - Roundhouse [2]
16/11/68 Manchester College of Science and Technology
23/11/68 Sheffield University
29/11/68 Richmond Athletic Club
10/12/68 London – Marquee Club
13/12/68 Canterbury – Country Club
16/12/68 Bath – Pavilion
19/12/68 Exeter – Town Hall
20/12/68 London – Fishmongers Hall, Wood Green

First US tour

26/12/68 Denver Coliseum
27/12/68 Seattle – Center Arena
28/12/68 Vancouver – Pacific Coliseum
30/12/68 Spokane – Gonzaga University Gym
31/12/68 Oregon – Portland
02/01/69 Los Angeles – Whiskey A Go Go
03/01/69 Los Angeles – Whiskey A Go Go
04/01/69 Los Angeles – Whiskey A Go Go
05/01/69 Los Angeles – Whiskey A Go Go
09/01/69 San Francisco – Fillmore West
10/01/69 San Francisco – Fillmore West
11/01/69 San Francisco – Fillmore West
12/01/69 San Francisco – Fillmore West

1 Billed as The Yardbirds
2 Their first show billed as Led Zeppelin

13/01/69 San Diego – Fox Theatre
15/01/69 Iowa University
16/01/69 New Orleans
17/01/69 Detroit – Grande Ballroom
18/01/69 Detroit – Grande Ballroom
19/01/69 Detroit – Grande Ballroom
23/01/69 Boston – Boston Tea Party
24/01/69 Boston – Boston Tea Party
25/01/69 Boston – Boston Tea Party
26/01/69 Boston – Boston Tea Party
31/01/69 New York – Fillmore East
01/02/69 New York – Fillmore East
02/02/69 Toronto – Rockpile
07/02/69 Chicago – Kinetic Playground
08/02/69 Chicago – Kinetic Playground
14/02/69 Miami – Thee Image
15/02/69 Miami – Thee Image

Second UK tour
01/03/69 Plymouth – Vandike Club
03/03/69 London – BBC Maida Vale
05/03/69 Cardiff – Locarno
07/03/69 London – Bluesville 69 Club, Hornsey Wood
10/03/69 Edmonton – Cooks Ferry Inn
12/03/69 Leicester University

Second Scandinavian tour
13/03/69 Copenhagen – Brondby Pop Club
13/03/69 Copenhagen – Gladsaxe Teen Club
14/03/69 Stockholm – Koncerthaus
14/03/69 Uppsala University
15/03/69 Copenhagen – Gladsaxe Teen Club
16/03/69 Copenhagen – Tivoli Koncertsal

Second UK tour continues
21/03/69 London – *How Late It Is* (TV show)
22/03/69 Birmingham – Mothers Club
25/03/69 Staines – *Supershow* (film recording)
28/03/69 London – Marquee Club
30/03/69 Southall – Farx Club, Southall
31/03/69 Edmonton – Cooks Ferry Inn
01/04/69 London – Klooks Kleek, Hampstead

253

05/04/69 London – Roundhouse
08/04/69 Welwyn Garden City – Cherry Tree
12/04/69 Tolworth – Toby Jug
14/04/69 Stoke-on-Trent
17/04/69 Sunderland

Second US tour
18/04/69 New York – University Jazz Festival
24/04/69 San Francisco – Fillmore West
25/04/69 San Francisco – Winterland Ballroom
26/04/69 San Francisco – Winterland Ballroom
27/04/69 San Francisco – Fillmore West
29/04/69 Los Angeles – Whiskey A Go Go
30/04/69 Los Angeles – Whiskey A Go Go
01/05/69 Irvine – Crawford Hall
02/05/69 Pasadena – Rose Palace
03/05/69 Pasadena – Rose Palace
04/05/69 Santa Monica – Civic Center
05/05/69 Santa Monica – Civic Center
09/05/69 Edmonton – Gardens
10/05/69 Vancouver – PNE Agrodome
11/05/69 Seattle - Aquatheatre
13/05/69 Honolulu – Civic Auditorium
16/05/69 Detroit – Grande Ballroom
17/05/69 Athens – Ohio University
18/05/69 Minneapolis - Guthrie Memorial Theatre
21/05/69 New York – Syracuse
23/05/69 Santa Clara – Pop Festival (afternoon)
23/05/69 Chicago – Kinetic Playground (evening)
24/05/69 Chicago – Kinetic Playground
25/05/69 Columbia – Merriweather Post Pavilion
27/05/69 Boston – Boston Tea Party
28/05/69 Boston – Boston Tea Party
29/05/69 Boston – Boston Tea Party
30/05/69 New York – Fillmore East
31/05/69 New York – Fillmore East

Third UK tour
08/06/69 Newcastle City Hall
13/06/69 Birmingham Town Hall
15/06/69 Manchester Free Trade Hall
20/06/69 Newcastle City Hall

21/06/69 Bristol – Colston Hall
25/06/69 Paris – Antenne Culturelle (French TV Recording)
26/06/69 Portsmouth – Guildhall
27/06/69 London – Playhouse Theatre (BBC recording)
28/06/69 Bath – Festival
29/06/69 London – Royal Albert Hall (2 shows)

Extra dates
10/10/69 Paris – Olympia
12/10/69 London – Lyceum
13/10/69 Holland – Haarlem

Third US tour
05/07/69 Atlanta – Atlanta Pop Festival
06/07/69 Newport – Newport Jazz Festival
08/07/69 Florida – Miami
09/07/69 Florida – Tampa
10/07/69 Florida – Jacksonville
11/07/69 Baltimore – Laurel Pop Festival
12/07/69 Philadelphia – Spectrum
13/07/69 New York – Singer Bowl
16/07/69 Detroit – Olympia
18/07/69 Chicago – Kinetic Playground
19/07/69 Chicago – Kinetic Playground
20/07/69 Cleveland – Musicarnival
21/07/69 New York – Central Park
25/07/69 Milwaukee – State Fair Park
26/07/69 Vancouver – PNE Agrodome
27/07/69 Seattle – Pop Festival
29/07/69 Seattle – Kinsmen Field House
30/07/69 Salt Lake City – Terrace Ballroom
31/07/69 Oregon – Eugene
01/08/69 Santa Barbara – Fairgrounds
03/08/69 Houston – Music Hall
04/08/69 Dallas – State Fair Festival[3]
06/08/69 Sacramento – Memorial Auditorium
07/08/69 Berkeley – Community Theatre
08/08/69 San Bernardino – Swing Auditorium
09/08/69 Anaheim – Convention Centre
10/08/69 San Diego – Sports Arena
16/08/69 Asbury Park – Convention Hall

3 It has been speculated that this show did not take place

17/08/69 Wallingford – Oakdale Theatre
18/08/69 Toronto – Rockpile (two shows)
21/08/69 Framingham – Carousel Theatre
22/08/69 Florida – Dania Pirates World
23/08/69 Florida – Dania Pirates World
24/08/69 Jacksonville – Veterans Memorial Coliseum
29/08/69 New York – Singer Bowl
30/08/69 New York – Singer Bowl
31/08/69 Dallas – International Pop Festival

European dates
03/10/69 Scheveningen – Circus Theatre
04/10/69 Rotterdam – De Doelen
05/10/69 Amsterdam – Concertgebouw
10/10/69 Paris – Olympia Theatre
12/10/69 London – Lyceum Ballroom
13/10/69 Haarlem, Holland

Fourth US tour
17/10/69 New York – Carnegie Hall (two shows)
18/10/69 Detroit – Olympia Stadium
19/10/69 Chicago – Kinetic Playground
24/10/69 Cleveland – Public Auditorium
25/10/69 Boston – Boston Gardens
26/10/69 Charlotte – Independence Coliseum
30/10/69 Buffalo – Kleinhans Music Hall
31/10/69 Providence – Rhode Island Auditorium
01/11/69 Syracuse – War Memorial Auditorium
02/11/69 Toronto – O'Keefe Centre (two shows)
04/11/69 Kitchener – Memorial Auditorium
05/11/69 Kansas City – Memorial Hall
06/11/69 San Francisco – Winterland
07/11 /69 San Francisco – Winterland
08/11/69 San Francisco – Winterland

French date
06/12/69 Paris – L'Ecole Centrale

Fourth UK tour
07/01/70 Birmingham –Town Hall
08/01/70 Bristol – Colston Hall
09/01/70 London – Royal Albert Hall

13/01/70 Portsmouth – Guild Hall
15/01/70 Newcastle – City Hall
16/01/70 Sheffield – City Hall
24/01/70 Leeds – Town Hall
17/02/70 Edinburgh – Usher Hall

First European tour
24/02/70 Helsinki – Kulturhous
25/02/70 Gothenburg – Konserthuset
26/02/70 Stockholm – Konserthuset
27/02/70 Amsterdam – Concertgebouw
28/02/70 Copenhagen – K.B. Hallen[4]
02/03/70 Brussels, Belgium
03/03/70 Cologne, Germany
04/03/70 Hanover, Germany
05/03/70 Frankfurt, Germany
06/03/70 Nuremburg, Germany
07/03/70 Geneva, Switzerland – Victoria Concert Hall
08/03/70 Munich, Germany – Cirkus Kroner
09/03/70 Vienna, Austria – Koncerthalle
11/03/70 Hamburg – Musikhalle
12/03/70 Dusseldorf – Rheinhalle
14/03/70 Montreux – Jazz Festival

Fifth US tour
21/03/70 Vancouver – Pacific Coliseum
22/03/70 Seattle – Center Arena
23/03/70 Portland – Memorial Coliseum
25/03/70 Denver – Coliseum
26/03/70 Salt Lake City – Salt Palace
27/03/70 Los Angeles – Forum
28/03/70 Dallas – Memorial Auditorium
29/03/70 Houston – Hofheinz Pavilion
30/03/70 Pittsburgh – Civic Centre
31/03/70 Philadelphia – Spectrum
01/04/70 Boston – Boston Gardens
02/04/70 Charleston – Civic Center
03/04/70 Macon – Coliseum
04/04/70 Indianapolis – Coliseum
05/04/70 Baltimore – Civic Centre
07/04/70 Charlotte – Independence Coliseum

---

4 Billed as 'The Nobs'

08/04/70 Raleigh – Dorten Arena
09/04/70 Tampa – Curtis Nixon Hall
10/04/70 Miami – Convention Hall
11/04/70 St Louis – Kiel Auditorium
12/04/70 Minneapolis –Metropolitan Center
13/04/70 Montreal – Forum
14/04/70 Ottawa – Civic Centre
15/04/70 Winnipeg, Canada
16/04/70 Evansville, Indiana – Roberts Stadium
17/04/70 Memphis – Mid-South Coliseum
18/04/70 Phoenix – Arizona Coliseum

European Interlude
22/06/70 Reykjavik – Laugardalsholl Sports Centre
28/06/70 Bath Festival
16/07/70 Cologne – Sportshalle
17/07/70 Essen – Grugahalle
18/07/70 Frankfurt – Festhalle
19/07/70 Berlin – Deutschlandhalle

Sixth US tour
15/08/70 New Haven – Yale Bowl
17/08/70 Hampton – Hampton Roads Coliseum
19/08/70 Kansas City – Municipal Auditorium
20/08/70 Oklahoma City – Coliseum Fairgrounds
21/08/70 Oklahoma – Tulsa
22/08/70 Fort Worth – Tarrant Convention Centre
23/08/70 San Antonio – Hemisphere Arena
24/08/70 Missouri – St Louis
25/08/70 Nashville – Municipal Auditorium
26/08/70 Cleveland – Public Hall
28/08/70 Detroit – Olympia
29/08/70 Winnipeg – Arena
31/08/70 Milwaukee – Arena
01/09/70 Seattle – Center Coliseum
02/09/70 Oakland – Coliseum
03/09/70 San Diego – Sports Arena
04/09/70 Los Angeles – Forum
05/09/70 Honolulu – International Center
06/09/70 Honolulu – International Center
09/09/70 Boston – Boston Gardens
14/09/70 New York – Rochester
19/09/70 New York City / Madison Square Garden (two shows)

Fifth UK tour ('Back To The Clubs')

05/03/71 Belfast – Ulster Hall
06/03/71 Dublin – Boxing Stadium
09/03/71 Leeds University
10/03/71 Canterbury – University
11/03/71 Southampton – University
13/03/71 Bath Pavillion
14/03/71 Stoke – The Place, Hanley
18/03/71 Newcastle – Mayfair Ballroom
19/03/71 Manchester University
20/03/71 Sutton Coldfield – Belfry
21/03/71 Nottingham – Boat Club
23/3/71 London – Marquee Club
01/4/71 London – Paris Theatre (BBC recording)

European mini-tour

03/05/71 Copenhagen – K.B.Hallen
04/05/71 Odense – Fyns Forum
10/5/71 Liverpool University
05/07/71 Milan – Vigorelli Stadium[5]

Warm-up shows

07/08/71 Montreux – Casino
08/08/71 Montreux – Casino

Seventh US tour

19/08/71 Vancouver – Pacific Coliseum
20/08/71 Seattle – Center Coliseum
21/08/71 Los Angeles – Forum
22/08/71 Los Angeles – Forum
23/08/71 Fort Worth – Tarrant Convention Center
24/08/71 Dallas – Memorial Auditorium
25/08/71 Houston – Hofheinz Pavilion
26/08/71 San Antonio – Municipal Auditorium
27/08/71 Oklahoma City – Civic Auditorium
28/08/71 St. Louis – Arena
29/08/71 New Orleans – Municipal Auditorium
31/08/71 Orlando – Civic Auditorium
01/09/71 Florida – Hollywood Sportatorium
03/09/71 New York – Madison Square Garden

---

5 Show abandoned after twenty minutes owing to rioting crowd

04/09/71 Toronto – Maple Leaf Gardens
05/09/71 Chicago – Amphitheater
06/09/71 Boston – Boston Gardens
09/09/71 Hampton – Beach Coliseum
10/09/71 Syracuse – Onadaga War Memorial
11/09/71 Rochester – Memorial Auditorium
13/09/71 Berkeley – Community Theater
14/09/71 Berkeley – Community Theater
16/09/71 Honolulu – International Center
17/09/71 Honolulu – International Center

First Japanese tour
23/09/71 Tokyo – Budokan Hall
24/09/71 Tokyo – Budokan Hall
27/09/71 Hiroshima – Shiei Taiikukan
28/09/71 Osaka – Festival Hall
29/09/71 Osaka – Festival Hall

Sixth UK tour
11/11/71 Newcastle – City Hall
12/11/71 Sunderland – Locarno
13/11/71 Dundee – Caird Hall
16/11/71 Ipswich – St Matthew's Baths
17/11/71 Birmingham – Kinetic Circus
18/11/71 Sheffield University
20/11/71 London – Wembley Empire Pool[6]
21/11/71 London – Wembley Empire Pool
23/11/71 Preston Town Hall
24/11/71 Manchester Free Trade Hall
25/11/71 Leicester University
29/11/71 Liverpool Stadium
30/11/71 Manchester – King's Hall Belle Vue
02/12/71 Bournemouth – Royal Ballroom
09/12/71 Coventry – Locarno
15/12/71 Salisbury – City Hall

Australia / New Zealand tour
16/02/72 Perth – Subiaco Oval
19/02/72 Adelaide – Memorial Drive
20/02/72 Melbourne – Kooyong Tennis Courts
24/02/72 Auckland – Western Spring Stadium

---

6 The so-called 'Electric Magic' shows

27/02/72 Sydney – Showgrounds
29/02/72 Brisbane – Festival Hall

Warm-up shows
27/05/72 Amsterdam – Oude Rai
28/05/72 Brussels – Vorst National

Eighth US tour
06/06/72 Detroit – Cobo Hall
07/06/72 Montreal – Forum
08/06/72 Boston – Boston Gardens
09/06/72 Charlotte – Coliseum
10/06/72 Buffalo – Memorial Auditorium
11/06/72 Baltimore – Civic Centre
13/06/72 Philadelphia – Spectrum
14/06/72 Long Island – Nassau Coliseum
15/06/72 Long Island – Nassau Coliseum
17/06/72 Portland – Memorial Coliseum
18/06/72 Seattle – Coliseum
19/06/72 Seattle – Coliseum
21/06/72 Denver – Coliseum
22/06/72 San Bernardino – Swing Auditorium
23/06/72 San Diego – Sports Arena
24/06/72 Berkeley – Community Centre
25/06/72 Los Angeles – Forum
27/06/72 Long Beach – Arena
28/06/72 Tucson – Community Center

Second Japanese tour
02/10/72 Tokyo – Budokan Hall
03/10/72 Tokyo – Budokan Hall
04/10/72 Osaka – Festival Hall
05/10/72 Nagoyashi – Kokaido
09/10/72 Osaka – Festival Hall
10/10/72 Kyoto – Kaikan #1 Hall

Return to Montreux
27/10/72 Montreux – Casino
28/10/72 Montreux – Casino

Seventh UK tour

30/11/72 Newcastle City Hall
01/12/72 Newcastle City Hall
03/12/72 Glasgow – Green's Playhouse
04/12/72 Glasgow – Green's Playhouse
07/12/72 Manchester – Hard Rock
08/12/72 Manchester – Hard Rock
11/12/72 Cardiff – Capitol Theatre
12/12/72 Cardiff – Capitol Theatre
16/12/72 Birmingham Odeon
17/12/72 Birmingham Odeon
20/12/72 Brighton Dome
22/12/72 London – Alexandra Palace
23/12/72 London – Alexandra Palace
02/01/73 Sheffield – City Hall
07/01/73 Oxford – New Theatre
14/01/73 Liverpool – Empire Theatre
15/01/73 Stoke – Trentham Gardens
16/01/73 Aberystwyth – King's Hall
18/01/73 Bradford – St George's Hall
20/01/73 Southampton University
21/01/73 Southampton – Gaumont Theatre
25/01/73 Aberdeen – Music Hall
27/01/73 Dundee – Caird Hall
28/01/73 Edinburgh – King's Theatre
30/01/73 Preston – Guild Hall

Third European tour

02/03/73 Copenhagen – K.B.Hallen
04/03/73 Gothenburg – Scandinavium Arena
06/03/73 Stockholm – Kungliga Tennishallen
07/03/73 Stockholm – Kungliga Tennishallen
10/03/73 Oslo
11/03/73 Rotterdam
12/03/73 Brussels
13/03/73 Frankfurt - Festhalle
14/03/73 Nuremburg – Messenhalle
16/03/73 Vienna – Konserthaus
17/03/73 Munich – Olympiahalle
19/03/73 Berlin – Deutschlandhalle
21/03/73 Hamburg – Musichalle
22/03/73 Essen – Grughalle

23/03/73 Cologne
24/03/73 Offenburg – Orthenau Halle
26/03/73 Lyons – Palais des Sports
27/03/73 Nancy – Parc des Expositions
01/04/73 Paris – Palais des Sports
02/04/73 Paris – Palais des Sports

Ninth US tour

04/05/73 Atlanta – Braves Stadium
05/05/73 Tampa Stadium[7]
07/05/73 Jacksonville – Civic Center
10/05/73 Tuscaloosa – University
11/05/73 St Louis – Kiel Auditorium
13/05/73 Mobile – City Auditorium
14/05/73 New Orleans – Municipal Auditorium
16/05/73 Houston – Arena
18/05/73 Dallas – Memorial Auditorium
19/05/73 Fort Worth – Tarrant Convention Centre
22/05/73 San Antonio – Hemisphere Arena
23/05/73 Albuquerque University
25/05/73 Denver – Coliseum
26/05/73 Salt Lake City – Salt Palace
28/05/73 San Diego – Sports Arena
31/05/73 Los Angeles – Forum
02/06/73 San Francisco – Kezar Stadium[8]
03/06/73 Los Angeles – Forum
06/07/73 Chicago – Auditorium
07/07/73 Chicago – Auditorium
08/07/73 Indianapolis – Arena
09/07/73 St Paul – Civic Centre
10/07/73 Milwaukee – Arena
12/07/73 Detroit – Cobo Hall
13/07/73 Detroit – Cobo Hall
15/07/73 Buffalo – War Memorial Auditorium
17/07/73 Seattle – Coliseum
18/07/73 Vancouver – PNE Coliseum
19/07/73 Philadelphia – Spectrum
20/07/73 Boston – Boston Gardens
21/07/73 Providence – Civic Center

---

7 The band broke the Beatles' then-world record for concert attendance and gross at this gig, with an audience of 56,800 and a take of $309,000
8 The band broke their own world record for a gross at a single gig (set at Tampa Stadium on May 5th) by raking in $325,000 here

23/07/73 Baltimore – Civic Center
24/07/73 Pittsburgh – Three Rivers Stadium
25/07/73 Boston – Boston Gardens
27/07/73 New York – Madison Square Garden[9]
28/07/73 New York – Madison Square Garden
29/07/73 New York – Madison Square Garden

Warm-up shows
11/01/75 Rotterdam – Ahoy
12/01/75 Brussels – Vorst National

Tenth US tour
18/01/75 Minneapolis -Metropolitan Sports Centre
20/01/75 Chicago Stadium
21/01/75 Chicago Stadium
22/01/75 Chicago Stadium
24/01/75 Cleveland Coliseum
25/01/75 Indianapolis Arena
29/01/75 Greensboro Coliseum
31/01/75 Detroit – Olympia Stadium
01/02/75 Pittsburgh – Civic Arena
02/02/75 Pittsburgh – Civic Arena
03/02/75 New York – Madison Square Garden
04/02/75 Long Island – Nassau Coliseum
06/02/75 Montreal – Forum
07/02/75 New York – Madison Square Garden
08/02/75 Philadelphia – Spectrum
10/02/75 Washington – Capitol Center
12/02/75 New York – Madison Square Garden
13/02/75 Long Island – Nassau Coliseum[10]
14/02/75 Long Island – Nassau Coliseum
16/02/75 St Louis – Missouri Arena
27/02/75 Houston – Coliseum
28/02/75 Baton Rouge – Louisiana State University
03/03/75 Fort Worth – Tarrant Convention Center
04/03/75 Dallas – Memorial Auditorium
05/03/75 Dallas – Memorial Auditorium
07/03/75 Austin – Events Centre
10/03/75 San Diego – Sports Arena

---

9 These three concerts were recorded and filmed for the *Song Remains The Same* LP
   and movie
10 Rolling Stones guitarist Ron Wood joins the band for an encore of 'Communication
   Breakdown'

11/03/75 Long Beach – Pacific Arena
12/03/75 Long Beach – Pacific Arena
17/03/75 Seattle – Coliseum
19/03/75 Vancouver – Coliseum
20/03/75 Vancouver – Coliseum
21/03/75 Seattle – Coliseum
24/03/75 Los Angeles – Forum
25/03/75 Los Angeles – Forum
27/03/75 Los Angeles – Forum

UK return
17/05/75 London – Earl's Court
18/05/75 London – Earl's Court
23/05/75 London – Earl's Court
24/05/75 London – Earl's Court
25/05/75 London – Earl's Court
10/12/75 St Helier, Jersey – Behan's Club[11]

Eleventh US tour
01/04/77 Dallas - Memorial Auditorium
03/04/77 Oklahoma City - Myriad
06/04/77 Chicago Stadium
07/04/77 Chicago Stadium
09/04/77 Chicago Stadium[12]
10/04/77 Chicago Stadium
12/04/77 Minneapolis – Metropolitan Center
13/04/77 St Paul – Civic Center
15/04/77 St Louis – Missouri Arena
17/04/77 Indianapolis – Market Square Arena
19/04/77 Cincinnati – Riverfront Coliseum
20/04/77 Cincinnati – Riverfront Coliseum
23/04/77 Atlanta – Omni
25/04/77 Louisville – Kentucky Fairgrounds
27/04/77 Cleveland – Richfield Coliseum
28/04/77 Cleveland – Richfield Coliseum
30/04/77 Pontiac – Silverdome[13]
18/05/77 Birmingham – Jefferson Coliseum
19/05/77 Baton Rouge – State University
21/05/77 Houston – Summit

---

11 This impromptu club date was the band's first performance since Plant's car accident in August
12 Show abandoned after an hour owing to Jimmy Page feeling unwell
13 Set a new world concert attendance record of 76,229

22/05/77 Fort Worth – Convention Centre[14]
25/05/77 Washington – Largo Capitol Centre
26/05/77 Washington – Largo Capitol Centre
28/05/77 Washington – Largo Capitol Centre
30/05/77 Washington – Largo Capitol Centre
31/05/77 Greensboro – Coliseum
03/06/77 Tampa Stadium[15]
07/06/77 New York – Madison Square Garden
08/06/77 New York – Madison Square Garden
11/06/77 New York – Madison Square Garden
12/06/77 New York – Madison Square Garden
13/06/77 New York – Madison Square Garden
14/06/77 New York – Madison Square Garden
19/06/77 San Diego - Sports Arena
21/06/77 Los Angeles – Forum
22/06/77 Los Angeles – Forum
23/06/77 Los Angeles – Forum[16]
25/06/77 Los Angeles – Forum
26/06/77 Los Angeles – Forum
27/06/77 Los Angeles – Forum
17/07/77 Seattle Kingdome
20/07/77 Tempe – Activities Center
23/07/77 Oakland Coliseum
24/07/77 Oakland Coliseum

Knebworth warm-up shows
23/07/79 Copenhagen – Falkonertheatre
24/07/79 Copenhagen – Falkonertheatre

The UK return
04/08/79 Knebworth Festival
11/08/79 Knebworth Festival

Fourth European tour
17/06/80 Dortmund – Westfalenhalle
18/06/80 Cologne – Sporthalle
20/06/80 Brussels – Vorst National
21/06/80 Rotterdam – Ahoy
23/06/80 Bremen – Stadthalle

---

14 Bad Company guitarist Mick Ralphs joined the band for encores
15 Abandoned after twenty minutes owing to heavy rain
16 Keith Moon of The Who joined the band to drum on encores

24/06/80 Hannover – Messenhalle
26/06/80 Vienna – Stadthalle
27/06/80 Nuremberg – Messezentrumhalle[17]
29/06/80 Zurich – Hallenstadion
30/06/80 Frankfurt – Festhalle
02/07/80 Mannheim – Eisstadium
03/07/80 Mannheim – Eisstadium
05/07/80 Munich – Olympiahalle[18]
07/07/80 Berlin – Eissporthalle

Proposed Twelfth US Tour[19]

17/10/80 Montreal – Forum [*cancelled*]
19/10/80 Landover – Capitol Center [*cancelled*]
21/10/80 Landover – Capitol Center [*cancelled*]
22/10/80 Philadelphia – Spectrum [*cancelled*]
23/10/80 Landover – Capitol Center [*cancelled*]
26/10/80 Cleveland – Richfield Coliseum [*cancelled*]
27/10/80 Cleveland – Richfield Coliseum [*cancelled*]
28/10/80 Cleveland – Richfield Coliseum [*cancelled*]
29/10/80 Detroit – Joe Louis Stadium [*cancelled*]
01/11/80 Buffalo – War Memorial Auditorium [*cancelled*]
03/11/80 Philadelphia – Spectrum [*cancelled*]
04/11/80 Philadelphia - Spectrum [*cancelled*]
06/11/80 Pittsburgh – Civic Arena [*cancelled*]
07/11/80 Pittsburgh – Civic Arena [*cancelled*]
09/11/80 St. Paul – Civic Center [*cancelled*]
10/11/80 Chicago Stadium [*cancelled*]
11/11/80 Chicago Stadium [*cancelled*]
12/11/80 Chicago Stadium [*cancelled*]
13/11/80 Chicago Stadium [*cancelled*]
15/11/80 Chicago Stadium [*cancelled*]

---

17 Abandoned after fifteen minutes owing to John Bonham eating too many bananas
18 Bad Company drummer Simon Kirke joins the band for encores
19 Billed as 'Led Zeppelin: The Eighties – Part One', these dates were announced by Peter
    Grant on September 11th 1980. The band was rehearsing for them at the time of John
    Bonham's death, following which they were cancelled.

APPENDIX FOUR

THE SWAN SONG DISCOGRAPHY

ALBUMS

06/74	**Bad Company** *Bad Company* (SS-8410)
11/74	**Pretty Things** *Silk Torpedo* (SS-8411)
02/75	**Led Zeppelin** *Physical Graffiti* (SS-2200)
04/75	**Maggie Bell** *Suicide Sal* (SS-8412)
04/75	**Bad Company** *Straight Shooter* (SS-8413)
12/75	**Pretty Things** *Savage Eye* (SS-8414)
02/76	**Bad Company** *Run With the Pack* (SS-8415)
03/76	**Led Zeppelin** *Presence* (SS-8416)
09/76	**Led Zeppelin** *The Song Remains the Same* (SS-2201)
03/77	**Bad Company** *Burnin' Sky* (SS-8500)
04/77	**Detective** *Detective* (SS-8417)
04/77	**Dave Edmunds** *Get It* (SS-8418)
04/78	**Detective** *It Takes One to Know One* (SS-8504)
09/78	**Dave Edmunds** *Tracks on Wax 4* (SS-8505)
03/79	**Bad Company** *Desolation Angels* (SS-8506)
07/79	**Dave Edmunds** *Repeat When Necessary* (SS-8507)
08/79	**Led Zeppelin** *In Through the Out Door* (SS-16002)
02/81	**Midnight Flyer** *Midnight Flyer* (SS-8509)
04/81	**Dave Edmunds** *Twangin'* (SS-16034)
04/81	**Sad Café** *Sad Café* (SS-16048)
11/81	**Dave Edmunds** *Best of Dave Edmunds* (SS-8510)
02/82	**Midnight Flyer** *Rock n Roll Party* (mini LP) (SS-11002)
02/82	**Jimmy Page** *Death Wish II* (soundtrack) (SS-8511)
06/82	**Robert Plant** *Pictures at Eleven* (SS-8512)
08/82	**Bad Company** *Rough Diamonds* (7900011)
11/82	**Led Zeppelin** *Coda* (7900511)
04/83	**Wildlife** *Wildlife* (7900781)

PROMO LPS

1978	**Detective** *Live From The Atlantic Studios* (LAAS-002)
1978	**Dave Edmunds** *College Radio Network Presents Dave Edmunds and Rockpile* (PR-230)
1982	**Robert Plant** *Pictures at Eleven – An Interview with Alan Freeman* (SAM-154)

SINGLES

11/74 **Pretty Things** *Is It Only Love? / Joey* (SSK-19401)

04/75 **Led Zeppelin** *Trampled Underfoot / Black Country Woman* (SS-70102)

05/75 **Pretty Things** *I'm Keeping… / Atlanta* (SSK-19403)

07/75 **Pretty Things** *Joey / Bridge of God* (SSK-19401)

01/76 **Pretty Things** *Sad Eye / Remember the Boy* (SSK-19405)

05/76 **Pretty Things** *Tonight / It Isn't Rock 'n' Roll* (SSK-19406)

06/76 **Led Zeppelin** *Candy Store Rock / Royal Orleans* (US only) (SS-70110)

07/76 **Dave Edmunds** *Here Comes the Weekend / As Lovers Do* (SSK-19408)

10/76 **Dave Edmunds** *When Or Where? / New York's A Lonely Town* (SSK-19409)

04/77 **Dave Edmunds** *Ju Ju Man / What Did I Do Last Night?* (SSK-19410)

06/77 **Dave Edmunds** *I Knew the Bride / Back to Schooldays* (SSK-19411)

03/78 **Maggie Bell** *Hazell / Night Flighting* (SSK-19412)

09/78 **Dave Edmunds** *Deborah / What Looks Best on You* (SSK-19413)

11/78 **Dave Edmunds** *Television / Never Been In Love* (SSK-19414)

03/79 **Bad Company** *Rock 'n' Roll Fantasy / Crazy Circles* (SSK-19416)

04/79 **Dave Edmunds** *A1 On the Juke Box / It's My Own Business* (SSK-19417)

05/79 **Maggie Bell** *Hazell / Night Flighting* (picture disc) (SSK-19412P)

08/79 **Dave Edmunds** *Girls Talk / Bad Is Bad* (clear vinyl) (SSK-19418)

09/79 **Dave Edmunds** *Queen Of Hearts / Creature from the Black Lagoon* (SSK-19419)

10/79 **Dave Edmunds** *Crawling from the Wreckage / As Lovers Do* (SSK-19420)

12/79 **Led Zeppelin** *Fool In the Rain / I* (US Only) (SS-71003)

01/80 **Dave Edmunds** *Singing the Blues / Boys Talk* (SSK-19422)

03/81 **Midnight Flyer** *Rough Trade / Midnight Love* (SSK-19423)

04/81 **Dave Edmunds** *Almost Saturday Night / You'll Never Get Me Up* (SSK-19424)

07/81 **Dave Edmunds with The Stray Cats** *(I'm Gonna Start) Living If It Kills Me* (SSK-19425)

10/81 **B.A. Robertson and Maggie Bell** *Hold Me / Spring Greens* (BAM-1)

04/82 **Midnight Flyer** *Waiting for You / Rock 'n' Roll Party* (SSK-19426)

09/82 **Maggie Bell** *Goosebumps / Key To Your Heart* (SSK-19428)

09/82 **Robert Plant** *Burning Down One Side / Moonlight in Samosa* (SSK-19429)

09/82 **Robert Plant** *Burning Down One Side / Moonlight in Samosa / Far Post* (12-inch) (SSK-19429T)

01/83 **Maggie Bell** *Crazy / All I Have to Do Is Dream* (MB-1)

09/83 **Wildlife** *Somewhere In The Night / Sun Don't Shine* (B-9842)

APPENDIX FIVE

THE EARLY ATLANTIC PRESS RELEASES

ATLANTIC RECORDS SIGNS ENGLAND'S HOT NEW GROUP, LED ZEPPELIN, IN ONE OF THE BIGGEST DEALS OF THE YEAR

Atlantic Records has signed the hot new English group, Led Zeppelin, to a long term, exclusive recording contract. Although the exact terms of the deal are secret, it can be disclosed that it is one of the most substantial deals Atlantic has ever made. Agreement for the group's services was made between Jerry Wexler, Executive Vice President of Atlantic Records, and Peter Grant, manager of the group.

Led Zeppelin consists of four of the most exciting musicians performing in Britain today. They are Jimmy Page, leader of the group and lead guitarist; John Paul Jones, bassist, pianist, organist, arranger; John Bonham, drums; and Robert Plant, lead vocal and harmonica.

Jimmy Page is a former member of the Yardbirds, the group that spawned the careers of two other great musicians, Eric Clapton and Jeff Beck. Page joined the Yardbirds in 1966 and stayed with the group until it disbanded in the summer of 1968. Prior to joining the Yardbirds he was one of the busiest session men in London.

John Paul Jones is considered one of England's finest arrangers, as well as an outstanding bass player. He is the arranger of Donovan's 'Mellow Yellow', 'Sunshine Superman' and 'Hurdy Gurdy Man', and of the Rolling Stones' 'She's A Rainbow'.

Drummer John Bonham created a sensation with his drum solos while accompanying Tim Rose on his British tour in early 1968. Vocalist Robert Plant is considered one of England's outstanding young blues singers, and has been involved in singing blues since he was 15. All of the members of the group are in their early 20s.

The pulsations surrounding Led Zeppelin have intensified ever since the group recorded its first (and as yet unreleased) album, which was produced by Jimmy Page, just a month ago in London. Top English and American rock musicians who have heard the tracks have compared the LP to the best of Cream and Jimi Hendrix, and have called Led Zeppelin the next group to reach the heights achieved by Cream and Hendrix. This Led Zeppelin LP will be released by Atlantic early in January.

Led Zeppelin is the eighth British group to be signed by Atlantic during the past 24 months. The others are Cream, the Bee Gees, Julie Driscoll / Brian Auger & The Trinity, The Crazy World of Arthur Brown, The Marbles, The Magic Lanterns and Jimmy James & the Vagabonds.

JIMMY PAGE, 23 – lead guitar, pedal steel guitar, acoustic guitar

One of Europe's foremost musicians, Jimmy Page embarked on his career at the age of 15, devoting equal time to playing with various groups while studying at a London art school. His forte was to become session work, and the studio experience he gained from backing up such artists as Mick Jagger and Keith Richard, The Kinks and Donovan, to name a few, gave him a sound knowledge of production, put to extremely good use in the first Led Zeppelin album.

Jimmy joined the Yardbirds in 1966. His first performance with them occurred in London at less than five minutes notice when Paul Samwell-Smith fell ill just prior to a performance and Jimmy offered to replace him for just that one show. The Yardbirds wanted Jimmy to stay but he refused their offer, choosing instead to return to his own busy schedule which sometimes included as many as three recording sessions a day. However, when the Yardbirds offered him a US tour, Jimmy Page reversed his decision, stating that maybe the time had come for him to start playing some of his own stuff. He played bass for that tour, and switched to lead guitar only after Jeff Beck fell out of several dates through illness. When Jeff recovered, he and Jimmy Page played dual lead, which continued after they returned to England and throughout a successful Rolling Stones tour. Anxious to get back to his own session work, Jimmy was ready to leave the Yardbirds in 1967. But Jeff Beck quit instead and Jimmy stayed on until the entire group split to go their separate ways in the summer of 1968.

A remarkable point in Jimmy Page's career came when he produced an Eric Clapton single for Andrew Oldham's Immediate Records two and a half years ago, after Eric had left the Yardbirds. They went into the studio and cut 'Witch Doctor', backed with 'Telephone Blues', said to be one of the finest blues tracks ever recorded in England. As a musician, Jimmy and Eric played together on an album titled *Blues Anytime*, now a collectors' item in England. Jimmy Page, the only unmarried member of Led Zeppelin, lives in a house supported by stilts in Pangbourne on the River Thames. He owns a 20 foot motor launch, fully equipped with an 8-track stereo tape system, and has a studio in his home where he writes and the group sometimes rehearses. His house is furnished in 17th and 18th century antiques and has a huge four-poster bed.

JOHN PAUL JONES, 22 – bass, organ, piano

A sought-after arranger of great repute in England, John Paul Jones is the former bass player with Jet Harris and Tony Meehan, who broke away from Europe's top instrumental group, The Shadows, in the early 60s, and found great success on their own. Today Tony Meehan is a producer at British Decca, and until John Paul Jones joined Zeppelin the pair of them continued to work together on various recording sessions.

Like Jimmy Page, John Paul Jones has arranged and played bass with several leading artists in the studio, his most memorable offerings being the arrangements on Donovan's 'Mellow Yellow', 'Sunshine Superman', 'Hurdy Gurdy Man' (both the single and different tracks on the album), and for the Stones' 'She's a Rainbow' and two tracks on *Their Satanic Majesties Request*. John Paul Jones played organ on the current Jeff Beck *Truth* album, and made one of his rare professional appearances playing bass for Dusty Springfield during her stint at London's Talk of the Town.

Though his brilliance as an arranger and musician brought him fame, John Paul Jones is in agreement with Jimmy Page that session work can be stultifying. The mood that he now creates in his playing proves beyond any shadow of a doubt that he needed to make his move when he did.

JOHN BONHAM, 21 – drums
Still too young to have an illustrious career behind him, John Bonham created a sensation with his drum solos while accompanying Tim Rose on his British tour in 1968. In Jimmy Page's words, "I went to see him and couldn't believe how he was living his music. He's extremely inventive, more so than any other drummer I've heard. He does his drum solo with his hands. When he gets into a trip, the audience goes with him."

John Bonham comes from the industrial town of Birmingham. It is not the hub of British music, but in order to get his experience he played with as many groups as he could in the area, and eventually joined one of the top local outfits, the Band of Joy. The Tim Rose jaunt brought John well deserved national acclaim and opened the door to the next chapter in his success story. Married and still living in Birmingham, John is, according to Jimmy Page, 'the champion beer drinker in England'.

ROBERT PLANT, 21 – lead vocals, harmonica, occasional bass
"Robert Plant's voice is so powerful that when the speakers broke down during our first date in Sweden, you could still hear his voice at the back of the auditorium over the entire group. When he records, we have to put screens around him."

Robert Plant has been into the blues as long as he can remember. While in his teens his roots were country blues, and then he moved on to city blues a la Otis Rush and Buddy Guy. However, his interpretation of today's blues is his own thing, totally different from anything heard before. Like John Bonham, Robert hails from Birmingham and was a member of the Band of Joy, now defunct. He also played on several occasions with Alexis Korner, who fathered the blues revival in England. It was singer Terry Reid, a friend of Jimmy Page's, who suggested Robert for Led Zeppelin, and there was no need to look further.

[*Bob Rolontz, November 1st 1969*]

LED ZEPPELIN - THE BEGINNING

Led Zeppelin began in a small, stuffy rehearsal hall, mid-London, late 1968. "Four of us got together in this two-by-two room and started playing. Then we knew – we started laughing at each other. Maybe it was from relief, or maybe from the knowledge that we knew we could groove together. But that was it. That was just how well it was going." Jimmy Page, master guitarist, former Yardbird, was watching his thoughts, his ambitions, his concealed desires as a musician, take shape in a new supergroup, Led Zeppelin.

"The statement of our first two weeks together is our album. We cut it in 15 hours, and between us wrote 8 of the tracks. Our main problem was knowing what channel to take it along musically. Everyone in the group had such a high musical content we thought each of us would be into our own thing. But it all fell in together. We'll probably always be faced with the fact that individually, each member could cut his own album going in his own direction and it would be great. But all those ideas in one outfit, well, that's pretty fantastic too."

The formation of Led Zeppelin was no easy task. When it became generally known that Jimmy Page was putting a group together, he was inundated with calls from musicians all over the country. When the Yardbirds finally split up in the summer of 1968, Jimmy was ready to take bass player Chris Dreja with him into Led Zeppelin. Chris eventually backed out of the arrangement, choosing instead to go into management. "When I joined the Yardbirds, my main reason was to give myself the opportunity of playing my own music. Before that, my only interest was session work. I began to feel limited not being able to express myself. When I left, it was for almost exactly the same reasons. The group split because everyone began to feel the need to go in his own direction. The pity is, there would have still been great potential."

It was all down to Jimmy Page, alone, on a one-man campaign to make himself heard. As a session guitarist he was, and still is, one of the finest in England, contributing his work to tracks by such stars as the Stones, Donovan, and latterly, Joe Cocker, who took the Beatles' 'With A Little Help From My Friends' to such a smash. "I was working on the Donovan album *Hurdy Gurdy Man* with John Paul Jones who did some of the arrangements. He asked if I could use a bass guitarist in Led Zeppelin. John is an incredible arranger and musician. He didn't need me for a job, but he felt the need to express himself and figured we could do that together. Sessions are great, but you can't get into your own thing. Both myself and John felt that in order to give what we had to offer we had to have a group. He wanted to be part of a group of musicians who could lay down some good things."

"I can't put a tag to our music. Every one of us has been influenced by the blues, but it's one's interpretation of it and how you utilize it. I wish someone would invent an expression, but the closest I can get is contemporary blues. I want us to be raw and basic. That was the whole thing that made the Yardbirds happen. To go into your own thing is fine, but it has to be a form of experimentation that evolves from a basic sound that everyone else knows and can relate to. Perhaps that's why the blues is so big. You can recognize the roots."

It took about two months for Led Zeppelin to emerge. The name was conceived by Jimmy Page when he was still with the Yardbirds, and each member of the group took a shot at recording on his own. Jimmy penned 'Beck's Bolero' for Jeff Beck. Today it's a Beck standard, then it was a track on which the Who's Keith Moon played drums. "When we were kicking around group names, I suddenly remembered Led Zeppelin, which I had come up with at that time." That, too, would have been a supergroup, but every musician to his own bag, and for Jimmy Page, it's John Paul Jones, John Bonham and Robert Plant to make Led Zeppelin an example of great music. And this is a group that won two standing ovations and two encores on their first date in London, with only six hours of rehearsal behind them.

It's the greatest trip any selection of musicians can take their audience on, the greatest feeling of being into a scene, one which America is ready and waiting for.

[*June Harris, January 1969*]

LED ZEPPELIN – A BIBLIOGRAPHY

Bonham, Mick
John Bonham: The Powerhouse Behind Led Zeppelin (Southbank, 2005)

Clayson, Alan
Led Zeppelin: The Origin Of The Species (Chrome Dreams, 2006)

Cole, Richard / Trubo, Richard
Stairway To Heaven: Led Zeppelin Uncensored (Simon & Schuster, 1993)

Davis, Stephen
Hammer Of The Gods (Sidgwick & Jackson, 1985)

Godwin, Robert
Led Zeppelin: The Press Reports (CG Publishing, 1997 / 2003)

Huylett, Ralph / Prochnicky, Jerry
Whole Lotta Led (Citadel, 2005)

Kendall, Paul (ed.)
Led Zeppelin In Their Own Words (Omnibus, 1981)

Lewis, Dave
Led Zeppelin: A Celebration (Omnibus, 1991)
Led Zeppelin: The Tight But Loose Files (Celebration II) (Omnibus, 1991)

Lewis, Dave / Pallett, Simon
Led Zeppelin: The Concert File (Omnibus, 2005)

Mylett, Howard
Led Zeppelin (Granada, 1976)

Mylett, Howard (ed.)
On Tour With Led Zeppelin (Hamlyn, 1993)

Mylett, Howard / Bunton, Richard
Led Zeppelin: In The Light (Proteus, 1981)

Welch, Chris
Peter Grant: The Man Who Led Zeppelin (Omnibus, 2001)

Welch, Chris / Nicholls, Geoff
John Bonham: A Thunder Of Drums (Backbeat, 2001)

Yorke, Ritchie
Led Zeppelin: The Definitive Biography (Virgin)